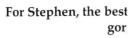For Stephen, the best
gor

Introduction

When most people think of Cambridge they'll visualize an affluent city of academia, populated with students, lecturers and professors. House prices soaring sky high and private schools in abundance. They'll associate it with the wealthy middle classes or perhaps London commuters, who can't quite afford to live in London, or maybe prefer the pace of life in Cambridge. Images of canal boats and punting on the pretty Cam come to mind, the touts peddling for fares for the punt operators. Rowers, Joggers and fitness fanatics filtering through the commons, tourists trailing past the usual hotspots vying for their iconic holiday snap, blocking pavements and infuriating locals, or ice cream vendors in pride positions outside the colleges, and more than anything cyclists everywhere. I grew up in Cambridge during the 70's and the Cambridge I am going to tell you about is not what you would have expected at all.

In 1974 Cambridge was in the thick of a crime wave, statistics showed a 36 percent increase in violence, beatings and muggings. The streets and commons were more dangerous than Glasgow, one in 333 people were at risk of becoming a victim of violent crime. Cambridgeshire's Chief Constable Mr Frederick Drayton Porter appealed for "The full support of the courts," in dealing with criminal activity. Cambridge was earning a reputation as one of the most violent cities in the country. The family I grew in up contributed generously to those statistics.

Some names have been changed to protect the identity of those in my story that survive.

Prologue

1975

Snow had fallen overnight, I'd been expecting it. Everyone had been saying it was coming and I'd gone to bed praying they were right. There'd been a few other winters with snow that I could remember. Waking up, the bedroom looked brighter than usual at this time, even the air smelt different. This was only my sixth winter, it was only three months since my sixth birthday. Looking out the window, the snow was a thick blanket across the back garden. It was piled up in the guttering of the shed roof. Only the precise markings of bird's feet had disturbed the even, perfect covering. Studying the trail of footprints, I marvelled at how sharply they were defined, so delicate, they could almost have been stencilled into the snow. Today was the day. At school every week on Mondays they had "Show and tell", you could take in anything and have a few minutes after registration, to tell the class about your object. Usually it was a favourite toy or a book. Sometimes it would be a milk tooth and the story of it coming out. If I had a wobbly tooth, Granddad always joked about tying string from the tooth to the door handle, and slamming the door shut to wrench it out. Tomas always said "Never sleep with your head under the pillow or the tooth fairy would take away all your teeth while you slept, but leave you a fiver".

This was going to be my moment, no one else would ever have taken in what I had. Nobody else would have such a story to tell. They'd be astonished, I could already imagine the silence and their huge eyes, with mouths hanging open from the impact of the wonder I was going to give them. The nervous excitement was almost too much, I wasn't sure if I should. If they found out at home I'd be in big trouble, nobody needed to know, they wouldn't ever know! I could take the ashes from the little carved table in the front bedroom and get them out the backdoor and down the side of the house. When I left for school, I could collect them and make my way across the road and down the street to school. It wasn't far. If I put them in a carrier bag that would make it easier to slide the ashes along by the handles of the bag, like a sleigh in the snow. I'd put them right back where they were as soon as I'd get home.

That morning I was full of haste and furtiveness. It was sharp, crisp and fresh, the weather seemed premeditated to assist with the frame of mind I was in. I was so alert, the cold warranted the need for swiftness. My nose was bright red and dripping with the cold. My top lip was already beginning to sting, and feel chapped. The air was so cold that every breath was a plume of steam like the kettle that whistled on the stove top at home. I shrugged on my school uniform and putting my elasticated green and black stripy tie on, tucked it under my shirt collar. I felt a sense of urgency to get ready for school for once. The hairbrush was dragged through my hair. The stench of cigarette smoke made me cough, stinging my eyes as it was sucked in and puffed out in my direction. If I squirmed too much and shied away from the brush when it got caught in the tangles, I'd get a whack across the back of the head with it. It was easier to wince and bear it as much as possible. Without any gloves, I'd put a pair of my school socks over my hands to protect them from the cold. They were just like the mittens that some of the girls wore.

They'd like me and want me to be their friend after today. They'd see, I was interesting, funny and smart. At last the other children would realise what a remarkable friend I might be. It was a struggle dragging the casket down the street, the handles on the carrier bag were beginning to stretch under the strain. It needed to be bumped up and down a couple of kerbs and the bag was splitting around the corners of the casket. I stopped to examine how my precious cargo was coping and wasn't sure but, I thought it looked like some grey powdery stuff was leaking out. No, it couldn't be. That wouldn't do. It must be the snow turning to slush already in places. My heart raced with trepidation. I was anxious I'd get a telling off. Maybe I shouldn't have taken it. A few of the other children, with their parents, gave me questioning glances as I trudged on past them. My hair felt like a balloon had been rubbed all over it from the frost in the air, and my nose was so cold it hurt. It was a mission, but I was determined, despite the dampness, I could already feel seeping in through the soles of my shoes and making my toes throb.

Once in the playground, the whistle blew, and so, I joined my classroom queue. Someone asked me, "What's in the bag?" and scowling I retorted "You'll see at Show and Tell, won't you!" With pride I walked over to Mrs.Childerly. Tugging on her sleeve said, "Mrs.Childerly, Mrs.Childerly, please. I've got something...I want to do Show and Tell, can I please?!" Mrs.Childerly was one of the nicest teachers, with silver bobbed hair that always looked so neat and shiny. She had a rounded figure, and always seemed so calm and kind. She never shouted and always comforted an unhappy pupil. Surprised to see this particular child suddenly being so forward, and showing such enthusiasm Mrs. Childerly exclaimed "Why of course you can! First of all we must let Katie Witt Show her brownie badge to the class and then it'll be your turn". That was alright, not much longer.

Those few minutes longer seemed an age, the wait was excruciating. Not only was I unsure if this was right, I felt as if I had to go through with it now. The numbness in my toes was now a burning itch, I tried rubbing my toecaps against the back of one knee. It was my turn.

"Today I want to show you all something I've brought in, this box has some ashes in it. They are the ashes of a dead man called Dick. He was my Mum's boyfriend and my Dad killed him."

Chapter 1

Kicked out

When Mum dies, I don't think I'll grieve for her. I'll mourn for the women we could have been. I'm probably mourning for her now and she's still alive, living like a shop dummy propped up in the corner of the sofa with my bully of a stepfather, in a house more like a mausoleum. Carolyn had a stroke when she was only 55 years old. Now she'll sit up and pretend to beg while Tomas waves a bag of marshmallows in her face saying "Look at what I've got for you for later, your favourite…What do you say?" he'll taunt and tease her in to begging. Carolyn isn't affected by the stroke in a way that makes her mentally slower or less sharp than you or I, she just wants to please him. He'll often refer to meal times as a "Feeding frenzy", calling Mum a gannet. Tomas met Mum and moved in when I was six, my brothers, Spencer and Antony were nine and five. Tomas's son, Shaun, our half -brother was born when I was nine.

1985

Growing up I couldn't wait to leave that house, only sixteen, I wasn't prepared, when the choice was made for me. Returning home after a night out, the front door had been locked to me. I'd been later and later getting home, because I'd started dating. Old enough to have a full time job and a boyfriend, but not old enough to have a key. Yet I was expected to abide by Tomas's curfews. Warned too many times already, I should have known it was coming. Maybe it was just designed to teach me a lesson. If I'd cried and banged on the door to be allowed in, accepted a scolding before being sent to the dog house for a week, I'd

7

eventually have realized the error of my ways and submitted to Tomas's regulations, things might have been different. Taken aback, I was stunned that they'd actually lock me out. My defiant pride wouldn't let me knock, especially as my boyfriend was watching from the kerb in his car, waiting to see me indoors safely. If he'd only dropped me off and driven away, I might have reacted differently. When I knew I wasn't getting in, I went back to him, "They've locked me out. Gone to bed and I can't get in." Appalled he asked "Can't you knock? Won't they come down and let you in?" He hadn't met them yet, if he had, he'd have known the answer already. "No. If I knock Tomas will ignore it, it's to teach me a lesson." He was compelled to take me home and entreat his parents to let me stay the night there. They were incredulous, unbelieving that any parent would lock a sixteen year old girl out of the house at night.

When I did knock the next day, Mum opened the door and without a word, put a suitcase containing my clothes on the doorstep in front of me, then shut the door. It was a surreal moment, it felt like a physical blow, if she'd slapped me across the face. I couldn't have been more stunned. The shock had me questioning myself frantically "What on earth was I supposed to do? Where would I go? Who would help me?" Tomas had told Antony and me for as long as I could remember, "When you're sixteen you're out. Our job will be done. You can look after yourselves. I did it. I was fifteen when I left home, I had a job and was working already. You can't stay here forever!"

Looking after myself seemed very unlikely. I was unemployed, I'd left school without sitting my GCSE's. Mum had insisted that I applied for a job at the local Budgens, where she was working. Insisting that I should leave school, "After all they're looking for staff now, and what's the point of exams and qualifications? You'll only get married and end up having kids" she concluded. I'd got the sack within a few months after stupidly taking the odd tenner here and there to top up my weekly income. Losing the job was probably a contributing factor in my being chucked out. After giving Mum and Tomas two thirds of my wages for rent, I wasn't left with much. Making friends at work, I'd wanted to begin socializing, get out, do stuff and meet people. I wanted to live. Suddenly I was able to buy a few nice things without being dependent on Nana Sheila clothing us from the Sally Ann. I didn't have to steal sanitary towels from Mum's dresser anymore or have Tomas shout at me for taking them, "Your Mum's run out of pads again! You keep stealing them! Why don't you make your own? Use your old tights and toilet paper, that's what women used to do!?" Well I might have done if he didn't complain about how much loo roll we got through too. If that wasn't bad enough I spent too long in the bath as well, He'd be shouting up the stairs "Come on you fat slug! What the fuck are you doing up there? Picking the black heads on your cunt?" He said it as casually as an operator at a boating lake would say "Come in boat number sixty nine, your time is up". Only it was harsh. It hurt me badly. The lump in my throat could last for days.

Those were my teenage years. Mum was quite a strong woman in some ways then. Occasionally they'd argue. Tomas would have to jump up off of the sofa, where he'd been laying moments before with his fly undone, to free his enormous belly from constraint, while he watched the horses on TV. An argument would begin either about money, or his domination of the TV and his lack of attentiveness to the home (he was not very, how shall I put it…adept at DIY) His reaction to this sudden quarrel was, jumping up, and in an almost Neanderthal movement with balled fists, pull up his jeans before grabbing his car keys, trying to tug his shoes on while shouting "I'm not fucking listening to this! I don't have to put up with this!" Then Mum would grab my brother Shaun by the elbow

9

and shout back at Tomas "Well if you're going, you can take him with you, he's yours too!" Shaun would start to cry and suck his thumb. She'd have him in his coat and be pushing him to the door behind Tomas. In what seemed seconds, as quickly as the wind can change direction, they'd be laughing and he'd be telling her "I love you, I love it when you get angry, you've such fire about you". Within moments, they'd be holding each other, Mum pretending to push him away, looking flushed and indignant. They loved each other, but Antony and I couldn't stand to be left alone in the same room with him. When we were younger, before Shaun was born, Antony and I had to be in bed by six o'clock in the evening. We shared a bedroom, and would hear Mum and Tomas talking and laughing downstairs, or the TV prattling in the background. They liked it when we were out of the way for the evening, sometimes we'd hear them having sex. Antony and I'd talk to each other about our hopes, dreams and wishes. I wished that the wallpaper was made of sweets that you could lick off of the wall and it'd just be replaced with another one. An everlasting sweetie wallpaper, like something out of "Willy Wonka's Chocolate factory". Antony would ask me if I thought Mum was a witch, or sometimes we would have a funny five minutes playing "Silly buggers". This involved climbing out on the bedroom window ledge and walking along it to the next window along and back into the bedroom. Our knuckles would be white, skin stretched over them, as we gripped the window frame. That was adrenalin pumping, nerve wracking stuff. It involved nerves of steel. Later as the night drew in and darkness came, Antony would fall asleep. In the night, I'd realise I was suddenly desperate for a wee. Terrified of the dark, and also frightened Tomas would shout up the stairs if I left our room for the toilet, I would try to wake Antony so he could watch over me. He'd grumble sulkily, and so I'd steel myself to creep out of bed, then folding the rug back on the carpeted floor pee under it, before folding it back in to place. Eventually, Mum detected the stench of urine in the room, the carpet had to be pulled up and replaced. We had a dog called Shadow at that time, he was always soiling where he shouldn't, so it couldn't be ascertained whether one of us was the culprit or the dog. We always had dogs and cats, growing up. Often they didn't stay too long. Shadow was dysfunctional and couldn't be trained, at least not with Tomas's approach. He kept shitting in the house, and Tomas, holding the dog by his head and ears, would grind Shadow's face into his own mess. When that method didn't work and the shitting continued, Tomas resorted to kicking Shadow. He was as unhappy as Antony and I. Admitting defeat, Tomas eventually had the dog rehoused, or at least that's what we were told.

I didn't like school. Taking cold toast for lunch in an old quality street tin, didn't add to its appeal. I remember, sometimes if a pupil forgot to take their lunch or dinner money, it was possible to go and see the bursar, who would give you a voucher to get a hot meal. But that involved sending a letter home to your parents and they'd be expected to repay the cost of the meal. One of my earliest memories at school, was moving across town with Mum to begin again and starting school at Queen Edith's. That was before Tomas met Mum or Antony came back to live with us, he'd been living with Spencer at our paternal grandparents. Mum had given Spencer to Nana and Granddad to raise because she didn't want him. Antony was only ever there indefinitely. My first day beginning again, involved having an episode in the dinner hall, full of children, teachers, lunchtime supervisors and dinner ladies. The cacophony of noise, with chatter the clanging of plates, and utensils, the uniformity of queuing and the children seated in lunchtime table "Families" proved too terrifying. I ran. Two supervisors had to pursue me down the corridor, trying to hide in one of the classrooms and pushing the door shut, they were too strong, and I was just a kid. They had to push the door open, while I braced myself against them on the other side. "What are you doing, you silly girl!" then "Grab her legs and I'll take her arms!" one of the women shouted. I'll never forget her, she was like a harridan on a warpath. They carried me like this back to the dining hall, I was crying all the way "I want my Mum, I want my Mum!" They sat me at a table with force, and eventually, aware of the silent watch of the other children, I calmed myself, embarrassed already, worried that I was making myself look stupid.

Antony came and lived with us when Mum and me moved to the other side of town. He'd only been staying with Nana and Granddad temporarily. He'd gone there with Granddad, when Dad had killed Dick. They said "We can't manage both boys". I was so excited that he was coming to be with us. We'd been staying with Mum's mother and her boyfriend Brian. Brian was lovely. He only had one arm, the other was a stump. He'd rest the stump in his coat pocket so that people couldn't tell there was no hand attached. One of my few encounters with the possibility of goodness in men, was Brian. He was kind and gentle to me. Nana Sheila was quite a brassy but handsome woman, always dying her hair jet black, it was permed, almost Afro like. When she wasn't dying her hair she was painting her nails. Even after eight children, a few abortions and a divorce she was still an attractive woman. Staying with them for a few weeks until we were rehoused was quite a nice time for me, and I think for Mum too. There was lots of laughter, Nana Sheila had a sense of fun and was a little bit wild. There was always music playing and Nana would dance around to it with a cigarette burning away between her fingers. They all smoked including Mum. This side of the family were quite wild, and early on Mum really did have the "fire" in her too. Nana and Brian were always getting ready to go out, and sometimes Mum would go too. The house was a hive of activity, with my uncles coming and going with their girlfriends. My aunts were already settled in relationships, one had moved away to America. The eldest Catherine had been born when Nana was only thirteen, she'd met a Polish refugee and got pregnant. Nana had been sent as an evacuee from London to stay in one of the surrounding villages on the outskirts of Cambridge. She stayed with Aunt Min, who became Nana's surrogate mother when she became pregnant and her family refused to have her back. Aunt Min raised Nana as well as Catherine, as though they were her children. Aunt Min was soft with Nana, who was a naïve girl, because, despite already having got caught out with her first pregnancy, she went on to get pregnant a second time out of wedlock, with her second child, Melvyn.

As I was growing up I always understood that my Mum's family were notorious in Cambridge. Melvyn was the first of my Nana's sons, she went on to have three more, John, Nigel and Mark. Each one had been to prison and each one was known to be violent. They were well known for committing burglaries, robbery and drug dealing. The decent people in the neighbourhood did their best to avoid interaction with the Pride family. It was common knowledge that they peddled drugs and albeit the culture of the time, to experiment freely, that didn't make them everyone's cup of tea. There were always gatherings at my Nana's house and it was often raucous. If there were not parties at the house, everybody would be getting ready and heading off to an "all-nighter" somewhere. My Mum wasn't an innocent either. She'd go along too. As for my aunts, Catherine had already married and distanced herself from the family. The family considered her above her station in life and "up herself". Mum was a damaged divorcee with a history already, Linda was seeing a man that looked to be making something of himself. This was the friend that had originally introduced my parents to each other. Susan had already emigrated after meeting and falling in love with an American.

13

Even Fred, my Nana's dog, roamed wild then. He didn't get taken for walks, he took himself. It was an ongoing problem, Fred had an issue with people on bicycles, he'd run after them and grabbing their trouser hem between his teeth, he'd try to yank them off of their bicycle's at their ankles. Endless times the local policeman had to come and complain about Fred, "If you don't keep him in or on a lead, the dog warden will catch him". He'd try to be good humoured about it, though I think he had little choice but to be. Knocking on the Pride family door, with a complaint was no mean feat. When Antony came to visit us during our time there, he loved it if Fred pulled his jean trousers by the ankles. If we encouraged and urged Fred on, he'd oblige by dragging him around the garden on his back until his jeans slid half way down and Antony's hysterical laughter turned to indignation, then tears.

It was a lively, cheerful time for a while after the terrible events that had led us to stay at Nana's. She liked me to scratch her back in the evenings for her, murmuring "Don't stop, Oh that's nice, right there, oh just over to the left a bit". Brian would read to me and tuck me into bed at night. Once he caught me trying to sleep with a new pair of shoes Mum had bought me, hidden under the sheets. That made him laugh, but somehow, he didn't make me feel daft about it. If he had a bubble bath, I'd sit and chat to him, it never felt inappropriate because I was completely at ease with him. He was a ladies man. Nana would one day have a break down, because of his fondness for women. I guess she wasn't as tough as I supposed.

One evening, the ice cream van had arrived in the street and Nana gave me some money to go and get a "Mr.Whippy". I was so pleased. Excited to buy an ice cream, that I forgot my shyness in the anticipation of having that creamy, deliciousness in my mouth! I went out to the van by myself and can remember walking away from the van, enjoying this simple treat with real relish. Walking without really thinking, I realized I wasn't sure which direction I'd come from or if I was going back the right way. Each way I turned, looked the same .I was lost. Completely confused now and terrified no one would miss me, or come to find me. I ended up slumped at the side of the road crying, the ice cream melting in my fist. The daylight began to fade and the evening was beginning to draw in. I really wanted Mum. I kept thinking "I mustn't talk to strangers". There was an advert on TV at the time with a ginger cat and a boy, it was animated and the cat meowed in cat language, which the boy could interpret. He'd told the viewer "Charlie says "Never talk to strangers" and" Always ask your Mummy before you go anywhere". It was perhaps only half an hour later when a young woman on a moped saw me. Pulling up to the kerb, she asked me "Are you ok? You look as if you're lost?" I bawled "I'm lost and I don't know where I live! I want my Mum!" She was so nice, taking pity on me, she walked me alongside her moped to the nearest phone box. I think she must have phoned the local police man. There were houses belonging to police officers in our neighbourhood. We recognized them by their blue front doors. Once she told him my name, he would have no doubt known where I belonged. She walked me back home, where she returned me unharmed, red eyed and with a quivering bottom lip.

The most upsetting thing was Mum's anger when I got back. She'd been frantic, looking high and low for me. Brian was still out looking. Rarely did she show me any anger, but that evening she shouted at me, "Don't you ever do that to me again!" and "How could you get lost? The bloody ice cream van was only outside on the street!" She opened the oven door and took out the dinner that she'd been keeping for me and with one swift under arm fling, she threw it against the wall beside my head.

Each of my uncles were quite attractive men, they were wild yet charming at the same time. Melvyn was the oldest, though short and sturdy, he possessed an aura of danger. There was something magical and seductive about him. Mark was the youngest, he was mixed race, although he would deny it vehemently if anyone dared to suggest it, which his brothers would teasingly do. A skinhead, he was cultivating one of the popular images of that time, and it seemed to coincide with his refusal to accept his possible parentage. Mark and the middle brothers John and Nigel all idolized Melvyn, because he always had beautiful girlfriends (attracted partly because he was always high and stoned and could provide an endless supply of uppers, downers or whatever it was they craved). They were his entourage, admiring of his popularity, and mindful that he never seemed short of money. He had been married for a brief while to Anna. They had two sons together, but Melvyn couldn't make it work. With his thieving, drug fuelled lifestyle and stream of girlfriends, Anna eventually divorced him, finding solace in Jehovah instead. Melvyn tried to maintain some contact with his sons, but time passed, the drug taking had him in its grip. The contact decreased in degrees, until it was non-existent. During Melvyn's stints in and out of "nick" as my family would call it, he'd paint. He painted the most incredible scenes. Nana Sheila had some of them in her house on the walls. One that has always stuck out in my mind, was filled with rich, splendid colours in deep hues of purple, maroon, jade green and pitch black. It was of a black woman, sleek and feline, singing in to a microphone. The skyline behind her was breathtakingly surreal and before her was a satellite. With all those powerfully striking colours, it could have been a Martian landscape. Melvyn had such a talent, potential and promise to be so much more. All of the men in my family had such potential. The potential to be wonderful, dynamic and wholesome people. Or perhaps that's only an illusion that was delivered through acid drops.

Chapter 2

The bosom of the family

Mum was born Carolyn Joy Pride, she was the third of Nana Sheila's children, with a mass of curly, unruly hair. "Carol" they often called her. She was a quiet, modest child that had a rebellious streak and was the only one of the girls that would challenge Nana. By the time Carolyn was twelve, she was already bringing up the younger children in her family. Nana was usually getting herself dressed up and going out most evenings. Catherine the eldest was lucky because she was brought up by Aunt Min. Melvyn was already a bit of a wide boy, Jack the lad character, which usually got him a belting from Carolyn's Dad, Leonard. I never knew Leonard. Nana and he were already separated by the time I came along. Fortunately for me I guess, as he'd been sexually abusing at least one of his daughters, although only one of them would admit to it. The others would admit that he'd made obvious advances and overtures, but didn't want to divulge any further about the extent of his affection towards them. Nana often worked waitressing, which meant working odd hours where Leonard was left with the children. The boys would get beatings for any misdemeanour, that involved a hard slap around the head or if the crime was deemed severe enough, Leonard would take off his belt and beat them with that. As a consequence, Nigel had learning difficulties at school. It was later realized he was actually quite deaf in one ear.

Nana wasn't only waitressing. They suspected, and have often since, speculated that she was probably giving sexual favours for money, as a way of increasing the household income. I can even recall one old man in a street near to where she lived, banging on his window one day as we walked by together. He was waving some money at her through the glass. She waved cheerily back at him while tugging me along briskly beside her. Sheila had a reputation for liking the company of American servicemen in particularly. While she was out either waitressing, or boosting her purse in what was a well-known red light district at the time, Carolyn would be looking after John, Nigel, Mark, Linda and Susan. They loved her. They didn't turn to Sheila for comfort or attention, it was Carolyn they'd turn to. Pressing their faces into her skirt to sob or hide from the upsets that so many times needed soothing.

On a Sunday afternoon, Leonard hadn't come back from the pub when he should have for his Sunday lunch. Sheila, being furious, marched down to the pub with his roast, and ceremoniously plonked it on the bar in front of him. "If you aren't coming back for your dinner, after I've spent all morning cooking it, I'll fucking bring it to you!" When Leonard returned home later, he beat Sheila for having made him look foolish in front of his drinking partners. Carolyn tended to the little ones, while this kind of scene played itself out. It was a usual occurrence.

So Sheila, worked hard and fooled around. She did her best to find enjoyment where she could from her real life, while Leonard was at liberty to supervise the children how he saw fit. Sheila always maintained that she hadn't any suspicions that Leonard was doing anything improper with their daughters.

Carolyn kept house, cleaning, cooking, washing, ironing for eight at a time when washing was done by hand. She was changing nappies, bathing her younger siblings, dressing them, getting them ready for school and giving them love, while little was given to her in return. Carolyn was the giver. She's often remarked since "In life there are those that give and there are those that take".

At sixteen Melvyn and Carolyn were like partners rather than brother and sister and some would even wonder if perhaps they were a little too close to be only siblings. Knowing each other like the backs of their hands, aware of each other's strengths and weaknesses, they were really the parents in the family, and would fly to each other's defence, if confrontation arose. The rest of the children doted on them, and still have done so until recently. Melvyn was a small, but strong, and handsome young man by this point, and Carolyn was old enough now to notice some of the other young men that he was hanging out with. Leonard, wasn't so quick with the belt or his fists now that Melvyn was older. He'd warned Leonard in no uncertain terms "If you take that belt to me one more, I will take it from you and beat the shit out of you with it".

Melvyn started stealing. He was taking and selling drugs, John, Nigel and later Mark, the baby of the family would all follow his lead. It was at this time that one of Melvyn's friends was already seeing Linda and introduced a mutual friend to Carolyn. David Charles. My Dad, Dave. He was charming, cocky and full of self-confidence. He seemed fearless and sure of himself, and he took a shine to Carolyn. They began spending time together, but it was generally within a crowd or among other friends. Melvyn tried warning Carolyn that Dave was bad news, he wasn't to be trusted and could be unpredictable. It was usually Carolyn, Dave and Linda with her boyfriend that arranged to go out together. All was going well enough, and as young people have a hankering to do, the two couples decided they wanted to get away for some fun by the coast one weekend. They devised a plan so that the girls could spend the weekend away from home without their parents feeling concerned. They went to Brighton. It was an exciting weekend and the girls were giddy with the sense of freedom, feeling adult, desirable and alive. It was short lived, however, and when they returned home the cat was out of the bag. Somehow Leonard and Sheila had caught them in their lie. Carolyn being the oldest was to blame, she was always the testy one, always the one to back chat and argue with Sheila. Sheila knew Leonard seemed to favour her.

Sheila was insistent in her interrogation of Carolyn "Did you sleep with that Charles boy?!" "Come on tell me the truth, I know you're lying, you've had sex with him, haven't you?!"

Carolyn was indignant, she couldn't believe that Sheila would assume she was so easy, she felt that Sheila was tarring her with her own brush. They shouted and nearly came to blows, Sheila kept gripping Carolyn by her arm and calling her names. An appointment was made for her to see the doctor, and she was duly marched by Sheila to the surgery. It seems implausible now. In this day and age would this happen? Could it? Would it be allowed? But back then it seems it was perfectly acceptable to take your daughter to the doctor to have her examined to see if her hymen was still intact! It was confirmed that, in fact, Carolyn was untouched. She wasn't a liar, and was left burning with shame and resentment. She had told Sheila nothing had happened, and had sworn "The honest truth", that she had done nothing wrong, but her word had not been enough. "Now you know I was telling the truth. The doctor has told you I haven't done anything with him, but you wouldn't believe me! You know what I'll do now? I will bloody well have sex with him!" Sheila was at a loss, she didn't know what to say or how to appease Carolyn. Whether she regretted what she'd done I'll never know.

I can only wonder if Sheila was jealous of Carolyn, and if she thought that Leonard favoured her and there was something more to his love of Carolyn than she was prepared to admit to herself. Carolyn has always said that Leonard never touched her in that way. She always said that in many ways she almost blamed Sheila for his behaviour towards her sisters and the brutality that the boys received. She believed that Sheila feigned ignorance because it suited her to do so, while she was out most nights with one new boyfriend or another. She believed that Sheila's behaviour drove Leonard to vent his frustration on the children. I believe that both parents had individual responsibilities as adults and human beings to care and provide for their children in a loving, caring, protected and nourishing environment. I am a mother now, I have a daughter. I love her. She is certain of that.

Carolyn continued seeing Dave, She was pregnant within the year. Spencer was born when she was seventeen. Leonard and Sheila went to see Dave's parents. Mr and Mrs Charles, who insisted that the right and honourable thing should be done and that David must marry Carolyn. They had a registry office wedding and so she went to live with her new parents in law until the couple could be housed. One thing that has remained throughout her life she consistently imparted to us, was that Nana and Granddad were decent, kind and gentle people. And they were, Nana and Granddad were the rock in my childhood. They are the rose tint in my nostalgia glasses and my glass half full. I want to be that kind of grandparent one day. If you are a grandparent and you are reading this, I hope you are that for your grandchildren.

In the summer of 1967 David was sent to Borstal training, for the robbery of a wallet. Other incidences of larceny and housebreaking were taken into consideration. He had left school at fifteen and although trained as a plumber, that was not the future destined for my Dad. They had just been housed in a lovely little two up and two down terraced house in Cambridge on Green's Road. Carolyn was four months pregnant. This was meant to be the start of their married life. Nana and Granddad, now familiar enough to be Edie and Les, settled Carolyn in to her new home. They decorated and furnished the house for her, and visiting regularly made sure she had everything she would need. They would take her back to theirs for weekends and their friends, neighbours and family pampered and attended to her. Carolyn was liked and cherished as the expectant new mum that she was. It was the kind of attentiveness that all new mum's should receive and be entitled to expect. However what should have been a wonderful time for any new mum was overshadowed by angst already. David had already been behaving unreasonably and showing signs of aggression and selfishness. His true character was going to emerge more as time went on. Edie and Les reassured Carolyn that Borstal would set David on the right track, he just needed some discipline and some time in detention to make him see sense. He wasn't a bad boy at all, it was just all a lot for him to adjust to, getting married, and becoming a Dad all so suddenly. But it was going to be alright "She would see".

It wasn't alright. Spencer was a home birth, born before Dave came home from Borstal, and Carolyn was finding it difficult. Alone with a new born, despite her experience bringing up her siblings, and the support from her parents in law. Spencer was a melancholy baby that cried continuously. She couldn't console him. He was bottle fed, as she couldn't bring herself to have him suckle from her breasts. The few times she had tried, the very sight of his mouth desperately trying to latch onto her nipple was enough to have her cringing in trepidation at the thought of it. Besides, giving him the bottle was easier for everyone. Even though she suspected Edie and Les were a little disappointed in her failed attempts at the expected feeding method, she felt that Edie secretly enjoyed being able to participate in feeding Spencer. More and more Carolyn allowed Edie and Les to take charge of her first born. Edie had only had David, there had been other failed pregnancies, miscarriages and a still birth while Les was away during WWII. It was always poignant to them that they hadn't been able to have more children. Edie and Les doted on Spencer.

David was home, uninterested in fatherhood or Marriage, the benefits of marriage were quite appealing however. Sex was available on tap, though Carolyn wasn't especially vigorous or an eager partner in the bedroom.

Chapter 3

Spuds, cigarettes and alcohol

1967

Night after night Carolyn was subjected to David's sexual demands. He'd had lonely nights to compensate for, she was forced to have sex in any position he chose, and whenever he chose. Should she complain or attempt to deny him access to her body, she was slapped hard across the face, thumped and kicked. "It's like fucking a sack of spuds with you!" Dave would declare. She would sob into her pillow and behind the bathroom door. The power he had over her in strength and the authority in his position as her husband simply seemed to fuel his appetites. When he was sated and it seemed he was satisfied the desire for cigarettes and a drink would take hold. If there were none to be had in the house he would demand that Carolyn get up and go to the local grocery store and get some. "I don't have any money Dave, you already had what money I had for food this week." Carolyn would tell him. Sometimes she would try to hide what little money she had ferreted away in a jar or a pot in the house. He would fly into a rage and throw things, smash ornaments, rip open cupboard doors, taking them off their hinges. Then when that was fruitless he would turn on her. One of these rages, involved him dragging her by her hair over to the kitchen sink. Putting the plug in, he began running the tap to fill the bowl "If you don't tell me where the money is right this minute, you bitch, I swear I'll fucking drown you!" His eyes bulged and spittle sprayed from between his clenched teeth as he twisted her head by the hair to force her to look at him. "Dave, stop! Please stop! I haven't got any money! It's all been spent!" Carolyn was already gripping the rim of the sink to try and brace herself for what was to come.

With sheer anger, Dave almost lifted her off of her feet by yanking her hair, as he pushed her face first into the water, the tap still flowing, water overflowed the sink and spilled to the floor. He held her head under the water. It was only briefly, maybe seconds, but it was enough. Carolyn's legs kicked from under her and slid around the floor. She surfaced gasping for air as with an almighty wrench David pulled her head up and cracked her skull against the mouth of the tap. Carolyn reeled. It was the panic that had caught her breath more than the water she was still choking on. If ever she had wondered where the line "Seeing stars" had come from, she knew now. Blood was running down her face and into the collar of her dress. Dave threw her down on to her backside. He saw the blood trickling from the roots of her hair down her cheek.

"Oh Fuck, Carolyn, look at what you've made me do, come on, come on girl let's stop this now and get you cleaned up". He pulled a tea towel from the hook on the back of the kitchen door and bent down to staunch the flow of blood on the back of her head. She was too stunned and shaken to sob, she wasn't really sure if she could answer him. "There you are you silly cow, all of this fuss over nothing, it'll be alright". Spencer was screaming from his cot at the foot of their bed upstairs. Carolyn knew she had to go to him. He needed her attention.

She went to see her doctor almost on a regular basis. He did his best to patch her up with butterfly stitches and told her not to wash her hair for a few days until her scalp had time to heal. She had visited him previously with bruised and cracked ribs. He was alarmed and begged her to go to the police, but Carolyn knew there was nothing that they could do. Dave was her husband and this was just a domestic dispute. There had been a couple of incidents already where the neighbours had heard the ructions next door and called the police. They came and told them to keep the noise down. Once they threatened to put Dave in the cells overnight if he didn't calm down. When they left she got another beating.

Time and again Carolyn left Dave and went to Edie and Les, they would take her and Spencer in and nurse her until she was well again. They didn't want to believe that their son was as bad as she was telling them, yet the evidence was there to be seen. They would beg her to go back and give him another chance. "He didn't mean it. He doesn't know what he's doing. He loves you really. He's sorry. It won't happen again". They said these things on so many occasions it was almost a mantra in Carolyn's own head now. It was decided that perhaps it would be easier if Spencer stayed with them, if only in the short term. It would surely take some of the pressure off the young newlyweds without a baby to fret about, as well as adjusting to married life. They needed some time to be together as man and wife that was all. Les even had a phone installed at the house for them so that they could ring any time of day or night. So Carolyn returned home, without Spencer. She practised being an obedient and dutiful wife. She cooked, cleaned, washed and ironed. It was reminiscent of another time.

One night Carolyn was already in bed. She was sound asleep and didn't think Dave would be home that night. Earlier on he'd been quite excited about going out with his mates, was hyped up and it seemed he'd already been drinking and taken some uppers. He was being charming and kept pulling her to him and hugging her from behind. She cringed at the contact, but couldn't let him see it. He told her to iron a shirt for him and polish his shoes. He went up for a strip wash and was singing to himself, strutting around, admiring his good looks in the wardrobe mirror. When he went out Carolyn sighed with relief. All the usual indicators were there, that he wouldn't be back until the next day. She would make the most of the evening without him, would have a wash and take herself to bed early. She would be able to read undisturbed. Not long after getting under the eiderdown, she was drifting off.

There was a loud peal of laughter and muffled noises of movement coming from downstairs. Carolyn sat bolt upright, she muttered to herself in a half awake fugue "What on earth's going on?" Silently she slid out of bed and tip toed to the door. She stopped, and pulling it ajar as quietly as she could, strained to hear what was happening. Again muffled sounds. Someone was talking and she could make out Dave's voice. Deciding to get closer to hear better, she started gingerly down the stairs avoiding the steps that she knew creaked. The living room door was ajar and the table lamp was giving out a subdued glow that gently spilled into the hall way. Carolyn felt like she was in some surreal world, half between waking and asleep. With her big toe Carolyn nudged the door enough for it to glide open a few inches more and as she peered into the room she heard a giggle and saw rising up and down at a steady pace, Dave's bare backside rhythmically appearing and disappearing above the back of the sofa as he plunged in and out of his impromptu house guest. Carolyn's eyes widened in horror and, flinging the door back to its full extent, she ran around the sofa. The woman screamed at the sight of her in her nightdress as Carolyn flew at them, grabbing at Dave and screaming with despair "What the fuck is this? What the fuck are you doing? You dirty bastard, you bloody dirty pair of bastards!" "How could you, how could you!" The woman was scrabbling around on the sofa, desperate to get her clothes back on and looking as white as a ghost. "Get out! The pair of you! Get out of my house…" Before she could finish Dave turned her around to face him and with one almighty sweep gave her a resounding back handed slap across her face. "Who do you think you are? To come down here and talk to me like this. This is my house, you don't wear the trousers here. I do. Now mind your fucking business and take yourself back upstairs to bed!"

It was tough, everyone in the street knew that Carolyn was a battered wife and if she encountered any of them on her way to the shops or back she would avoid eye contact. It was so embarrassing, she felt such shame. When she did feel brave enough to raise her eyes to say hello, sometimes they would look away and feign having not seen her, because they were embarrassed for her. Even the local shopkeeper knew all about her. She'd lost count of how many times she'd had to ask for tick, and how many times he'd had to prompt her to settle up. There had even been times when Dave had kicked her out of bed to go to the shop in the dead of night, and she'd had to bang on the grocery door in her dressing gown until the shopkeeper answered. "What is it now Carolyn?!" he'd ask, wearily rubbing his eyes and peering through the crack of the door. "I've got to get some cigarettes for Dave Mr. Ramsey. I'm so sorry, but I can't go back empty handed. Please, I promise to pay you back as soon as I can. I'm really sorry to get you up like this". The shop keeper would grudgingly fetch the cigarettes, and write it on the pad he kept by the register. He had seen the bruises on Carolyn's face enough times. He didn't want her to go back with nothing.

Often Carolyn would make that call to Les and he would come. Dave would be having one of his rages and Les would talk him down and get him on an even keel again, sometimes Dave was the one to call. He would plead and wheedle for either Les or Edie to lend him some money, to see them through the rest of the week. Considering his parents were already feeding and clothing Spencer they were generous to a fault. Carolyn would visit Spencer at theirs and sit on the rug in the living room marvelling at his sitting up and tentative attempts to crawl. He was safer here. It was healthier for him and he seemed so much happier, though it hurt her to leave, her heart felt as if it would burst.

Chapter 4

I am born

1969

Life continued. Spencer was walking now and he was adored by Edie and Les, turning away from Carolyn to them when she came to visit. He had a full head of wavy blonde hair and chocolate brown eyes, with little chubby legs and plump wrists. Carolyn took heart in seeing how well he was and how attentive Edie and Les were. They were such lovely grandparents, but they couldn't accept that Dave was a monster. They still believed he would mend his ways, and it was almost as if they believed Carolyn could straighten him out. With time he'd outgrow his selfish ways and would grow into a good father and husband.

It was Carolyn's twentieth birthday. Spencer was two years and four months old when the doctor confirmed that she was pregnant again with me. She was terrified. Another baby! What would she do? How would she cope? Would she have it? She couldn't get rid of it. How would Dave react? It was his bloody fault anyway! She was fearful of telling him. So she decided to wait, until they were with Edie and Les again. Edie was overjoyed, Les more cautious and concerned. Dave, strangely, behaved like it was wonderful news and draped his arm around her shoulder, saying with a smug grin, "So I'm going to be a Dad again".

The next nine months were relatively peaceful. There were some moments of aggression but the beatings were far reduced and not as bad as they had been. Carolyn bloomed, and she somehow still managed to look beautiful, despite living in a permanent state of fear. Edie and Les came to visit regularly and even Sheila called once or twice. With this renewed contact with her Mum Carolyn made some visits to stay with them at weekends. Dave enjoyed the time she was out of the way to have his bursts of freedom. He would go on a complete bender, drinking all weekend and take whatever drugs he could find.

Carolyn enjoyed the contact with her family again. Melvyn was around at that time, as he was having one of his stints out of prison. Out of prison, however, did not mean out of trouble. The house was alive with the activity of a large family, her brothers, coming and going all the time. Lots of banter and laughter, but lots of arguments and fighting among themselves was the norm too.

One Sunday morning, having had a lie in, Carolyn was getting ready to go home. It was always difficult to make herself go back. She was quite heavily pregnant now and struggled to get into her dress. Having managed to get the zip halfway up her back, she decided to go and find Linda and get her to help. "Good morning love, what have we here then?" It was Leonard. She felt on her guard instantly. In all the time Carolyn was growing up, he had never laid a finger on her, but she knew he had fiddled with Susan and Linda was too scared to say if he'd done anything to her. "Looks like you're having a problem getting yourself dressed. Come over here and let your old Dad do you up". She hesitated, before stepping towards him, he put his hands on her shoulders and spun her round, facing her back now his hands on her hips his, voice became softer, and huskily he said "D'you know what? If you weren't my daughter I'd quite fancy you myself". With that he pulled the dress together at the neck so that the zip would glide more easily, zipped her dress up, and then ran his hands down her arms at her sides. Carolyn stepped quickly away from him, gathered her things and left to return home.

At home, Dave was still out, who knew where. Les phoned and said he'd got some curtains for her from Robert Sayle, He worked as a carpet fitter there, and they were an end of line pair and he'd picked out as a perfect fit for her living room. He came over and fitted them for her. She made him a cup of tea and they had a piece of cake that Edie had sent with him. "Edie's at home with the boy". Les said. "She's getting dinner ready, but sent some of her cherry Madeira for you". Carolyn Sobbed, it just burst like a bubble from her throat. Les awkwardly put an arm around her "There, there, don't get upset now. I don't know, you women. Hormones, that's what it'll be." He patted her back gently and tried to console her. "Now don't go getting yourself upset, you've got the baby to think about".

I was born, early November 1969. The same year that Neil Armstrong, Buzz Aldrin and Michael Collins landed on the moon. Men were making incredible advances, but for many women their situation was as archaic as it had ever been.

Both Carolyn and David were still only twenty years old. Between 1970 and 1975 David's alcohol and drug intake increased as did the amount of offences that he was committing. His drug of choice was LSD. Within eight months of my birth he was arrested for the possession of an offensive weapon. Already having a record, he was given a three month suspended sentence and within two months was arrested yet again for the same offence. For this he duly served his three month's suspended sentence. In both cases he had been carrying a knife.

I was only four months old when Carolyn conceived again. Antony was born in December 1970, around the

33

same time that Dave returned home from prison. I was just one year old.

Carolyn had a hard labour with Antony. The pregnancy had been difficult, she had problems balancing, and she fell several times. It was something of a respite that Dave was away at the end of the pregnancy. The labour was long and as with Spencer and me, she had Antony at home. Sheila was with her and the midwife was called. Carolyn writhed in agony on the bed, bathed in sweat and riddled with anguish. Sheila held her hand and tried to keep her calm. The mid wife told her to stop pushing, but she couldn't resist the urge, it was too strong. She tore and Antony was delivered. He didn't make a sound, the midwife held him up by his legs saying "If he starts to turn blue, you'll know he's dead". Then she gave his bottom a spank and with that he let out a piercing wail of unhappiness that seemed in outrage at having to come into this world. Carolyn was exhausted, she turned her face to the wall and her tears flowed silently into the pillow.

David returned the next day. No one knew where he had been the night before, no doubt he was still celebrating his release, but everyone could guess what he had been doing. He arrived back appearing highly strung and agitated, behaving as if he was in a hype about something. Sheila was there to greet him and told him that Carolyn had given birth. He began to head upstairs to their bedroom, where Antony was asleep beside Carolyn in the bed. Sheila anxiously followed saying, "Don't disturb her Dave, she's had a bad time of it. It wasn't an easy birth, she really ought to rest!" Dave continued stalking up the stairs oblivious of her. Sheila tried to get ahead of him and step in front of the doorway, but he was too quick. He marched into the room and up to the bed, his face already a mask of sneering resentment and disgust. He lent over the bed and Carolyn, startled, awoke. She curled an arm around

Antony and tucked him in against her. "So you've had him then, who does this one belong to? He can't be mine, because you don't fucking open your legs to me you bitch!" Sheila ran into the room and was shouting, "Stop that now Dave. Don't be so bloody ridiculous, of course he's yours! You're not thinking straight, coming back here looking like that and who knows what you've taken. You're drunk!" But even as she tried to stop him, he had climbed on the bed beside Carolyn. She had her back turned against him and curled into the foetal position with Antony wedged against her womb, where she wished he could stay. Dave was standing on the bed now, in his boots, and towering over her he shouted "You're a fucking lying slag. That kid is nothing to do with me. So don't think you can fool me!" he kicked her and swung his leg back to kick again. Sheila screamed and ran at Dave. Carolyn lay as still as she could and tried to create a defence around Antony with her arms and thighs as barriers. Sheila had hold of Dave's trousers belt and managed to drag him off the bed, he over balanced and toppled onto the floor. In the midst of all this commotion, there was a loud banging at the front door. Both David and Sheila froze, her face contorted with anger and fear, while he was quickly composing his expression. His eyes, wide and wild only seconds before, now veiled and guarded. Already his jaw was tensing and his mouth clenched shut. There was more banging, and the letter box was pushed inwards as Les called "David! We know you're there, let us in!" David stood, and straightening himself up, looked at Sheila and said "If you know what's good for you, never come between me and her again." A smile spread across his face but failed to reach his eyes, as he pushed past her and went to open the door.

Carolyn would endure nine years of these torments with David, he would also, take pleasure in being spiteful with us as we grew. We were not specifically beaten in the way Carolyn was, the cruelties were less vicious. Maybe that was because we were slighter and it would have got worse as we grew. As an example, we didn't have a bath in our little house. So Carolyn would bathe us in the kitchen sink. The memory stays with me even now, of being naked in the sink and him soaking the tea towel in the water beside me, wringing it out and then using it to flick at me and sting me until I cried. Carolyn had to plead with him to stop "That's enough Dave, stop! She doesn't like it!" He would laugh and prance around the kitchen flicking the tea towel at me, and then her.

It was Antony who became David's favourite child as the years went by, perhaps because he was the only one of us to attempt any understanding or sympathy for our Dad.

Chapter 5

Godwin Close

Antony came back to live with Mum and me, when we were making our new start in 1975. He was four. We weren't sure yet if he would need to have counselling. It was difficult leaving Nana Sheila and Brian, but at the same time, Mum and I were excited about having our own home. I never thought it was odd that Spencer lived with Nana and Granddad Charles and I never questioned why Antony had been living with Dad. It all seemed normal to me. I knew I wanted to be with Mum, there was never any question of me being anywhere else. She never made me feel as if I wasn't where I belonged. Moving into a new house and having Antony with us was exciting. Mum explained that Nana and Granddad would be looking after him temporarily until we were properly settled. It felt lovely, like some of the families I saw on TV. We would still see Nana Sheila and Brian and it was agreed that we would visit Nana Edie and Granddad regularly too. Mum was happy, but sometimes I thought she seemed quiet and didn't give lots of cuddles. I craved more cuddles from her.

My uncles came to visit a lot. Nigel and John, Melvyn quite often if he wasn't away, but Mark especially. He was Mum's youngest brother and he came nearly every other day, sometimes also staying over. He was very close to Mum and very jealous of his time with her. She was more a mother to him than Nana Sheila. We also had a dog called Ricky, an Alsatian crossed with a Great Dane. Ricky was huge, loveable and gentle, he would bark if anyone came to the door, and strain on his lead when we walked him. His size and enthusiasm was enough to deter any potential aggressor. We felt safe having him as a faux protector, in reality he was a softy.

One of our first nights in the house, before Antony had moved in, early one morning I was lying in bed with Mum and there was an almighty crashing noise of pots and pans hitting the floor in the kitchen. We were both startled and didn't know what on earth it could be. Mum put on a brave show for my benefit and said we should go and investigate. Off we went downstairs in our nighties, Mum first, me behind, clutching her hand. I could see she was just as scared as me, pressing her back against the stair wall as she moved downwards. We went along the short hall to the kitchen and found that the tiered, wire saucepan rack had fallen over, all the pans haphazard across the kitchen floor. There were no windows or doors open, or any sign as to how the pans had fallen. Mum said "That'll be Dick. He's upset and angry, and he's trying to let us know he's here". I didn't really understand "What does that mean Mum? I thought Dick was dead? He won't come here will he?" Mum looked slightly rueful for having said it "No, I'm being silly. Dick is dead and he's in the spirit world now. But sometimes spirits like to let us know that they are nearby even if we can't see them. So they make loud noises and sometimes bang doors." I was worried, I didn't want anyone banging doors in this house. "He won't hurt us…Will he Mum?"

Mum believed in spirits. She said she had been able to see things since she was a child, and she believed she had a sensitivity to things that others did not see. Growing up this was going to become a theme that would ultimately cause problems and more heartache for her, but also confusion and despair for us.

So Antony came to live with us permanently. We were both going to be enrolled at the same school. I would be going to Queen Edith's just across the road from where we were now living and Antony would follow me. We went to bed together at night and shared the same room. Antony would sometimes wake us up in the night, and he'd be upside down in the bed, under the covers, screaming. Mum would come running into the room to try and comfort him, he would shake and sob as he awoke and she would tell him all was well "Its ok you're safe now". He couldn't remember what it was that had upset him so much. He didn't remember granddad having to put a coat over his head and lead him away from Dad's house. We got up and had breakfast together in the mornings. We were bathed together and we were learning to ride bikes together. Granddad had bought us a bicycle each. Both fast learners, we were good at most practical things. Riding our bikes was spectacular! We thrilled at the freedom we felt. Where we lived was a cul de sac so we could go outside and around our street again and again. There was a recreation ground that cut through from Godwin close, came out onto Spalding way, and not much farther on to nana Sheila's house. Occasionally Mum would walk there with us while we cycled. Sometimes we would cycle as far as the rec and back if we were feeling brave and adventurous. Antony was the more daring of the two of us. He loved to pull only his front brakes so that the back of the bike would rear up behind him. I tried doing that and ended up over the handle bars and in a heap on the floor. Godwin close was lined with trees all the way around the cul de sac, and in the spring the trees were absolutely full of pink blossom. I loved it! The whole street became paved with it, and I believed that there must be a God then.

Every day at my new school we said The Lord's Prayer and I had learnt it off by heart. We sang hymns and talked about being good Samaritans. I had a gingham school summer dress, the same as all the other girls. Granddad came to collect Antony and me every Friday, in his green Vauxhall Viva, and we went to stay with him, nana Edie and Spencer until Sunday evening. He would come in and have a cup of tea with mum first and they would have a chat, while we ran upstairs to pack our nightclothes, toothbrushes and a spare change of clothes. We didn't need to take toys with us, as there was always plenty to do at their house. Nana would cook sausage and mash for us, and make either a homemade rice pudding or semolina for dessert. Granddad would teach us how to play cricket and rounder's on Saturday morning before he settled in for the afternoon to watch "Grandstand". Spencer, Antony and I would play hide and seek. Spencer would make me hide and told me to count to a hundred, then they would come and look for me. They didn't always come and look, sometimes it was just a ploy to get rid of me, because Spencer said "You're a whinger and we want to play boys games. Girls can't play". Nana Edie worked at St. Catherine's College and would serve tables, once in a while she worked Saturday evening's, we would all bundle into the Vauxhall Viva to take her to work, while she was there, if it was winter, Granddad would pull the sofa up to the coal fire in the living room to keep us warm, then he would go to the kitchen cupboard and bring three white paper bags full of penny sweets out of hiding that he'd fetched earlier in the day. He smoked John Player's Specials and had probably got the sweets from the paper shop while buying his newspaper and cigarettes, as we still slept that morning. It was funny looking back, that he was softer and more affectionate when Nana wasn't there to witness it. It was as if he couldn't be gentle and silly with us in front of her. We would watch Saturday night viewing on TV. The likes of" The two Ronnie's ", "Starsky and Hutch" or "The Professionals". We would be half asleep and in our pyjamas, docilely sleepwalking or being carried back to the car, to go and pick Nana up again. She would wearily get in, still looking pleased to see us all the same, wanting to know how our evening was. Back at the house we would be shepherded up to bed, Spencer and Antony in the back room and me in their room in a single bed adjacent to their double bed. They would fret over the three of us, keep asking "Are you alright? Have you got enough covers? Are you going to be warm enough?" Even as they were laying blankets and overcoats on top of the eiderdowns on our beds. On Sunday we always had a roast and Sherry trifle or Lemon meringue pie. Nobody has since made a lemon meringue pie as good as Nana did. She would be up early on Sunday mornings baking, and always said it was a shame to have the oven on just for the roast, so that would be the day for making cakes. Before we went to bed on Saturday night she would remind us, "If you want to do some baking in the morning, you'll have to get up early and join me in the kitchen". Nana was a homely woman, with a proud bearing. Whenever we went to stay, she was always in the kitchen when we arrived, providing a delicious meal. She never questioned us about our home life, but always asked if mum was keeping well. Nana never said bad things about anyone, always smiling. She would stop in front of the hall mirror before going anywhere, to dab Yardley foundation powder on, would squint her eyes and apply lipstick, then blot her lips together to mute and blend the colour. The wardrobe in their bedroom had her hats on top of it, different colours and styles, some with veils. I had hours of fun trying on her hats in front of her dressing table mirror. After lunch on Sundays Granddad would take us to the Gog Magogs to walk in the woods. He would tell us to gather bird's feathers and leaves, so that when we got home, Nana and he would show us how to glue the feathers on card to make Indian headdresses and we would rub paper over the leaves with crayons to make intricate patterns. Life had started to get better.

Chapter 6

Speed Dating

1975

While Antony and I visited our grandparents at weekends, Mum was having a social life. I have never been able to fathom whether the relationship with my grandparents was a convenient one, so that Mum could get shot of us, and live it up at weekends, or if there was a genuine respect and fondness for them. Possibly it was a mixture of both. Mum had started to go out a lot more, and was looking healthy and strong. She had an air of vigour about her again. Buying new clothes and taking care in how she looked, there were patent platform shoes and boots in her bedroom closet, in shades of metallic hues. I would slip in and secretly try them on when she wasn't looking. My uncles popped in and out all the time, and mum went out with them at weekends. How she had come through the past few years and arrived at the lifestyle she was living now is almost inexplicable to me. To have been mistreated so badly, yet suddenly to be living such a wild and uninhibited lifestyle, and taking uppers or amps as they were called. I can only assume that she thought she was "self-liberating". We seemed to have men around us all the time. But where were they when she was being beaten time and again? No one came to intervene or maybe they felt interfere. Marriage was a bed you lay in, for better or for worse.

Melvyn was at the house often and his friends were showing a great deal of interest in her. Briefly she had a fling with a man called Mick. I didn't like him at all. If he came round and sat on the sofa near me, I would hold a cushion over my face and if he tried to speak to me I'd bury my face in it to block him out. He was married, but Mum didn't want him for keeps and anyway, he started to mess her around and was seeing other women besides her. Eventually, none too concerned, she told him "Don't think you can treat me like you treat your wife, so fuck off". The men that were on the scene were either intimidated by her apparent fierceness, or were drawn to what they thought they could tame. They knew the Pride family and their hot-tempered, fractious reputation.

Within the year mum met Tomas, which is in fact his nickname. He was born John William Moloney. His father was an Englishman and his mother Irish, and with that knowledge, to his friends he was forever to be Tomas. When Tomas first saw Carolyn he thought she had hair like a lion's mane. They met through Melvyn, as Tomas and he were friends. It was an all -nighter and everyone was getting high, drinking and dancing. The place to go was "The Still and Sugar Loaf". It was a club underneath the old Victoria cinema on Market Street in the centre of Cambridge. A trendy place to be, with a cellar bar that squaddies often frequented, there was a skeleton behind bars in a pretend jail for effect. It was always busy and fights often broke out, more often than not involving the Pride brother's. It was a heady time. People flocked to get intoxicated. Women wore miniskirts and closely fitting tops, with heels as high as they could stagger in. Men displayed chests with wide opened necked shirts, pointed collars and wide cuffs. Melvyn was always at the forefront, dressed in up to the minute clothes, looking sexy and behaving cool. Mum her other brothers, John, Nigel and Mark would be equally as fascinating. They're friends venerated them. Weekends were either spent there or at "The Dorothy". A venue renowned for having had "Small faces" and "Pink Floyd" showcase there. On one of these evenings, Tomas and Mum got talking and he asked her to dance. Later on he was off his face, none the less he asked

Melvyn if he could walk her home. Mum didn't feel threatened by him, as he was six years younger than her, only twenty one. There was something about him. He was a bit awkward, clumsy almost, in his obvious interest in her. He was trying hard to be cool, but there was an air of vulnerability about him that she liked, and he was a bit gauche. The tallness of him and his blue eyes, appealed to her, though he was almost a little too thin. But could he talk! And he was funny, really funny, with a sharp wit. When they got back to Godwin Close, she knew he thought she'd ask him in for coffee, but she virtually shut the door in his face with a "Yes, that'd be nice. Goodnight" as he stood on the doorstep asking if he could see her again. That was where it was to begin.

Antony and I became accustomed to this new face appearing at home. He was there more and more often and seemed to be there whenever we came back after the weekends. We tentatively liked him. He was always friendly and fun and mum seemed happy having him around. It was almost as if suddenly, he just lived there. We couldn't remember when it happened, and there wasn't a discussion or an introduction to it happening, but Tomas had moved in. It wasn't a big upheaval, and he didn't arrive with suitcases, as he didn't have very much. For a while it all rubbed along very well. We were quite a little family unit. Granddad would still come and fetch us, and he and Tomas got along fine. They had what seemed a mutual respect for each other. Granddad couldn't very well disapprove, when his own son wasn't around, and here was someone prepared to take us on.

Now things were becoming settled, we were on an even keel. Balance had been gained. It was decided, that perhaps, we should have contact with our Dad. Looking back now, I imagine it coincided with Tomas entering our lives. Nana and Granddad said Dad wanted to see us. Reflecting on that, I can hazard a guess that was only to assert to my Mum's new boyfriend, that we had a dad. As if we were belongings or products that he had sired, he needed to stamp authority on us and create a boundary for Tomas. But Mum wanted to do the right thing by Edie and Les, also believing we should have contact with our Dad. What harm could it do? He was behind bars. Antony, at any rate, absolutely wanted to see him. He reminded Tomas "We have a dad". Tomas agreed, we would still have our weekends at Nana and Granddads and if that meant we went to visit Dad on those weekends, then so be it. It suited them both to continue having their weekends without us, even if Dad was the compromise.

Our lives kept shifting and altering, as if seen through a kaleidoscope. Nothing ever panned out the way you expected. Even having Antony move in wasn't what I'd hoped. He didn't show me any affection and I didn't feel he even liked me. He would show off and brag about stuff all the time. He missed dad and often talked about him. Mum had been initially happy to have him home with us, but her interest in him wasn't as apparent now Tomas was with us. She used to watch him being dragged around the garden by Fred at Nana Sheila's and say to her "Isn't he beautiful! I just love him so much Mum".

The little toes on both of Antony's feet had grown so that they overlapped the other toes. He had worn such ill - fitting shoes, while living with Dad, that they had become crippled. It was impossible to separate them from the other toes, as they would simply curl back over. His toes are still like that today. Mum did try to persuade Antony that a doctor could make a hospital appointment and he could have them reset, but he refused and she didn't insist. The night terrors continued and now sometimes it was Tomas who would go to Antony in the middle of the night when he woke up screaming. He would hold him, saying "It's alright mate, there's nothing to be scared of, you're right here with me and I've got you". But he didn't want Antony to have counselling, and he said we could work out between us. We would deal with it as a family. When it dawned on the other parents at school that my Mum was one of the Pride's and that I was the daughter of David Charles, the friendships I had begun to make were soon cut short. Girls I had previously been invited to have tea with were suddenly being swept away with a protective arm after school, before invitations could be extended. They had seen the local news on TV and in the newspaper. Tomas was the one to console me when I sobbed at home, because a friend I thought I'd made suddenly wouldn't even speak to me, ignoring me in the playground, when once we had been holding hands, the best of friends.

It was on one of the weekends we were away, that Tomas surprised Mum. He had booked the registry office, chosen the ring, and arranged the date, and the time, booked a table for dinner and invited the immediate family. Without a clue she went with him into town. She had no idea. He had brought her a flattering brown, almost russet suit which she wore because he liked her in it. Maybe with some trepidation, or maybe because she didn't want to disappoint, whatever her thoughts were on that day, mum married Tomas. She stood outside afterwards in the bright sunlight of that March morning, Tomas's arm around her shoulders, her wild hair blowing in her eyes as she squinted at the camera, looking slightly sombre. Was her slight smile, only a half-smile, due to the glare of the sunlight in her eyes, or an apprehensive smile full of mixed emotions? What I do know is that she loved him.

Spencer, Antony and I were not invited or included at all. Antony and I came home to be told that they were married and that Tomas was our Step dad. That took a bit of explaining. We didn't know what that meant at all. We didn't know whether Tomas had told Nana and Granddad or if it was a surprise to them also. I was upset. I would have wanted to be there, and I was jealous. Who had been there? I stupidly thought that if you got married that meant bridesmaids. Did that mean Mum had some other little girl being a bridesmaid for her?

Chapter 7

Dustbin kid

Tomas was always a big funny character. He could talk the hind legs off a donkey and tell the most vivid stories. When he told a tale, he'd describe the people in detail and would get up and demonstrate their actions as he spoke. If Tomas was recounting a story, or moment from his day, he'd capture your imagination and you'd listen avidly. We would be rolling around with laughter. When we were growing up, sometimes if we were home for that weekend, he would play music, from whichever album it was that he might have bought that week, or an old favourite that he was in the mood for. If it was Meatloaf's "Bat out of hell" he would explain that it was a love song. Another example was Pink Floyd's "Another brick in the wall". He could be sensitive, and would write poetry for us, when he was coming down after a high. On the other hand, he could also fly off the handle at the slightest thing and get upset very quickly. You'd jump out of your skin when something displeased him, all of a sudden he would shout completely unexpectedly "Watch what you're fucking doing! Don't spill that drink, look where you're going!" Often it would be followed with a tirade about the carpet you might ruin or the how shitty that cup of tea was that you'd just made for him.

Mum would later tell me how she had rescued him. When they met, Tomas was an addict. He was hooked on LSD, as had Dad had been. Tomas, however, was never physically abusive. He didn't hit my Mum and he did seem to cherish her. She had helped him slowly withdraw from using, it was a pact that they'd agreed upon. If he wanted a relationship with her and wanted to live with us, and stay with us, then he would have to get clean. Having said that, he was allowed his misdemeanours at weekends. If they were going to have a night out, or he was going drinking with my uncles he might do some "Dexy's" or some sulphate. Mum would also dabble. Coming home on Sunday evenings after being in the care of my grandparents, the stark reality of home life could be very grim.

We would have had a couple of days of attentive nurturing. Drawing, making things with "Plasticine", baking cakes, playing rounders and cricket, followed by cuddles with nana on the sofa. We might have been learning finger knitting, or playing cards. It was always reliable and routine. There were rules and boundaries. If we were silly at the dinner table, talking with our mouths full, giggling and spraying food everywhere, or putting our elbows on the table, we would be sent to stand outside the backdoor until we had learned some manners. I argued with Granddad once because he told me to put my knife in my right hand. He said "Your knife always goes in the right hand, everybody eats with their knife in the right hand. Now stop messing about and do as you are told". I wasn't happy with that rule. "Who said we have to have the knife in our right hand Granddad? And what if I'm left handed? What if I can use my left or right hand?" He was annoyed at my facetiousness, and said "Get down from the table, go and stand outside the back door now!" I'd be so upset for annoying him and would really feel his disapproval. I wanted to be the apple of his eye "But Granddad! I didn't do anything wrong!" My bottom lip would be trembling and I would cry as I went and did as he'd instructed. It was never long before I'd realize if I went back in and apologized that would mean I'd learned some manners. On the way home on Sunday evenings, we often had conversations that involved us asking if we could stay with him and Nana, sometimes we would virtually be begging "Why Granddad? Why can't we stay with you!?" It was always the same. He would end up singing to us on our way home, trying to make us laugh and lighten the mood so that we wouldn't part unhappily. It was a silly song that he'd made up. "Well who's a silly? Youse a silly, I's a silly bugger!" He would remind us not to repeat it to anyone else, and certainly not Nana.

When we got home, the atmosphere was as if someone had died. The house would be dark, curtains nearly pulled, no joyful greeting for us. They would be irritated by us. We were full of the things we had done over the past couple of days and wanting to relay it back to them. They wanted us to be quiet. Our bath would be run, and we would get ready for bed almost as soon as we returned. Sometimes if they were feeling the munchies during their come down, we might be allowed to stay up long enough to take a list to the local Chinese to order a meal for them. If we were very lucky we might even get a bag of chips to share as a reward, and then bed. We felt unwanted.

Mum tried to explain to us that "Tomas is still only young, he needs looking after and he didn't have much love when he was growing up". She said we needed to try and understand him, and that we would understand more when we grew up. So Tomas would write us poems sometimes, and mum would read them to us when he wasn't around. Perhaps they were poems he wrote for her benefit, to convince her of his love for us. She was so proud of them. I wanted to believe he loved us, and I thought that if he could write such lovely things, that somewhere inside him, he did have a heart. I believed all I had to do was tell him I loved him, because all I wanted was somebody to tell me they loved me. "Tomas, do you know I love you? Because I do, I want to tell you that". He smiled at me and hugged me. When he hugged me it almost hurt, it was like being hugged by a bear, he gripped so tightly.

When Tomas was a child his mother and father would put him outside the back door in the dustbin. They would tell him if he didn't behave the bogey man would get him. They'd put the lid on the bin and go back indoors and shut the door. That is where they would leave him. I try so hard to remember this when I think of all the cruel things he has said to me and the awful things he has done. Cruelty comes in so many forms. People never think of the effect their words and actions will have on a child.

Chapter 8

Drought

1976

During 1976 we were all adjusting. Mum and Tomas were happy together, while Antony and I lived for the weekends. That year we had the hottest summer any of us had known. There were stand pipes and water rationing in some areas. It was awful trying to sleep at night, the heat was so overwhelming. Both Antony and I complained because we couldn't get comfortable in bed at night, and even a sheet without blankets, was too much. The windows were thrown wide, yet there was no breeze, it was so still outside. Riding our bikes around our neighbourhood after school, and when the holidays arrived, seemed the only way to keep cool. The breeze we created as we cycled, and the distraction was a relief. Often we would be at the little rec' through the passageway off our street, as there were swings there. Another opportunity for creating our own breeze. The sun had bleached our hair blonde and we had tanned arms and legs. It didn't occur to our parents to put sun cream on us before exposing us to its rays. Melanomas were, as yet unheard of. Nana Sheila had a white cat called Candy that had such badly burnt ears they looked like crisps, yet still the daft thing would bask in the sun. She was an affectionate creature that loved a fuss. I would sit on my haunches to stroke her, avoiding stroking her ears because running your fingers over them was not a pleasant sensation, for me or for her.

It was so hot that forest fires broke out in the south of England, and temperatures reached as high as 35 degrees. There were swarms of ladybirds. I rode my bike through masses of them and remember having to turn my face

51

away as I cycled to avoid getting them in my eyes. My armpits were sore from ladybird bites. They were swarming in search of food, as the spring had been so warm, that the aphid population that they fed on had collapsed. The soreness in my armpits was worse at night, it made trying to sleep even more impossible. Mum tried dabbing on Calamine lotion, but it didn't help.

There was a new family in our neighbourhood. They were black. We had heard Tomas comment "There's a bunch of chalkies moved in down the road, you'll see, it won't be long and the whole fucking tribe will turn up". This kind of opinion was a common theme in our house. Tomas was always spouting on about wogs, nig nogs and jungle bunnies. He always made some remark if Trevor McDonald was on ITN in the evening. It was an everyday occurrence for us to hear racist tirades from Tomas. Mum would often have to tell him to quieten down or say "That's enough now love!" It was on one of those hot summer afternoons, that Antony and I, while out on our bikes, rode through the rec', only to find a group of children from the new family swinging on what we thought of as our swings. As we cycled by we stared at them and they stared back, Antony shouted "What are you fucking looking at you nig nogs, why don't you go back where you came from!" They all stood, and we cycled as fast as we could peddle back home. We thought we had escaped confrontation and started to settle in for the rest of the afternoon before dinner, when mum said "What's going on out there?" She was peering through the net curtains at the front window in the living room, so we both strained to see what she was watching. Outside, on the grass verge opposite our house, were about twenty young black people. Brothers, sisters and cousins. They just sat, quietly all staring at our house. There wasn't any show of aggression or hostility. It was a display of strength and unity. They were shaming us, and I did feel ashamed. They were so proud and defiant. Mum looked at us and asked with a tight voice "What have you been doing?" Antony said "Nothing", while looking at the toes of his sandals, and I couldn't help but pipe up immediately with "It was him, he said bad things, called them names and told them to go back where they came from!" I couldn't stop myself. Antony and Spencer already called me a snitch or tell- tale. They didn't think I could keep a secret and that I was always telling the grown- ups on them. Mum was furious. She shouted at us "You shouldn't have said those things, you shouldn't bloody well repeat what Tomas says. Go to your room now, the pair of you!" We went, blaming each other. Mum had to go out and talk to them. She was nervous and embarrassed, but she went and apologised for us, and she didn't make us go and face them. Antony would have refused anyway. Somehow she eventually persuaded them that we would never behave that way again. Gradually, almost reluctantly, they dispersed and departed. They were the Cross family. Simon Cross would be in my class and one day would be my friend at secondary school.

Tomas was working as a slaughter man at an abattoir in Cambridge. He came home in the evenings, reeking of sweat and dried animal blood. It seemed to have seeped into the pores of his skin, and as he sweated the smell would intensify. Mum didn't even seem to notice! He would arrive home with knives wrapped in cloth, still in bloody overalls. Why on earth he didn't change before coming home I don't know, it just seemed perfectly normal back then. Sometimes he would bring home clear bags containing pigs' snouts and trotters, he'd call through to us "Samantha, Antony come and see what I've got for you! I've got you a new pet!" We'd run through to the kitchen with high expectations, excited and wondering if it was a new puppy or a box of kittens. There they would be, snouts and trotters hanging from the utensil rack. Tomas would laugh and get the bag down for us to examine

53

closely, he pointed out what was what and explained how he'd had to kill a lorry load of pigs that day. He often brought home different cuts of meat. The smell was repugnant to me, it would make me retch and I'd have to dash away gagging. It was the same if I went shopping with mum at our local shops where there was a butcher. There was sawdust on the butcher's floor and the smell there was the same as the smell of Tomas. We seldom brought food from a supermarket. There was one in the town centre, but the way we shopped then was to buy from our local stores within the community.

Ricky our dog, was a big part of our lives. Literally. If the letter box was rapped, Ricky was there, barking ferociously and standing on his back legs, huge front paws pressed against the glass in the door as he tried to get to our visitors before us. He wanted to be wherever we were. Mum was very fond of Ricky, as were Antony and I. Tomas wasn't so keen. Mum had allowed Ricky to dominate the bed and believe he was the alpha male in the house. That wasn't going to work, not for Tomas. Tomas had long shaggy hair now, wore huge flares and owned a t- shirt that said "Float like a butterfly, sting like a bee". Despite his declarations about Black people moving in to the neighbourhood, he seemed to have a contradictory respect for Muhammad Ali, whose one liners and quotes, not to mention prowess in the ring, had found a chink in Tomas's flawed psyche.

For a brief time after marrying Mum, when Tomas had been trying to occasionally visit his parents, and encouraged Mum to make an effort. They took it in turns to pop round. This time it was him, me and Ricky. We would walk to theirs and exercise our dog. He needed wearing out. We'd had a nice time, seen Tomas's parents and were coming home via a park near where they lived. It had been a good day. I was still anxious around Tomas without Mum and felt awkward. I wasn't much of a conversationalist, and still shy. It irritated Tomas if he tried to make conversation, if all he got were one word answers. "It's been nice hasn't it?" he asked "Did you enjoy today? Would you like to do this again?" I kept answering "Yeah". He would lose his temper and harshly say "Can't you say anything else!? You can fucking talk to me properly you know! I'm not going to bite you!" It made me want to cry and I walked along beside him, my chin on my chest, fighting back the tears. They had all told me enough times already what a cry baby I was. We continued walking, making our way to the swings, Ricky kept pulling on the lead, eager to get ahead, and be at the front. Tomas was swearing under his breath and yanking him back. When we came to the swings I jumped on and pushed off, leaning my body back and using my legs to swing out and gain momentum. I remembered Spencer showing me how and Nana and Granddad teaching me at the rec' near their house. I was picking up speed and getting a gentle rhythm going. It was fun. I began to feel a bit happier. Tomas tied Ricky to the post of the swing frame and said "Here, I'll give you a push". He started pushing me gently, and I was laughing. It was great. This is what Dads did with their little girls! He pushed harder and I swung higher, I was going faster and higher still. He was laughing with me and shouting "How's that?! You're going really high now! Are you enjoying it?" I looked down and the ground was speeding away from underneath me. Holding on tighter, I was beginning to panic. I tried to turn and look at Tomas, the chains twisted, and the swing jerked to the left with me "I don't like it!" I was screaming back "I want to get off, I want to get off!" At that moment Rick although leashed to the frame was still within reach of Tomas. He leapt up and launched himself at him. I was screaming with terror, Ricky was going for him, snarling, teeth bared and snapping at his face. His great paws were on Tomas's shoulders and he'd pushed him to the ground. Tomas threw him off, shouting

55

at him "Sit! Sit! You stupid mongrel. Ricky, Sit!" Ricky wouldn't sit but still glared at Tomas and barked loudly, remonstrating at him almost it seemed for pushing me too high and frightening me. Tomas grabbed the chains of the swing, bringing it to an abrupt halt "That's it now, that's enough. We're going home, come on, get off!" he pulled me by the arm and said "Whatever's the matter with you, you silly girl! I was only pushing you! All you had to say was stop!" He was furious. Other parents and children in the park were watching, mouths agape, looking at each other and exclaiming in hushed voices. Tomas untied Ricky, I went to stroke him and Tomas shouted at me "No, Leave him. He's a bad dog. A bad dog!" He lifted Ricky up by his collar with all his might, Ricky's back legs dangled off the ground and he looked as if he were trying to shrug out of his collar. Tomas punched him in the head, as if he were punching a man in a bar brawl. Ricky was yelping with fear and shock. Tomas wrestled him to the floor and they rolled around as he punched Ricky again and again. Ricky howling with anguish and fear, tried to get away and was cowering from Tomas as he dragged him up by the lead, back onto his feet. Finally both standing again, Ricky shying from him and looking at him from under his worried brow, Tomas dusted his jeans down and looked around him at the onlookers staring "What the fuck are you lot looking at!" he said, and with that we made our way home. The three of us, our heads hung low.

When the incident was retold to Mum, she was horrified. Tomas told her "It's me or the dog". He emphasized how Ricky had attacked him, he said Ricky couldn't be trusted, and that he didn't want him in the house. Eventually, after arguing and pleading at length, Tomas's persuasion won. Mum felt she had no choice but to agree that Ricky would have to go. Tomas said he would take him. He insisted that he had a mate at work that would have him. Mum was going to let Ricky go. We had got him to be our protector. He had given us our first sense of security when we were coming together as a family again, and now we were saying goodbye. When we came home from school he was gone. We never saw him again. We don't know what happened to him. Tomas jokingly told us that he'd taken him to the slaughterhouse and put a bolt through his head.

The visits to Tomas's parents also came to an abrupt halt, as had Ricky's existence in our lives. Tomas's parents didn't take to Mum. They thought she was no better than she ought to be. His mum (coming from a Catholic background) didn't approve of a divorced woman with three children getting her claws into her son. She alleged that Mum was no better than a prostitute. Meanwhile, when Mum made attempts for Tomas's benefit, to befriend and include them in our lives, her new father in law kept trying to send me outside to play so that he could make advances on her. When we did visit, if Tomas's Mum was at work, his dad would try bribing me with sweets and a rubber ball to go out and play, so he could try to touching up my Mum. She made me promise never to leave her alone with him if we had to visit. Eventually she refused to visit either of them anymore and when Tomas learned why he vowed never to see them again.

Chapter 9

The Cambridge conspiracy trial

1976

My family were making lots of noise about how dreadful my Dad was, how he was a coward and wasn't right in the head. He should never have been born. Antony and I were absorbing this information subconsciously in the background. It must have felt nice for them to have the moral high ground for a change. Suddenly they had honour and principles compared to the atrocity committed by my Dad. In comparison their offences were minor short comings. They believed there was honour amongst thieves and that they were "Robin Hood" figures, only they weren't taking to give to the poor. They took so that they could fuel their addictions and garb themselves in the trappings of successful racketeering entrepreneurs. My uncles deported themselves with arrogant conceit, an array of different girlfriends between them, the girlfriends and my Mum basking in the limelight of their notoriety throughout Cambridge. They were bankrolled by their misdeeds, which kept them fashionably turned out, and euphoric for the weekend all –nighters which would begin as soon as Antony and I were out of the way at our grandparents. There were often events, however, we were privy to. We had often witnessed Tomas and my uncles using a set of scales in the dining room to weigh up sulphate or amphetamines, before being shooed away.

It was a school day, begun with the normal routine, getting up in my nightie and making my way downstairs for breakfast with Antony in tow. Still bleary eyed and bedraggled from our beds, Tomas had already left for work. Mum was in the kitchen in her dressing gown, which was odd because she was cooking already. That wasn't part of the normal routine. Usually our nostrils were awakened by the waft of cigarette smoke reaching us before we saw her. Habitually her morning routine was to get herself a cup of tea before we were awake. She'd drink that accompanied with an Embassy No6, to bolster her in preparation for us descending on her as soon as we woke. This morning the smell of bacon greeted us. Catching movement from the corner of her eye, she saw us heading towards the living room ready to flop around on the sofa while we waited for breakfast. She came towards us hurriedly, "You two, don't go making too much noise. Your uncle Melvyn is in there. You behave yourselves and don't touch anything!" She spoke quickly with a hushed voice. We couldn't be suppressed though, Melvyn was there and we loved him. Immediately we were excitable, wide awake now, the residue of sleep vanishing in an instant. Pushing open the living room door we were falling over each other to see him, while mum admonished "What did I just say!" She followed in behind us. The curtains were still drawn and the dim living room light was on. As we entered the room the scene before us was like something from a fairy tale, Aladdin's cave. In front of us, the coffee table was overflowing with stacks of notes and piles of coins, Melvyn and Mum must've been counting the money before we got up. Beside the piles of cash were heaps of jewellery and coils of necklaces entangled together, and draped over the edge of the table. Scattered amongst the chains there were beautiful rings in all sizes, with gemstones twinkling in different colours, there were rubies, emeralds, sapphires and diamonds. Some of the jewellery had slipped to the floor around the table, and there were black bin bags in the armchair with more trinkets and notes spilling out. We were awestruck. We had never seen such an incredible sight. Melvyn was slumped on the sofa, half nodding off and half awake.

Smiling at us he was delighted to see us, slightly slurring he greeted us jubilantly "Hello Samantha and Antony, come and give me a hug." He was happy, an air of celebration was in the room, leaning forward he held an arm out ready for an embrace, and scooped both of us in to him. It was then I noticed the other arm lay motionless, hand palm up in his lap. Around his forearm was tied his belt with a needle hung, forgotten about, in the crease of the joint between his arm and elbow. It was very curious, I didn't understand what that was. Mum suddenly realizing, scooted around the coffee table to remove the needle and untied the belt. She pushed Melvyn backwards to settle against the sofa and told us "There, just sit next to Melvyn on the sofa and don't be a nuisance, he's tired. Been at work all night, haven't you Melvyn?" They laughed together and Melvyn asked Mum to light him a cigarette. Putting two cigarettes in her mouth and sparking up the lighter she waved it across both until the ends glowed red. Once alight the smoke streamed from her nostrils as she sucked then exhaled to ensure they were definitely burning. Leaning forward she pressed Melvyn's cigarette between his lips as he smiled vaguely, with his eyes half lidded. Antony and I slid out from under the crook of his arm now. We were keen to examine the haul on the table but mum chastised us again "Leave stuff alone! That's not to be played with…" Before she could finish, as she was flapping our hands away, Melvyn interrupted "Leave them be Carolyn, let them have a look." Turning his attention to us he said "You can touch, but don't mess up the notes and coins, we've spent ages counting that lot. Be good and I'll let you choose something." We were elated. Mum was about to protest when, sliding a wad of notes towards her, he said "If you make me a slap up breakfast, this is yours." She grabbed his face and planting a kiss firmly on top of his head, hastened back to the kitchen. As Melvyn hovered between sleep and consciousness he smiled benignly at us, enjoying the sight of me gingerly picking up chains and trying on rings. Antony stood watching, unsure, one hand down the back of his pyjamas scratching his bum, and the other hand with his thumb jammed in his mouth. Deciding to follow my lead, he started to finger through the jewellery on the table too. He was more interested in the coins and Melvyn gently asked him "Would you like some money? Hey, how about I give you some money to buy yourself some sweeties or a toy instead? How does that sound my little mate?" Antony nodded eagerly, managing to answer even with his thumb still in place "Yes please Uncle Melvyn!" Melvyn took Antony's hand from his mouth, dropped a handful of coins into it. Antony looked at Melvyn adoringly and hopped back up onto the sofa to snuggle up again. I was still probing through the mass on the table, looking for the one thing that would catch my eye. There was too much to choose from, and I was overwhelmed by it all. Melvyn chuckled at me. He knew I was struggling to make a choice and slurred dozily "Here, let me have a look, I'll find something just right for you. You're only a little old girl, you don't want anything too big." He sifted amongst the charms and finally, squinting and peering at one particular chain, he lifted it out from the rest. Holding it before my eyes draped over his fore fingers, there dangled the most delicately beautiful thing I had ever seen. It was the thinnest, lightest filigree chain and the pendant that hung from it was the littlest outline of an apple, complete with one tiny leaf sprouting from its stem. Inside the body of the apple one minute ruby was inlaid. "This is the one for you. Perfect for a little girl." Melvyn offered it forward to me and I took it, running directly to the kitchen for Mum to put it around my neck, without even pausing to say "Thank you."

That morning was probably one of the happiest moments of my childhood. Better than any Christmas morning. It was drilled into us not to tell a soul what we'd seen. We could tell our friends that our Uncle had given us money

61

for sweets, or bought me a necklace, but we mustn't ever describe the events of that morning, not even to Nana or Granddad.

On the 10th of November 1976 Melvyn appeared in court charged with six other men. They had all been operating as a team of burglars and were charged with committing a list of offences throughout East Anglia. It was one of the biggest criminal trials in Cambridge. There were a total of 28 charges and all seven men pleaded not guilty. Thousands of pounds in money and property had been taken from all over East Anglia. Jewellers, post offices, shops and chemists were the targets. Residents were affected too, household burglaries increased, people were waking up to discover their savings and valuables had been taken while they slept. The trial would last several weeks, the men were described as operating as a gang led by two leaders, who one was referred to admiringly as "The Man". One of the other members of the gang was Brian, my Nana's one armed ex-boyfriend. He was the one who, unwittingly, had drawn the attention of the police through his inefficiency. He'd generously taken a new girlfriend to see some of the haul they'd acquired and allowed her to choose some jewellery for herself. She later bragged to a friend, who then subsequently reported it to the police. Melvyn was arrested as he tried to escape from the scene of a burglary at the Co Op in Ely. He and an accomplice from the gang had accessed the hardware department to gather the tools needed to break the safe. Having made it away with the money via the roof, an alarm went off. Despite setting the car radio to the frequency used by the police, they were captured when road blocks were set up to stop them.

The case when it went to court was called "The Cambridge Conspiracy Trial." It was described as one of the biggest criminal trials in Cambridge and the headlines read "Men went on orgy of crime." Thousands of pounds in money and property had been stolen, the jury heard how safes had been attacked using explosives or hauled away and forced open. All of the men pleaded "Not guilty." Witnesses were brought in to tell the jury how the men were still conspiring even while on remand. An inmate from prison, who had been sharing a cell with Melvyn and another man told the court how Melvyn had explained he'd "Got caught after doing a safe." The witness described having overheard them organizing more offences on the outside to weaken the strength of the case. Forensics provided the most overwhelming evidence. Having taken clothing from the suspects, tests discovered pin head traces of glass and safe ballast. During sentences the men were given a total of thirty five years between them. The judge presiding looked across at the men and said sternly "The tragedy of it is that all of you are able men and you chose to use your talents for crime." Looking then to the court he pronounced "The people of Cambridge will now find it a little easier to sleep in their beds."

"The Man" was sentenced to seven years in prison. To Brian the Judge stated "You are a pathetic character, but you are not as harmless as you appear. I am satisfied that you are up to your neck in this conspiracy. I sentence you on the conspiracy charge to six years, and five years concurrent for other offences." Melvyn the fifth man to be sentenced was given six years and three years concurrent. The judge told him "You are and have been a thorn in the side of the police and the citizens of the city and county of Cambridge for too long."

Chapter 10

Cowboys and Detectives

Parents advised their children to stay away from us at school, and the few times Mum did come to school, they gave her wary, disapproving glances. We liked to dress up and play act. Having watched countless westerns such as "High Chaparral" and "Bonanza". Not having a throng of friends didn't prevent Antony or me from using our vivid imaginations and creating our own theatre. We pretended to be "Starsky" and "Hutch". Our bicycles would became horses or motorbikes, dependent on our make believe characters. Often I would initiate a game we would play, becoming a male lead like "John Wayne" and putting Antony in a nightdress so that I could rescue him as I rode into town on my horse. Antony would have to sit cross bar on my bike so that I could ride away into the sunset with him. Mum and Tomas were happy when we were out of the way, and we had lots of freedom as long as we were home for dinner. We invariably were, because we were always hungry. Our stomachs never let us down, they were our internal meal time gongs. When dinner was finished the routine was a cup of tea, then some biscuits in front of the TV before bed. Bedtime was 6pm every evening. During the summer months we would lay listening to the sounds of other children playing in back gardens. Whispering to each other, we would plan our lives and share our hopes and dreams, until Tomas would shout up the stairs, "Shut up! Don't make me come up there! You'll get a good hiding if I do!" The authority in his voice was enough to silence us. It was never necessary for him to hit us and he never did.

We all missed Melvyn, and we didn't see so much of our other uncles now. John and Nigel were each married and Mark came less often. Still a constant visitor, he would visit more during the day, while we were at school and Tomas was at work. He still looked to Mum as the mother figure who'd raised him, and he could have her to himself then. Melvyn was often mentioned and the adults loved to reminisce about the escapades he'd had, some they'd been part of, some they'd heard tales of. Antony and I listened avidly. We hero-worshipped him and listening to the grown-ups talking about him with such devotion and respect, we knew he must have some special kind of magic.

Dressed in jeans and shirts, we had an idea. Antony had toy guns and a holster, he wore one of the guns and I stuffed the other in the waist band of my jeans. We both donned cowboy hats, and taking two scarves from mum's bedroom drawers, we took ourselves out on our bikes. It was late afternoon. The day had been dry and dusty, just as we'd seen in the westerns. We cycled to our local shops in Wulfstan Way. We'd lost count of how many times we'd frequented the shops there, whether with Mum, or popping in on our way home from school. We knew every one of the shop keepers. We'd previously taken folded notes, holding the money from mum or Tomas for cigarettes, to the offy, which they were too lazy to go and fetch for themselves. There was Mr Cruickshank the butcher, where I would have to wait outside while mum bought our meat for the week, because the smell made me sick. Mike and Julie who ran the chippy, Mr Hall the hairdresser, and a formidable couple called Mr and Mrs Rowland that owned the "Maid Marian" grocery store. Starting at the "Maid Marian", throwing our bikes on the floor, wheels still spinning and tugging the scarves up over our faces, we pointed our guns at the shopkeeper "This is a stick up" Give us your money or your lives!" Stunned, red with indignation, Mr Rowland shouted at us "Get out! Go on clear off! I'll be telling your Mother about the pair of you! Go on now!" We scarpered, undeterred, across the road with our bikes to the next shop. Avoiding the butcher's for obvious reasons (and because they had meat cleavers) we headed to Mr Hall's. He chuckled at us humorously and opening the till, gave us a few coppers. This gave us motivation and urged us on to Mike and Julie's chip shop (we by-passed the newsagents, intending to head there last when we had our ill-gotten gains) Julie looked annoyed and gestured to us to leave, but Mike feeling a little more kindly towards us said "Aw they're only kids, mucking about. It's just a lark." He gave us a bag of fritters each. Onwards, peering through the off license door, we could see there was a queue at the counter. Not wanting too much of an audience we sat down on one of the bench's to enjoy our fritter's contentedly. Vinegar seeped through the bottom of the bag between my fingers and I'd poured on so much salt, that I desperately needed a drink. Collecting a small bag of penny blackjacks and fruit salad chews from the newsagents, we went home.

A few days later, when Tomas was told of our antics by one of the shop keepers, he was livid. We weren't allowed out to play on our bikes for days after that. Even baby-faced felons had to pay the consequences.

Chapter 11

The Keep

1975

Wandsworth Prison was built in 1851 and today is the largest prison in the UK. It is referred to as "The Grey Lady" because of its reputation for being haunted by a previous female inmate in a veil. Women inmates in Victorian times wore veils to protect their identities. Originally it was designed that each prison cubicle would have its own toilet facilities. These were removed to make extra space for more prisoners, this reintroduction to the humiliating routine of "Slopping out" their own waste every day until as recently as 1996. The last execution at Wandsworth Prison was in 1961. Previous inmates of notoriety include the likes of Charles Bronson and Ronnie Kray. In 2015 alone over £300,000 worth of drugs were seized with the aid of sniffer dogs inside the prison. Inmates include murderers, rapists and drug dealers.

Nana and Granddad were going to start taking Spencer, Antony and me to visit Dad. He was in Wandsworth Prison. If anyone was to ask us where our Dad was, we had to tell them he was in hospital. Nobody explained what we were to say was wrong with him. Granddad came and picked us up on a Friday night, as was the usual routine. There was a new mutual respect between him and Tomas. Despite, Tomas still being at work when Granddad came, occasionally they would meet.

At Nana and Granddads, Spencer was unimpressed by our reaction to seeing Dad. He had already been a few times and it didn't seem to be much of an issue with him. Often he would appear far more sophisticated than us. He didn't react to things the way we did, and was much more controlled. He was, however, demanding of Nana and Granddad, and they catered to his every whim. If he wanted to learn to play the trumpet, a brand new trumpet was bought. It would be there gleaming in its case and Spencer took great pleasure in showing it to us. By the following weekend, the novelty would have already worn off, and the lessons would fizzle out.

He was quite mean to us at times and it was usually him that decided which games we would play. If we played knights in the back garden, using the metal bin lids as shields, Spencer would decide I couldn't play, because I was a girl. However, the great thing about having an older brother, was that we had more freedom. We could go out on our bikes a bit further afield if Spencer were with us. Across the road from Nana and Granddads house you could get down an embankment to where the cattle market was held, it was close to the train lines, not far from Mill Road Bridge. In those days it was easy to play near train tracks, now there are all sorts of barriers, fencing and security to prevent such stupidity. There was an old air raid shelter or bunker, and we could play down there too. It was pretty scary though, because inside it was pitch black. You could walk through it from one end and come out the other side. If it had rained, it would get flooded, and you'd have to wade through. Spencer was always daring Antony or I to do it. We did a couple of times, with the aid of a torch. Spencer made dares, but seldom attempted them himself first. We were always the test dummies beforehand. The three of us were active, physically capable, busy bodies. Cycling, running, climbing, chasing and hiding from each other. Loving and hating each other. We shared the same dad and we were all going to see him together. Antony was excited, so pleased, he kept going on and on about it. I was mixed up. There were feelings of betraying Tomas, as he was the one looking after us, but these feelings also conflicted with wanting to see my Dad out of curiosity. After all he was my real Dad. The thought of seeing him, being in the same room as him, frightened me too. Granddad tried to allay all our concerns. It was alright, we would all be there together, and Dad was going to be happy to see us. He was missing us and wanted to see how much we were all growing up. I didn't trust dad. I did trust Granddad.

It was an early start. We were all up and taking turns to use the bathroom. Nana was making noises. Spencer and Antony giggled outside the door and she called out "Oh! I'm sorry! It's only flatulence". Spencer laughed and explained that flatulence meant farting. She emerged, slightly flushed and embarrassed, in a quilted dressing gown, with her hair net on, and rollers in her fringe "Hurry up, we all have to get ready. We've got a journey today and we mustn't be late". We all dressed up in our smartest clothes, while Granddad polished all our shoes on the back door step. He was wearing a chunky knitted cardigan that had leather elbow pads. His thinning hair was brushed smartly back off of his forehead, the "Brylcreem" was barely noticeable. I had a dress to wear and nana helped to put my hair in bunches .She wasn't very good at platting, which was the way I preferred to wear it. Mum was the best at platting, but Nana was gentle and would kiss the top of my head when it was done. Before we left, Nana paused in the hall mirror to apply her face powder and lipstick, as she always did before leaving the house. I wonder how she felt, going to visit her only child in prison. Between them my Nana and Granddad would never give up on my Dad. What he had done wouldn't stop them from loving him and forever trying to straighten him out. All in the Vauxhall Viva now, we set out. Nana with her supply of lime and chocolate eclairs stashed in her bag to keep us content on the journey, us already asking how far it was and how long that would take. On the way, we stopped at a layby for a toilet break, where there was a hill that sloped up and over into a field beyond. The three of us ran wildly up the hill to see what was on the other side and discovered a herd of sheep grazing. We hadn't seen sheep in the flesh before, only in books or on TV. We were puffing and panting at the top as granddad made his way to catch up with us. We pointed enthusiastically, jumping up and down and breathlessly chorused "Look Granddad! Sheep! They live here, there must be a farm here somewhere!" That hillside was going to become a familiar sight for us as our visits to Wandsworth Prison were going to become a routine. It was the place we would always stop, it was where we could stretch our legs and let off some anxiety and tension half way.

Wandsworth Prison, was a huge great hulking Victorian building. It was so solid and square in structure. With flat rooftops it looked like a fortress. Several police vehicles were parked outside, and it seemed it very menacing. My hand clutched Nana's, as we headed towards the queue of people waiting outside the enormous heavy wooden doors. They were families there, also to visit a son, brother, boyfriend or father. There was a glum hush about us, nobody really spoke to each other and there was no conversation. There was a rattling and clanking, and the door opened, as a prison guard finally came to shepherd us all in. I was already feeling worried. What if they didn't let us back out? How would we find the way back? Would they forget that we were in there? Would the prisoners be nice to us? I was scared. We were going to a place where bad people lived, they were being kept locked up there away from us, yet we were going to visit. The guard led us through security to another room, where there were several other guards. They inspected everybody's bags and assessed how we were behaving, and what we were carrying. Granddad was polite, they talked and laughed easily with him when he made a joke "Edith was going to bake a cake and try to smuggle a file in, but I told her you lot would want to eat it before it even got to David" he was a familiar face to them now, and they understood that the visitors resorted to this kind of joviality as a coping mechanism. The security checks done, we were now led to a room that had tables and chairs at even intervals around it. A serving hatch was opened and some women with tabards were behind it in a little tuck shop. There were chocolate bars and snacks, pale green cups and saucers, an urn, and the biggest tea pot ever. Spencer already knew the drill and went to sit down at one of the tables. Antony and I still clung to Nana, gently letting go of our grip she encouraged us to sit down. Antony was sucked his thumb and rubbed his nose with his forefinger, while I sat on my hands. There were guards in uniforms and hats around the room, a couple of them sitting at a table at the front. They watched all of us and spoke quietly to one another. We all waited in nervous expectation.

Eventually, a door opened and men began filing into the room, all wearing matching trousers and faintly checked pale blue shirts. They all had a coloured band worn across their chests, almost as if at school on sports day at school. The men took seats at tables, were greeted by their families, and the atmosphere lightened. There was a sense of relief, chairs scraped as people stood and smiled, hugged and clasped hands. Then, there was Dad, still the same swagger, heading to our table all smiles, arms wide. Spencer just sat there, having been before, but neither, Antony or I ran to meet him. Granddad and Nana stood, Granddad patting him on the back and Dad saying "Alright old fella? Good to see you Pops ", and pecking Nana on the cheek. She was weeping and trying to wipe the tears away with a tissue from her handbag "Aw now, none of that mum, no water works!" he said, then turning his attention to us, first Antony. "Here you are, my little man, come and give your Dad a kiss!" Antony went cautiously and was pulled into an embrace. His arms slid around Dad's neck, his feet on tip toes as he strained to get closer. It was the first time Antony had seen dad since the events of that awful, fateful night had put him here. Yet Antony unreservedly wanted to hold, and be held by him. He was the only one who didn't remind him of what he had done, his love for him was unfaltering. Dad, still with an arm around Antony, leant over to Spencer and ruffled his hair. Spencer hated it and almost recoiled from his touch, but Dad just chuckled humorously and turned his attention to me.

This was our big reunion, the moment I had been dreading. I'd been assured again and again by everyone that it was safe, Dad was different now. He wouldn't hurt anybody, he was seeing special doctors and they were helping him to get better. When he wasn't looking at me I could study him comfortably, unobserved by him, he was like an insect in a jar. I knew it was usual for children to love their parents, but when I watched him he made me feel sick with fear and anger. He turned to look at me, our eyes met, and I felt as if he could see right into me. Looking back at him, I was certain he could read the thoughts racing through my mind. I wanted to scream at him "I know you, I know what you've done! I hate you, I don't want you and I wish you were dead!" Still I sat on my hands, squirming in my seat. "Sammy, well…you're really growing up, don't you want to give your old man a kiss?" I wasn't "Sammy" that was another little girl, not me. Nobody called me Sammy. I was Samantha, Tomas always said so. That is who I was. I wished Tomas was there. My shoulders hunched up and I tried to sink into myself, bowing my head and peering at him from under my hair. I shook my head and looked at granddad with imploring eyes. Granddad pulled me towards him and said swiftly "She's a bit of a shy one, our Samantha. You'll need to give her a bit of time David. It's all very unusual for them, being here and seeing you after so long". I recognised the fleeting expressions across his face, and I could still remember what they meant. He hadn't changed, it was obvious even to me. Our visit was an awkward and uncomfortable meeting, the three adults sitting there talking about how Dad was getting on and he pretending buoyant optimism about spending his time there in productive ways. He was going to take up as many courses as he could while he was there and do his utmost to improve himself, mentioning further education and the opportunities he would have available to him. I don't know if he was sincere in his optimism at that point, and that dwindled away, or if it was only ever to allay Nana and Granddads concerns and to lessen the obvious distress they felt at his circumstances. Yet although I was only a child, I could detect the tone of relief in their voices and behaviour. They felt safer knowing he was there, and happier believing he would receive the medical attention he needed to mend his rationale and bring him back to logic and reason.

A routine I came to recognize at each visit, that I'd failed to see initially, was that every time, as if scripted, Dad would always say to Granddad "Pops, have you got a bit of spare change? The kids might like a treat, a bar of chocolate or a pack of crisps". At this point they would look at each, other sending some unspoken signal and granddad would rummage in his pocket for some loose change. He would push the coins across the table towards Spencer "Go and get yourself, Samantha and Antony a Kit Kat and a packet of chewing gum for your Dad". Spencer, sighing heavily, dolefully plodded over to the counter. The ladies there cooed and clucked as they saw him approaching. What no one seemed to notice was that when granddad had pulled the coins from his pocket, he had also pulled out the tiniest wad of notes folded again and again, until they were the tightest, smallest square he could make. Keeping his hand on the table he rested it lightly over the square. Our table had an air of expectancy about it, as we waited for our chocolate bars, and Dad waited for his exchange. The officers around the room and sitting at the front table, chatted to each other, yawning and wearily watching the clock. When Spencer brought back the treats, we greedily consumed our chocolate, as Dad unwrapped the foil from a stick of gum and pushed it into his mouth. Granddad casually removed his hand from the square of money, then Dad fluidly would brought his own hand around, to cover it, and then taking the foil from the gum, he folded that around the tiniest wad of cash, until it was as compressed as he could make it, before putting it in his mouth to seal with the gum and swallow. The exchange complete, conversation resumed. Once I had questioned what I'd witnessed, on the way home "Granddad, what was that you gave Dad? Why did he swallow it with his chewing gum?" I asked unknowingly. "That was nothing for you to worry about Samantha. It was just some money to help your Dad buy things like cigarettes". He was quite open with me, and explained to us all that it was a secret. We mustn't ever make a fuss about it while we were there, and were told that Dad only got a little bit of pocket money which wasn't enough to buy the things he needed. In hindsight I wonder if they were as naïve as us.

This was to be the pattern for our visits to see our dad. During the six years that he was away he sent us cuddly toys and strange pieces of art work, that were like 3D spiral graphs made from coloured threads, woven around multiple tacks on black backgrounds. They must've been the products of the many courses he'd said he'd attend to improve himself. When we returned home to Mum on Sunday evenings, I'd feel embarrassed and stupid. Tomas asked what it was I had tucked under my arm, I'd have to show him the latest gift from Dad, and he'd look scornfully at my new teddy bear or artwork, while I squirmed under his inspection of the gift. I was ashamed to bring it into the house, feeling like a traitor for having accepted it. I sporadically wet my bed at night from this time until I was twelve years old.

Chapter 12

Cottontails

At last, all our begging and pleading had gotten us somewhere. Tomas relented, agreeing that we could have pet rabbits. Real live rabbits, not dead ones that hung upside down by their bound legs, from the utensil rack in the kitchen. Antony and me were in high spirits, Tomas had been offered two rabbits and a large hutch, from someone he knew at work. It was very important that we understood, they would be our responsibility, we would have to clean them out and remember to feed them regularly. We crowed with delight when he said "Ok. You can have them, but remember you've promised to take care of them, not just for two weeks and then when you're bored of them you forget about them. If that happens, I'm warning you I'll get rid of them". We should have known what that meant, really. I was seven now, and Tomas emphasized that seven was the age of reason. I should be old enough to think things through and make decisions. I was sure I was old enough to look after two little rabbits, I could do it.

They were both a mixture of grey and white, with lovely little fluffy white tails, and long floppy ears. They looked exactly the same, and we couldn't tell them apart, which was disappointing and annoyed Antony "How are we supposed to know which one's which? I won't know which one's mine!" Despite his remonstrations, we settled on calling them "Salt" and "Pepper". Tomas had set the hutch up in one of the sheds in our back garden, the one nearest to the back door. Our garden was quite long and we had three sheds along it, each one different. The one nearest to the house was brick and had been built at the same time as the house. Two thirds of the way along the garden there was a metal shed, which was going rusty and had a broken window. The third shed was just before the end of the garden and made of wood. The garden itself reflected the sheds, the top half was well kept, with bushes around it and a small lawn. Mum had planted a rose that climbed the side of the shed wall, it had a wonderful scent. We would use this part of the garden in the summer and could sit out on a blanket. In the summer it was a great suntrap. Mum liked to sunbathe here, sheltered by the bushes from neighbours. I remember finding desiccated insects and burying them, while saying "The Lord's Prayer". The second third of the garden, around the metal shed was mud. It had been intended as a vegetable patch, but had become redundant. Before Tomas came along, when the soil was soft enough Antony and I would sit in it and make mud pies. Mum let us, and would laugh at how messy we got. She'd make us strip outside the back door before we ran upstairs to the bath. This part of the garden was fenced, but we could see over into the neighbouring garden. They had a cherry tree and a greengage tree. We admired the feat it must have taken, because both were covered in netting to prevent bird's eating all the fruit. The netting didn't prevent Antony and me from scrumping though. The couple next door got really fed up with us and complained to Mum about it. She told us "The lady next door doesn't want you keep stealing their fruit, you mustn't keep climbing over there. If Tomas finds out you won't hear the end of it". We felt very indignant that they didn't want us sharing their fruit, when there was so much of it. It seemed very unfair. They were an older couple with grown up children that had left home. The lady always wore bright red lipstick, so we called her "Mrs Lipstick Face from next door". Mum couldn't hide the laughter in her eyes when we told her what we'd named her "Don't you let her know that's what you call her!" We did, however come to a truce in the end. Mrs Lipstick

Face, said we could have as much of the windfall as we liked, but not take any fruit from the tree. That was alright with us, we just had to search a bit for the nice fruit, as lots of it was already beginning to rot.

The last third of the garden with the wooden shed was hardly ever used by us. There were a few spindly trees struggling to survive there, sparse grass, and patchy shrubs around the perimeter, that marked the divide between our garden and our neighbours. This last section backed onto the house behind us, but their garden was long also, so we were well set back from their house. Despite having three sheds, we only used the one nearest the house, and even then there was just an old wardrobe and an old window frame behind it, still with some broken shards of glass in place. There was plenty of room for our rabbit's hutch, and it meant during the winter we could easily duck out the back door to feed them and dive back in again to escape the cold. Tomas provided an old rug from somewhere that was large enough to cover Salt and Pepper's hutch at night.

Tomas was constantly asking us after school "Have you fed your rabbits today? Did you do it this morning? Have you bothered since you came in from school?" It was frustrating. I was trying very hard to remember, but I would forget in the mornings, in the rush to get ready for school. I was never awake enough to think about Salt and Pepper, and I was always in a hurry not to be late. Tomas always asked me, and Antony wasn't interested in them anymore, his chopper bike or "Bionic man" doll preoccupied him now. I kept doing things wrong, I'd feed them but forget to fill up the water bottle. I would put off cleaning them out, because the hutch was so large it seemed like a mammoth task. Nobody offered to help me and I couldn't work out what was the easiest, most suitable way to clean the hutch. I would try to pet Salt and Pepper, as I did love the feel of their fur under my fingers.

77

It wasn't easy catching one of them to hold and sometimes they would go for me, springing forward and almost growling, back paws thumping. When I did manage to get one by the scruff of the neck (like Tomas had shown me) it would almost box me with its front paws. Then when I had hold of one of them, I'd feel its heart racing so fast with sheer terror, the beat pulsing against my rib cage. As I was trying to soothe it, the terrified creature would scrabble against me to escape. I was beginning to feel the whole experience was very unpleasant. Having rabbits wasn't living up to expectations.

It was almost like a sixth sense. I had a strange feeling. It occurred to me while I was at school one day, I must remember today to check Salt and Pepper when we get home. Tomas would be pleased if I didn't need prompting. He had stopped asking recently, which was a relief. I think I was beginning to remember for myself. I must remember this time, water and food! It was odd that he had stopped asking, maybe he was going to trust me to think for myself. I felt grown up, he was going to be pleased with me, when he asked and I was able to say "Yes, I've done it already!" I walked home with Antony. It was the tail end of winter. Cold enough for a frost in the air. A grey day. Grey skies, and daylight with the palest of grey hues to it. Trees were just leafless skeletons, bushes and shrubs a mish mash of twigs and branches. Even spider's webs could been seen against the backdrop of such nakedness. We were glad to get home, opening the back gate we were already calling "Mum….Mum! We're home!" Antony ran into the house ahead of me, while I went to check Salt and Pepper first. The shed door was already opened. I knew Tomas must have been in already and checked them, or he'd left the door open as a visual prompt for my benefit. However, when I looked the rug was thrown back and the hutch door was ajar. I didn't understand, where were they? This was strange, had Tomas let them out? I was starting to feel fear and panic. I bet he'd given them away. I bet he'd done as he'd warned and taken them away from us, without even telling me! I rushed into the house, heading through the kitchen as Tomas and Antony were heading back towards me. Tomas looked angry "It's no use looking in there for the rabbits, I told you, what would happen if you didn't fucking look after them, didn't I? You didn't listen and you didn't believe me!" I couldn't believe it, he had given them away. Antony was crying, snot running from his nose, he slurped it up with his tongue and rubbed his eyes with his sleeve. Tomas said "Your rabbits are down the bottom of the garden, you didn't feed them and they didn't have any bloody water! They would've died of thirst and starvation anyway! But you don't have to worry now, because I've put an end to their misery!" He grabbed us both by our elbows and thrust us towards the back door "Go on, go and have a look, they're down the bottom of the garden!" with that he forced us out the back door, saying "Don't say I didn't warn you!" he slammed it shut.

Antony still spluttering, was trying not to choke on his own tears. I wasn't crying. I felt dizzy with fear and apprehension, and I felt the colour drain from my face. My whole body felt like it was shaking. We did as we were told, and headed slowly and falteringly down the garden. I was in front, Antony following me. We kept looking around. Were we going to find Salt and Pepper hopping around freely? Had Tomas let them go to run away as they wished? We knew it couldn't be that. We were kidding ourselves. "Where are they Antony? Can you see them?" I asked him. He was scanning the garden too, eyes darting from left to right "I can't see them, I dunno where they are". We continued cautiously making our way further down. In that last third of the garden, that we hardly ever used, the shrubs and trees were bare. Amongst the twigs and branches, that was where we found them. A bloodied claw hammer lay on the ground, Salt and Pepper lay where they had been flung. Their heads had been bludgeoned in, crushed by the force of the blows. Stunned, Antony and I just stared. We couldn't believe what we saw. We didn't look at each other. We couldn't look at each other. A sob broke the silence and I realized it came from me. I looked from Salt and Pepper to the hammer and could visualise the scene. Tomas in a fit of anger wielding the hammer, the rabbits hanging from his fist by their legs, bucking to get away. He would have swiped at them in annoyance, quick to still their plight and finish the job. My eyes scanned from the hammer around the garden. There were bits and pieces of what could almost have been jelly spattered in the mesh of twigs and branches, it was hanging in droplets and sitting in tiny globules in the sparse bits of grass. It was wet and glistening. It took me a while to process. I realized that it was Salt and Peppers brain and skull matter. I was crying, tears sliding down my cheeks, my sight blurring as my eyes filled too quickly. Antony was a blur as he ran down the garden back to the house "It's all your fault!" he screamed at me as he ran.

Chapter 13

Golden child

1978

Having pets in our house was always a dicey matter. We always had pets, they came and went in the early days. Sometimes, because they didn't fit and got passed on to other eager animal lovers with more patience, as in Shadow's case. Or sometimes because they left of their own free will, just up and gone never to return, at least that's what I hope. Mum and Tomas were much better at having pets when we all left home. There was a tortoiseshell cat that lived around the corner from us, she kept coming and sitting on our doorstep. Mum liked her, and encouraged her to stay. She got talking to the people who owned her originally, and they said her name was "Fluffy" and that she'd had her nose put out of joint, because they'd got another cat. They were happy for us to keep Fluffy if that's where she wanted to be. Mum told me cats are clever, they know things. If somebody is going to die in their household, the cat will move home and find a new owner, or if a baby is going to be born they can sense that also, and will want to move in.

I was eight when Mum told me that they were going to have a baby. I'd be a Big sister again. It was one of the happiest moments I'd ever had. She told me how I'd be able to help her look after it, hold and feed it. I was old enough to be such a help to her, and I felt so proud. It was such great news. Mum was the happiest I had ever seen her. She was different, there was a softness about her I hadn't seen before. Part of my happiness was due to the difference in her. Tomas was absolutely overjoyed, he was attentive and protective of her. The only thing was, that made him over anxious, so we couldn't get near Mum. If we tried to cuddle up with her he would shout "Mind what you're doing, be careful! Remember there's a baby in there now!" Antony was not happy at all. He would scowl at the mention of a new baby. That hurt Tomas's feelings and damaged the delicate bond that had only just begun to form between them. Spencer's reaction to the news of the baby was a disinterested shrug, his top lip curled in the vaguest of snarls "So what?" By this time he hardly ever saw Mum. He didn't come to the house. She didn't go to visit him. He never asked after her, it was as though they were acquaintances and nothing more.

Still living in Godwin close, Mum was blossoming along with the trees in our cul de sac. She looked glowing with health and was radiant with happiness. Tomas was attentive and adoring of her. He loved seeing her body changing and knowing that his child was growing inside her. I was fascinated by the changes too. There were few dramas in our family during Mum's pregnancy. She fell several times in the late stages, she was mystified, complaining that she felt so clumsy. Her centre of gravity seemed to have changed with the growing bump! It was a time of peace, the only issue of any concern being that Antony didn't want to know anything about what was happening, and would have preferred it if nobody mentioned that there was going to be a new baby. As Mum's belly got bigger, I'd press my ear to it, to see if I could hear a heartbeat, only to be surprised instead by a ripple of movement under my cheek, as the baby moved a fist or a foot, changing position. Mum, Tomas and me debated names, while Antony refused to participate. We continued going to Nana and Granddad's at weekends, holidaying every summer with them on the east coast. We always went to either St.Osyth's in Clacton or Lowestoft. Granddad had a brother that owned a chip shop in Kessingland, and we would visit him and his wife. He gave us cones of fritters drenched in salt and vinegar. The three of us loved those holiday's. We were like water babies, swimming every day, whether it was at the beach or the campsite pool. Always staying in caravans that Granddad had rented for the week. The anticipation building up to that week was enough to make Antony ill every year. He was such a peculiar boy, if he was excited about something, he'd get so wound-up that he always became sick, it happened before Christmas and birthdays too.

Driving to our holiday reminded me of driving to see Dad in prison. They were our only long journeys by car. I'd suffer with travel sickness, notwithstanding nana's lime and chocolate eclaires. Nana and Granddad would pack plenty of food, and cooked breakfast every morning. We'd have a choice, full English or toast and cereals. They would buy multipacks of mini cereals as a special treat, so that we could pick and choose each day. A picnic was prepared to take down to the beach or have beside the pool and the whole day would be spent there. We could swim to our hearts content, getting in and out, drying off in the sun, and going in again. Nana always ready with a towel, arms wide ready to engulf us, as we ran shivering to her. Our teeth chattering and dripping wet, Granddad would say "Dry yourself off properly, don't just wrap yourself up in the towel, that won't do the trick". He always knew the best way to do things. They would befriend other holidaymakers and chat with them. Their children would befriend us, and knowing nothing of where we came from, or who we were, for a week it was like being "Normal". In the evenings we'd go to the club house on the campsite, and taking part in the activities there, dancing and singing along to music, while the adults entertained us with jokes and encouraged us to take part in competitions. Nana and Granddad would sit nearby, smiling benevolently, clapping and cheering us on, urging us "Go on, join in. Don't be shy, have fun".

There was a counter selling sweets, rock, candyfloss and an amazing new drink, in all sorts of flavours and colours called "Slush Puppies". I'd ask Granddad if we could buy some nougat to take home for Mum, as that was her favourite. He always agreed. We would trail back to our caravan in the dark, exhausted, sated and entirely happy. Granddad would tuck us all in to bed in turn, while Nana got into her nightie before coming to kiss us goodnight. I was so tired I'd be barely aware of her stroking my cheek and saying goodnight.

Granddad always dropped off Nana and Spencer, before taking Antony and me back to Mum and Tomas. Spencer never came with us to see them. It was as if it was engineered to avoid it. It was a Saturday afternoon when we arrived home from holiday, that Tomas came to the door to greet us. It was unusual for him to do so, he told us that Mum had given birth to the baby while we were away and that, we had a new brother called Shaun. I was ecstatic and charged up the stairs to meet my new brother, Granddad following behind, Antony didn't want to come in, asking if he could go home with Granddad, Tomas and he tried persuading "Look, come and say hello to him, he's so tiny and you're his big brother". Antony didn't want to even look at Shaun, pleading to go with Granddad. This further deteriorated Tomas and Antony's delicate bond.

Chapter 14

Intoxication

1973

When Antony was born, the little two up and two down in Green's Road wasn't big enough to accommodate our growing family. We were moved to a relatively new council estate to the north of Cambridge. Building had begun there in 1967 and was still ongoing when we moved in. The area was a problematic place to live, there were numerous incidents of vandalism, and tenants complained about the lack of community facilities. The estate was originally a King's Warren, an expanse of land that was used as a game reserve, where hedges would've been grown, especially for the purpose of the huntsmen to corral the game and entrap them for the kill. This inspired the name "Kings Hedges" for the new estate.

The move to a new house, wasn't the turning over of a new leaf for Dave. His activities became more and more erratic. Already having been fined for causing Actual Bodily Harm, he went on to serve a three year probation for robbery. Even while in attendance at court, he was fined for using threatening language. Under the influence of alcohol he'd assaulted a police officer. Subsequently he was sentenced to six months imprisonment, taking into account he was in breach of the probation order that was almost spent. Its mind boggling to comprehend, how he had been managing to still hold down a job satisfactorily enough for his employers up until this point. He was constantly drinking heavily and consuming other drugs. Meanwhile, Carolyn was still taking his beatings, besides the sexual and verbal abuse, and all while trying to preserve some semblance of a normal family life.

When Dave was released this time, the population of the estate was growing fast as houses were completed. He found employment as a Progress Chaser at various sites. That's when he made it to work instead of his local drinking holes "The Jenny Wren" and "The Carlton Arms". Both pubs were notoriously grim and disorderly. With the estate not having much else to offer they held a certain glamour, and it's possible that this was where he and Richard Gilchurch first met. Richard was a cool customer, he was quite the hippy with long hair and a beard, while Dave, bucking the current trend, still wore his hair short and was always clean shaven. A friendship struck up between the two, they were near in age with Dave being twenty five now, and Richard or "Dick" as he was more commonly known, only two years younger. The pair had similarities in common, as both, despite being so young were already married, had children, and liked to experiment with drugs. Dave was invited to visit Richard's home to meet his family. Instantly Dave, a consistent womanizer, was attracted to Dick's wife Carole. She exuded an air of sexual confidence that aroused him, he liked her looks, dirty long blonde hair and shapely figure. Many of the men in the neighbourhood gave her admiring glances, and she was known to be flirtatious. This was in stark contrast to Carolyn, who flinched and shied away from his touch. It was a challenge to seduce this other woman, and it seemed his infatuation was reciprocated. Carole was animated by this newcomer on the scene. He was exciting, giving her lots of flattery and attention, which she hadn't been getting from her husband since starting a family. The attraction to Dick's wife cemented the friendship as Dave feigned more interest in Dick to get access to Carole. The near parallel between her name and my mum's is almost laughable in hindsight, he didn't need to worry about calling Carolyn by the wrong name.

An act of fate, conveniently gave Dave and Carole the opportunity to get to know each other more intimately, when Dick was arrested and had to serve a stint in prison. As with his new friend, his own history of offences and drug abuse were catching up with him. This allowed Dave and Carole to begin seeing each other. It started with Dave's continued visits after Dick's sentencing, and escalated when the temptation to become involved proved too strong. She shared his weakness for drugs and drink, and they were becoming besotted with each other. During this period my Mum was relieved that he'd found a new distraction. For a while the beatings would be fewer as his attentions lay elsewhere, and she'd see less of him for as long as this recent fling might last. The knowledge that this new "Carole" was supplanting his interest in her was a relief. These intervals of his infidelities, were what helped her to survive. They were like respite care for a battered wife courtesy of earthly intervention. Her days continued, with the usual chores and routines. The rituals kept her from becoming senseless. She continued, to nurse Antony and bring me up, chain smoking, as one cigarette burnt to the butt, the next already lit. The only uncertainty for the lovers was how Carole's husband was going to take the news of her adultery, if he were to find out.

Carole and Dave had a few months of uninterrupted pleasure. They surreptitiously spent as much time together as they could. Often they discussed having a future, as it was becoming more serious than a fling. Although drug fuelled and based on sexual chemistry, in their intoxicated minds, they believed they were falling in love. Dave was sometimes aggressive, he'd have jealous rages if another man showed an interest in her, or if he imagined she'd invited attention from elsewhere. He loved her too much and, so far, had enough control never to raise a fist to her. Carole decided the rumours that he beat his wife were exaggerated. Her anxiety about Dick coming home and discovering their betrayal and the fear that the budding relationship would come to an abrupt halt, stirred her into taking the shrewd initiative to confess to Dick while he was in prison. If he was given the truth while in that controlled environment, it would be better for all parties. That would allow enough time to gauge his initial reaction and have a plan of action. When her next visiting order arrived, Carole decided she would tell him.

Dick wasn't surprised. He'd suspected as much. Aware that Dave had still been seeing his wife, the truth was just a confirmation of his suspicions. Carole had been dropping his name during her visits, he knew Dave had a track record for having extra marital flings, and he knew his wife's libido. It didn't need a rocket scientist to figure out the rest. Logic didn't make it any easier to accept, however, knowing that another man had been enjoying his wife while he was detained was unbearable. With more restraint than Dave would ever possess, Dick managed to measure his response. It would do him no favours to over react in the presence of the wardens overseeing the visit. Carole didn't know how incensed he actually was.

Dad had virtually moved in with Carole by the time that Dick was released from prison.

Dick returned home to find the affair in full swing. An almighty row ensued that almost turned to violence. Dick wanted Dave out of his house and demanded that Carole surrender him as her lover, he was incensed that they thought they could carry on in his home. While Carole insisted that she loved Dave and wouldn't give him up, she calmed things down enough to persuade Dave to leave her with Dick, so that they could talk it all through and find a compromise. Dave left in an agitated state heading to the nearest pub, before going home to my mum to wait for news from Carole. In his absence Dick was more pliable, he was softer towards her, and eventually acquiesced to her wheedling. She had an idea that might be a solution for them all.

Chapter 15

Shattered

Mum knew it was a waiting game, it was only a postponement. Dave had been virtually living at the slag's house. I grew up often hearing her referred to as "The Slag". Mum said she was the town bike and that everybody had ridden her. I had no idea if that was true or if mum's judgement was only based on her experience of Carole. A new element in her otherwise unhappy existence was a friendship that had blossomed between Mum and our neighbour Gina. Gina was a mixed race single Mum who had moved in recently. She was slight and wiry with chin length hair, she often wore a slide in her fringe to keep it out of her eyes and she always had a smile. Gina permanently wore a tabard to protect her clothes while she was about the house, and even wore it to go to the shops. Mum would go and have coffee with her when Dave was out and Gina became her confidante. It was silly to pretend all was well when Gina was right next door and the walls were thin. Sometimes Gina would give her the money for a loaf of bread, or lend her a couple of cigarettes. "Why don't cha leave his sorry arse?" she'd ask Carolyn. "He ain't no good for ya woman. He gonna keep beatin' ya, and one of these days he gonna kill ya!" Carolyn hated hearing talk like this, she would rather they discussed the weather, music or what films were on at the "Kinema" that week.

"Gina, if I were to leave him, where would I go, I can't go back to my parents, they don't want me, and his parents just tell me to give him another chance!" She could feel the tears coming and pricking her eyes. Gina grabbed her hand. "There are women's shelters now ya know, tings are startin' to change for women like ya." Carolyn pulled her hand away "It doesn't matter what I do or where I go Gina, He'd come and find me."

One of my earliest memories has been etched in my mind forever, as if seared there by a branding iron. This happened around Carole's visit to see Dick in prison and tell him she was seeing my Dad. Disturbed by this he decided to go on a bender, drinking away the stress and restlessness. Unsettled knowing Carole was seeing Dick, he was twitchy with tension. He came home loaded with alcohol and all worked up. Not having been back for days, stumbling in the front door, we were all startled. Even he looked a little surprised that he was home. Antony and I were on the rug in the living room, we'd a tea set and were having pretend tea with my tiny tears doll. Antony jumped up, actually taking his thumb out of his mouth for once, running over to greet him straight away, pleased to see him, grabbing dad's leg and clinging to his trousers. Dad was oblivious. Mum asked "What are you doing here? Where've you been until now?" She already knew the answer, but her mouth ran away with her. The nerve of it, simply walking back in like he'd only been out for a few hours. "Edie and Les have been asking after you, I told them you're never here!" Dad looked at her with irritation, swaying towards her "I've been to see a man about a dog!" he sneered, finding himself funny, he snorted at his own joke "A man about a dog, that's a good one!" Still amused, he pointed a finger at Mum. Poking her in the chest said "You and my parents, always wanting to know my business "What you doing Dave? Where you going Dave?" He mimicked how they questioned him. "I can't fucking breathe without the lot of you having something to say about it". The laughter had subsided to a low mutter now, as he put his finger inside the collar of his shirt and tried wriggling it away from his neck, it suddenly seemed restrictive and he appeared stifled. Antony gave up, sitting back down beside me. Dad flung his arm widely to gesture around him, looking dolefully at Mum "Can't you send them upstairs to play? They just make a bloody racket. It's bad enough I have to listen to you fucking harping on!" We were still. Unsure what the next move should be, not wanting to draw attention to ourselves or arouse his anger. Mum was muttering under her breath something about "Doesn't turn up here for days, then when he does, nothing changes, drunk as always." We were frozen to the spot. My eyes were fixed on a cigarette burn in the pattern of the rug. I started counting how many spirals there were in the pattern. I felt Antony's fingertips reaching for mine. "What did you say? What did you just say?! You fucking whore, I heard you, you think I'm drunk! I can handle my drink, Can't a man have a fucking drink after a hard day's graft?! Spittle sprayed from his mouth as he roared at her. I couldn't hear them now over the sound of my heart beating. It was like an ocean was pounding inside my head. I was aware of the movement around me, but there was no sound. Antony buried his face into my lap, his thumb jammed in his mouth. Dad held Mum by the tops of her arms, I could see him shouting words at her. Her head was shaking fiercely. His face was almost touching hers, He looked like a dog baring his teeth at her. Mum strained to get away, turning her face, she looked directly at me, terror in her eyes. He was shaking her, her whole body juddered and her eyes left mine as they shook inside her head. Dad lifted her off the floor and hurled her against the glass cabinet in the corner of the room.

It was the stylish thing of the time to have a cabinet to store glasses in. Mum had admired Nana and Granddads. They'd bought one similar for Mum and Dad as a gift, and she'd gradually filled its glass shelves with pretty sets of glasses in various designs. They were fragile, with elegant stems, some were coloured in hues of deep red or pale pink. As she was propelled against the cabinet her body went straight through the double fronted glass doors. Cracking the wooden frame that held the glass in place, and shattering the panes of glass, the shelves, and all that was within. My hearing returned, as she came to a halt landing in a heap at the bottom of the cabinet. She'd instinctively tucked her chin into her chest and her shoulders hunched up around her ears. Glass glittered everywhere. Large shards and miniscule glints gleamed from the carpet. Mum's legs had shot out in front of her, dead straight, as if she had flung herself backwards intentionally. She stayed sitting. Dad completely spent now from his labours pitched himself face down on the sofa, leaving one arm trailing to the floor. I couldn't move, the floor wet beneath me, I'd wet myself. Antony's face still buried in my lap, his hands now covering his ears. "Mum?....Mum? Are you hurt?" I whispered so quietly I wasn't even sure she could hear me. There were scrapes, cuts and grazes all up her arms, blood oozing from some of them. I cried silently as Mum raised her head slowly, cautiously. As if she wasn't sure yet, if she even wanted to see the scene around her. She couldn't look at me. I don't know where she was then, and I hope to never know where that place was. Her face was expressionless, completely void of colour and empty. Slithers of glass tinkled, sprinkling away from her as she shifted and tried to move. Lifting her hands, she looked around for a place to push herself up from. Finding nowhere clear of the sharp fragments, she pulled her knees up and tried to push herself up legs first. A small whimper escaped her as her mind struggled to process how best to extricate herself. Finally, she managed to hoist herself on to her feet. There was a multitude of nicks and cuts up the back of her legs and finally, when she stood she swayed, as though about to collapse. Antony cleaved against me, releasing his grip I tried to scrabble on all fours through the glass, to go to her. She didn't want me. Wouldn't look at me. Dad grunted on the sofa. Wavering, I thought she's heading towards me. I thought, she's Ok, Mum's going to be OK. He hasn't hurt her. Onwards she weaved, past me, continuing into the hallway. Opening the front door, and leaving. The door slamming shut behind her. The worst thing that could possibly happen to us had happened. Our Mum had left, she'd left us with him. I started screaming, and Antony echoed my cries.

Dad was catatonic on the sofa. Together, we shuffled to the front door. Antony holding my hand, as I tried to turn the door knob. I couldn't get a grip. Each time I tried, my hands slipped. I realized I had cut myself and the blood had made my hands too slippery to get a grasp of the handle. Antony was inconsolable beside me "I want Mum, where's she gone?!" I couldn't think. All I knew was that she had left us and I didn't know if she was coming back. Opening the letterbox, I tried peering out. There was no one in sight, Antony strained on tiptoe to see too, but he wasn't tall enough to reach. Still we cried. My hands were sore. The little puncture wounds beginning to sting. I felt so hopeless. The awareness of my sores without a Mum to soothe them, made my desperation more urgent. Lifting the letterbox flap again, I screamed "Help! Somebody help! Please, we want our Mum!" Antony, spurred on by my shouts, joined me as we both tried to attract somebody's attention. This seemed to go on forever. Every second without our Mum, seemed a second further away she could be. I wanted to get outside the door to run down the street and look for her. Each second that slipped away, she would be harder to find. I could only just see through the letterbox, and had to keep shutting and reopening it, to call out again. We were becoming tired. It felt impossible, then Gina walked past. I have never felt so relieved to see anyone in my life, even to this day, as I did seeing her "Antony! Shout! Look, its Gina!" I bawled as loudly as I could "Gina! Gina! Help! Mum's gone!" Antony and I cried in unison.

Gina was on her way home from work, hearing our cries she came to the letterbox "What's happenin? What you babies doin?" She was shocked to see us looking so pitiful, she assured us she'd be back, but would go and get help. What she found on her doorstep was even more pitiful, it was my Mum. She'd had nowhere else to go

.

Chapter 16

Swapping

Between them, each with their own methods of persuasion, Dave's fits of rage and Carole's feminine wiles, they convinced their respective partners, that the best solution for all was if Carole moved in with Dave, meaning my Mum would have no choice but to move in with Dick. Mum knew Dick from before, when the two men had been friends. She didn't need much urging to agree with this sudden arrangement. Dave presented the idea to her, making sure she knew it was not a choice. Fearful of another attack or perhaps being ejected by force onto the street, she had thought Dick to be courteous and friendly whenever she had encountered him previously. It couldn't be worse than the abuse she suffered at Dave's hands. There was a thread of spite that ran through her thoughts too, let the slag have him, she'd find out what it was really like to live as his wife. Familiarity, and all that! One stipulation, however, was that Antony had to stay with Dad. He wanted Antony, he didn't want another man bringing his boy up and besides, Antony wanted to be with Dad. So the pact was made. Mum packed our few things and we left Antony behind, to move only a few streets away. I didn't understand what was happening. I was happy to leave Dad, I didn't understand why Antony wasn't moving too. They told me he'd wanted to stay, but none of it made any sense. I was going to live in another man's house.

No one explained it to me properly. I didn't see Antony very much and the man had a little girl with the same name as me, she would come and stay with us. They said we'd all call her Sammy so that we didn't get in a muddle, and my Mum was so nice to her that I felt jealous. I didn't have to call him Dad, he was Dick. Where I had shared a bedroom with Antony at home, here in this man's house I sometimes had to share with Sammy. We had twin beds, she'd get out of her bed in the night to come and sleep with me. But when she'd peed my bed in her sleep, she'd go back to her own bed. Dick kept telling me off for wetting the bed. Sammy wanted to cuddle up and be affectionate with me, then she would pull my hair or bite me. Mum told me she was only a toddler and that's what they do when they don't know any better. Dick liked to meditate and would sit in the lotus position. He would close his eyes to empty his mind and chant "Om….Om…Ommmmmm." I had no idea what the purpose of this was. Then he tried to include me in these strange practices "Now Samantha, if you come over here…try to do a handstand, then lower yourself onto your head so that you are standing on your head." I'd try repeatedly to stay upright long enough so that I could lower myself into a head stand, my arms quivering with nerves and exertion. Dad never did stuff like this with me. Dick explained "When you are upside down the blood rushes to your head, it suddenly supplies a rush of oxygen to the brain, which helps you to think more clearly and cleanse your mind before meditation." Then he'd suggest "Maybe if you try doing a hand stand against the wall it will be easier to go into a head stand, let's try that!" It seemed incredible. Previously my Dad was throwing Mum into walls and here was this man teaching me how to use a wall to enable my meditation technique. I couldn't help liking Dick, he was kind to me and gentle with Mum.

For a few months this new arrangement worked quite well. Mum was never obviously happy. There was calm and a sense of safety. I couldn't let her out of my sight, too afraid she would leave me. She didn't seem settled. Restless and misplaced, she'd sit in the kitchen smoking one cigarette after another, always with the back door ajar, for a quick escape route or hasty exit, I'm not sure which. Cross legged and fidgety at the breakfast table she would continually swing her foot up and down, it was like a clock pendulum. Often she'd be waiting for Dick to return, but he was becoming unreliable. Sometimes I'd ask "What are we waiting for Mum?" and she'd say "We're waiting for Dick to come home." He had a job driving a van making deliveries for a butchers, this enabled him to have freedom throughout the day to stop off and see his wife and their daughter. Mum wasn't to know, though probably had some suspicions, Dick's desire to restore his and Carole's relationship had been reawakened. He was going to visit her while Dave was out at work. When he collected or returned their daughter, he'd seen the tell-tale bruises, listened to Carole's anguish about Dave's displays of aggression towards her. With a sympathetic ear, he was trying to coax her into rekindling some affection for him.

Somehow, it became knowledge to Dave that Dick was making attempts to visit Carole more frequently than sharing child care alone necessitated. It may have been Carole herself that taunted Dave with the attention of her estranged husband, there will have been an amount of gossip and rumour attached to it too. It's apparent also that Dick was goading and making jibes at Dave, making him insecure and causing trouble. Each visit to the house was an opportunity to provoke Dave, plant suggestions and create paranoia. Dave believed he would do anything to win back his wife's attention and was greatly distressed that she might leave him to return to Dick.

Mum was angry and frustrated. Doubt, mistrust and suspicion were creeping in. She was finding herself interrogating Dick, quizzing him about his routine and asking him "How'd it go today? Anything interesting happen? Was it busy?" The flimsy trust she'd allowed herself to have in him was faltering. When probed, he lost his temper with her, which gave him reason to storm out. Resentment was everywhere, it was palpable even to me, though I was only four years old. One evening I was sitting on a rug in the living room in front of the TV with Mum "Coronation Street" on. She always let me watch it with her, bedtime was when it finished. Tonight Mum was in a funny mood. She sat with her legs tucked under her, and pulling me on to her lap, wrapped her arms around me, and hugged me tightly. It was wonderful. In that moment she was right there in the room with me, nowhere else. Nothing else had her attention. Her eyes were focused on me, not an image in the corner of her mind or a thought somewhere far away in the distance. Feeling confident I said "Mum, do you love Sammy?" I wanted to know so desperately. "Is that what you think?" she laughed "Do you think I love her? Are you worrying about it?" I shrugged, awkwardly, waiting for an answer, cupping her face with my hands and trying to make her face me, so I could look into her eyes. "I don't like Sammy Mum! She wets in my bed and is horrible to me!" My lip trembled, fat tears welled up, waiting to spill down my cheeks. Mum held me as close as she could "How about if you and me take Sammy down to the woods? We'd tie her up to a big oak tree, where no one could find her, she'd scream and scream, then a big bad wolf would hear her and he'd come and gobble her up!" She tickled me under my ribs and we fell around on the floor laughing together. When the laughter subsided, she stroked my hair and said "I love you Samantha".

Spencer's birthday was coming up very soon. Nana and Granddad were unhappy with the dynamic between the two couples. It was very improper. They couldn't understand what on earth was happening these days. Everyone seemed to do whatever they liked. Since the introduction of the pill in 1961 marriages didn't last. Women were unfaithful. Free love and promiscuity was infecting decent people. It wasn't right, for better or worse, through thick and thin, that's what marriage was. You made your bed and you should lie in it. Edie and Les were disappointed in Dave. They hadn't brought him up to miss work, get drunk, and philander with other women, forgetting about his responsibilities. Les tried to talk to him, teach him the choices he should be making and encourage him to at least maintain contact with his children. They wanted the three of us to have some contact with each other as well. It was important to them that we knew who our siblings were. Besides not seeing so much of Mum now, while having to accept Dad's new woman was difficult for them. It was her phoning for help now, instead of Mum.

Nana and Granddad proposed that getting the three of us children together with Carole and her daughter, would help us to engage and accept our new extended family. The only hiccup was how to convince Dick to miss having Sammy for an evening and let her take part in the festivities. What could go wrong? A children's party, some harmless fun for the kids.

Chapter 17

A coat to shield his eyes

1974

Dad pretended to like the idea of a children's party, even though he didn't really care if we all got along or not. Having Antony living with him was alright, he'd a soft spot for him. Otherwise, he wasn't making any effort to stay in contact with either Spencer or me. Which was how Mum and me preferred it. For him, however, there was a certain attraction in organizing a party to include Dick's daughter. That appealed, if only for the purposes of aggravating Dick. It would give Dad pleasure to throw a party, rub it in everyone's faces that Carole and he were together, show Dick he was surrogate father to their child now. Still Dick thought he could win Carole back, kept showing his face and causing upset. It was time for a little stage-managing, using the façade of a children's party to gain leverage. Dad would gain the upper hand and show Dick exactly how things stood. He was the one in control. Around and around in his mind it churned. Anticipating an argument, he fully expected it.

On the 29th November Dad pulled a sickie with work, which was getting to be more of a regular occurrence. He couldn't trust leaving Carole at home alone, as no doubt Dick would be sniffing around, if he thought the coast was clear and she'd let him in, so the two of them could hark back over old times. Well it wasn't going to happen if he had anything to do with it. Making the most of an impromptu day off, he opened a bottle of cider. His hands shook with the need for a drink, his mouth parched, he licked and smacked his lips together in expectation of the first gulp. Pouring the cider he actually licked the rim of the bottle neck, put the full glass on the table and rubbed his hands together gleefully before guzzling that first glass down in one long, greedy draught. Some dribbled from the corners of his mouth and he swiped the back of his hand across his lips, bristles from the mornings unshaven growth rasping as his hand swept over them. This was when he was happiest, the alcohol seeping into his bloodstream. His hands would steady, his mind seemed to clear, and he could think more quickly. It all made more sense after a drink. They were all out to play him for a fool, but they didn't know how much he saw, and he didn't miss a trick. "Fucking games behind my back, I'm smarter than the lot of them". He mumbled to himself, and digging out a bottle of whisky, he poured himself a generous chaser and swilled it back.

He continued drinking into the afternoon, feeling empowered. His inhibitions fell away and his confidence increased. He'd have that chat with Dick, rehearsing the conversation in his mind. Carole had stayed in bed until nearly lunchtime, she'd been down a couple of times to have a cigarette. Sammy was with Carolyn, and Antony had been left to his own devices. He was such a good kid, no bother at all. Dave was proud of how he would entertain himself, he didn't need looking after, always pushing toy cars around on the living room floor, or drawing. Carole was always saying he was a handful, her way of punishing him was to shut him in the cupboard under the stairs. Maybe that's what had done the trick, what had made him so well behaved. Well, he was as happy as Larry now, silently driving his cars around the coffee table legs. Carole came downstairs eventually, yesterday's mascara smudged under her eyes and thickly clumped in her lashes. She looked rough "For fuck's sake, look at the state of you! Eyes like piss holes in the snow you've got!" Head flung back on the arm of the sofa he pointed at her. Carole gave him a withering look. "Oi!

102

Don't you fucking give me that look, you bitch, I'll come over there and wipe it off your face for you!" He bawled at her before swallowing another gulp of cider. Scornfully Carole mocked him saying "That's if you can stand after all you've been drinking." He hauled himself up clumsily and lumbered over to her, she had turned her back on him to put the kettle on, cursing herself already for having spoken hastily she tensed, hoping he was just fetching another drink. As she turned to look at him, he landed a slap across the back of her head and her forehead slammed into the cupboard door "Shut your mouth, or I'll shut it for you, your pathetic husband's not here to go running to now!" Regaining her equilibrium Carole moved to the other side of the kitchen to put some distance between them. Antony having stopped pushing his cars, was furiously sucking his thumb and staring at them with eyes as wide as saucers. She went to the cigarettes, only to find the packet empty, the ashtray overflowing "Dave you've finished the fags." She looked from Antony to him "And what are we going to do about food? He's going to want feeding. Aren't you hungry?" That was the tipping point for Dad. "How the fuck can I go and get food?! I'm supposed to be at work you dumb cunt! If I get seen I'll get sacked!" His voice reverberated around the kitchen as he shouted at her, then balling his fists he started lumbering towards her again, Antony scuttled across the floor crablike to shield himself by the side of an armchair. Before he got too close Carole held her hands up in surrender "Alright Dave, alright! Of course you can't go out. I don't know what I was thinking, I'm being stupid! I'll go." She waved her hands at him to ward him off and placated him "You relax, have a little snooze on the sofa and I'll go to the shops, by the time you wake up I'll have a nice dinner on the table. Come on what do you say? I'll look after you, you work hard and you've deserved it." Pacified now, a smile spread across his face, the tension in him diminished. The unwinding was visible.

103

"Go on, put your feet up." Carole ushered him into the living room. Antony still unnoticed by either of them hid, peering out at them from around the armchair. Dad settled down onto the sofa and grappled with Carole, trying to open her dressing gown and pull her down with him "Why don't you come for a little lie down too eh?" It was a half-hearted attempt. He was fighting slumber as he sunk into the sofa once more. Carole couldn't wait to extricate herself, no sooner than she had, his eyes drooped and his head lolled, ready to descend into a stupor. Carole hurried to call Les and Edie. She was afraid that when he woke he'd be worse, that was the usual pattern.

Granddad went, he always did. Whether it was Mum or Carole, it never changed. Dad never changed. The boy was there and he needed to make sure he was alright, it was a terrible state of affairs. He took some groceries with him and a packet of Embassy No6. It would help if Dad had a cigarette when Granddad tried talking some sense into him. He'd go and stay for a while. When he felt sure Antony was settled and all was peaceful again, he would leave. Edie and he were despairing. It seemed never ending and there was only so much they could do! He arrived to find Dad had just woken up. "Aww! Bloody hell, she didn't have to call you Pops!" He sat on the edge of the sofa shoulders slumped, feeling both drunk and hung over, disgruntled because he wouldn't be able to continue drinking now Les was there "Just for a change, I wanted to let my hair down and have a day off, but she had to ruin it!" He stood, seeming much steadier, recovered slightly from his earlier splurge. Granddad could see he was in a black mood. Where was Antony? Toy cars were scattered around the floor, and scouring the room for the boy, he saw his foot sticking out from down the side of the armchair, socks hanging half off. He was asleep, his thumb had slipped from his mouth, and a thin dribble of drool had trickled down his cheek. As Granddad scooped him up it stretched briefly like a slender thread of elastic. The motion roused Antony and, realizing it was Granddad, he clasped his hands around his neck, and pushed his face into his shoulder. "Granddad!" The cry was muffled. Antony wide awake now started chattering "Granddad, they shouted, I didn't like it!" Granddad soothingly held him, swaying him gently on his lap. "It's over and done with now, it's alright again, just a silly argument, nothing to fret about." Antony knew that if Granddad was there it was going to be alright. "Come and play with my cars! Look Granddad I was making a road!" Les knew he would have to stay a while.

Dad was feeling less drunk and more hung over, he ranted on to Les "I'm pissed off Dad. Her ex keeps coming around, thinking I don't know what he's up to! The pair of them! Talking about me behind my back, when I'm not here to defend myself. I'm going to pull him up about it. He wants her back and she's leading us both on! " Les tried to reason with him "Dave, calm down, you're being paranoid. He has every right to make arrangements with her about seeing their child. You've got to be rational."

It was an unfortunate coincidence that this evening Dick arrived outside, Carole hearing his car made the unwitting mistake of telling Dad "Dick's here." Dad already excitable, impulsively told her "Ask him if I can have a word with him." Fearful of provoking more argument, she obediently went to the front door, with Antony in tow and told Dick "Dave wants a word with you." Dick replied "I'll be round in a minute." Carole left the front door ajar. Feeling uneasy, and suspecting there would be a quarrel, she took Antony by the hand and led him back to Granddad in the living room.

Everything was about to change in a matter of minutes. Dick had arrived at around 8pm. Carole, Les and Antony were in the living room. Dad called out "Come in, old mate." This was in the hallway. It would seem Dad was waiting for Dick with a knife, which he had taken from the kitchen. He must have lunged at Dick and a fight ensued, they wrestled fiercely and Granddad came out to try and intervene. Granddad always said he never saw the knife, yet he cut his hand, presumably trying to take the knife from Dad. In the next instant Dick was laying prostrate on the floor and Dad was shouting at Carole "Go and get an ambulance!"

Dad had stabbed Dick five times, four times in the back and once in the side. Granddad made Dad help him carry Dick through to the living room, where they removed his shirt. I can only guess it was to try reveal his wounds, and assess how bad his injuries were. Someone had returned the knife to the kitchen and left it on the draining board. The police arrived before the ambulance. While one officer attended to Dick, another asked Dad "What had happened?" Dad said "He came to the door and a fight started." When asked "Who is he?" Dad replied "I don't know." He became hysterical and kept repeating "Can't you help him, he can't die!" An officer asked him "Is this the knife?" he answered "Yes." Asked "Whose is it?" he said "I don't know." The officer said to him "You stabbed him, didn't you?" My Dad replied hysterically "I didn't mean to hurt him! Do something! Can't you do something?!" He was frightened now, repeatedly crying "Can't you help him? Don't let him die. He mustn't die. Keep him alive." Yet still when asked "Who is it?" Dad insisted "I don't know." It wasn't until later that he would tell them it was Dick Gilchurch. By 8.25 pm Dad was taken into custody. Dick was taken away in the ambulance but couldn't be resuscitated. Antony was there the whole time. He saw them carry Dick into the living room and when the ambulance men came in to carry Dick away, Granddad put a coat over Antony's head so that he wouldn't witness anymore.

In the back of the police car, Dad tried to drink a miniature bottle of whisky which Carole had given him. He'd tried to smuggle it away, and the police had to remove it from him as he desperately sought to undo it and pour it down his throat. Screaming he now "He's not going to die, he's not going to die! It's not me, you know me! He shouldn't have brought that knife with him!" He tried to say Dick was the one in possession of the knife. Dad's brain was desperately trying to piece together a plausible plan, even in this moment of disaster he still tried to divert blame. Once at the police station he was taken to the interview room where his statement was taken and recorded.

"It was my knife. He grabbed it and lunged at me. It was one big bundle. He took the knife off me. There was a scuffle. He came for me and fell on it. The bastard kept hold of the knife, I don't know how. I didn't want the cunt to die. We scrabbled, the knife went into him. I felt it go. I tried to keep him alive, the kiss of life and everything. I didn't want the bastard to die, I am giving you it all. I said "Keep away, don't cause me any trouble!" He snatched the knife from my hand. It was just a threat. I didn't mean to use it. The knife was just there to warn him. You've got me now. I said "Look Dick, I don't want you to cause any trouble, go home." I don't stab anybody. You know me, belted them and that. I didn't mean to do the geezer, he asked for it."

The Sergeant in attendance said that Dad became hysterical again at this point, and then turned from hysteria to violence. The officers present had to restrain him, he was like a trapped animal, and other officers had to be called to help. Dad screamed "It was his knife, his knife!" Later he would claim to have previously asked the police for help because he was being provoked by Dick. This claim was never substantiated. A detective chief superintendent visited Dad the following day to report that Dick had died "Richard Gilchurch is dead, stabbed several times." Dad cried "He's not dead is he?! Tell me he's not dead!" The detective chief superintendent told him solemnly "He's dead. You must be quite sure of that, and stabbed with a knife that I am told came from the kitchen drawer in your house." Dad pleaded "No I didn't do anything! I got the knife to make him go. That's all. Tell me he's not dead!" The chief inspector told him "I can't do that. Why did you get the knife from the kitchen drawer?" Sobbing Dad continued to plead "To make him go! To make him go! He was going mad." He went on to allege that Dick had tried to take the knife, it had all been an accident and the knife had "Just gone in him." The chief inspector said to him "It couldn't have just gone in, he was stabbed five times." When the photographs taken at the scene were examined they showed that Dick had cuts to his hands in accordance with him having tried to defend himself.

Chapter 18

The penalty

1975

Dad was held at Leicester Prison while he waited for his trial date. Carole must have had some genuine affection for him still, as she visited him practically every day. The trial was set for March 5th. The clerk of the court explained to Dad that he was charged with murder and asked how he pleaded. Dad replied "Not guilty, but guilty to manslaughter." His defence highlighted that the most probable verdict that a jury would return was manslaughter on the grounds of provocation. It wasn't possible for the prosecution to prove that Dad had not been provoked. It was left to the jury to decide.

The defence appealed to the jury to take into consideration expert medical advice, that suggested Dad's brain had rapid mental deterioration over the course of the previous 18 months. Everything that could be used to gain the sympathy of the jury and reduce his sentencing was dredged up. The world that Dad lived in, the wife swap, that between the foursome, and in both homesteads, there were drugs and the influence of drugs. After Dad had joined Carole, his drug taking and alcohol consumption had spiralled. They reiterated that Dad's first reaction to assist Dick after stabbing him, negated that it was premeditated and intended to take his life. The statements of the officers at the scene were used to emphasise the distressing state of hysteria that he was in.

"The officers were confronted with a man in extreme agitation, high hysteria, culminating in the cells, they had to quell him somehow from the lunatic that he was in their hands. Those officers who first arrived at the scene were faced with a state of chaos. While in the police car an officer had to dissuade him from babbling on by saying "Now look, this is a serious matter, please hold onto yourself, let us get to the police station, then you can be interviewed."

A consultant psychiatrist was called to help understand the medical issues regarding Dad's mental stability, unbeknown to anyone he had been to seek help, and he'd asked to be admitted to a mental institute in Cambridge. The doctor had attended a home office committee in connection with the problem of drugs, and had specialist training in the diagnosis and treatment of mental illness. Only one month before the attack Dad had been referred to the doctor for help. On the day of the appointment Dad arrived but the doctor was unable to attend. Eventually Dad saw him at a rearranged appointment. The doctor described how Dad admitted to drinking prior to the appointment to "Summon the courage to meet him." The doctor described how he had smelt the alcohol on him. When asked by the judge what his expert opinion was regarding Dad's mental state he replied "In my original examination he showed signs of deterioration in judgment, in insight, in concentration and memory, which is consequent with his indulgence. I should also mention when I examined him on November 4th in prison, he was almost unable to give an account of himself, it took a long time to get him settled enough for a reasonable examination." The judge asked "Has his brain been permanently damaged by his addiction?" to which the doctor confirmed "Lysergic acid does, as with other drugs, over a period of time. He has probably damaged his brain. Maybe not irretrievably, but certainly for some time to come."

More revelations, as it was disclosed that Dad had suffered a neurosis for years and had previously been prescribed a powerful tranquilizer called "Largactil". When he was 13 he'd had a head injury that left him unconscious for a whole day. The judge asked the doctor if he believed Dad had a psychopathic element in his genetic makeup or if his behaviour was the result of his addiction. It was revealed that Dad had been taking drugs since he was 14 years old. Cocaine and LSD. The doctor believed that alone was enough to deteriorate a person's character and personality.

The defence pleaded that the court had a duty not only to punish him, but also that it was in the interest of the public to rehabilitate him. He should be prepared to return to society cured of his addiction. The judge read out the verdict.

"David Charles, this is a terrible story that has been unfolded in front of me. I am told you have been taking drugs, and hard drugs, since you were about 14, and have reduced yourself by that over-indulgence and over-indulgence in alcohol to the man who killed Gillingham on this night. I accept, as is clear to you from the fact that you are not facing a murder charge now, that there was some provocation that you received from Gillingham, both preceding this tragic night and to some extent on the night in question: the extent of that is impossible for me to assess. What is clear, and what is in front of me, is what you did to him. Whatever provocation was suffered, you took a knife to him and inflicted those terrible wounds of which I have seen the photographs, four in his back, one in his front, and that was a violent and savage response to whatever violence he was offering you. I have listened with the greatest care to what the doctor has said, and I have no doubt that the effect upon you of prolonged drug-taking has led you to behave as you behaved on that night, and as you have behaved over a large number of years. I

111

cannot shut my eyes to the fact that in a number of offences since 1967 you have shown violence of one sort or another over a period of 4 or 5 years, and this was another eruption of violence on this particular occasion. I take into account as best I can what has been said so fully on your behalf by your defence, but it seems that you were affected by drink on this night, possibly by drugs (there is no evidence of that). But you have reacted as you did, and I am unable to accept that your mind was a blank, as your doctor says, on that night. It may well have been that you were provoked excessively to do what you did, but the nature of your response was grossly excessive in my view. I have got to consider what sentence to pass upon you. I think this was a very bad case of manslaughter indeed, and the sentence I pass upon you is one of 10 years' imprisonment,"

Dad wrote to appeal that the sentence was too severe, he continued to insist he'd been provoked, that his mental health had been affected by the provocation. The judge responded by telling him "This is a lenient sentence, you have written to complain about."

Those four to five years of violence were the first years of Spencer's, mine and Antony's lives. 1974 was the last year of Dick's life and the last year that Sammy had a father. Dick was cremated, and his ashes were given to Mum, in recognition of her as his common law wife.

Chapter 19

Starting again, again

1980

The council moved us after Mum had badgered and beleaguered housing officers to transfer us to a bigger house. I was eleven now and it was becoming awkward, having to share with my 10 year old brother. My bed had been moved into the dining room so that Shaun could share with Antony. It was done in preparation for the housing officer to see our situation. It worked, we got a transfer. Wulfstan Way was only a couple of streets away from our old house, we'd be staying in the same neighbourhood. There wasn't the same excitement as moving to Godwin Close, but I looked forward to having my own bedroom, with anticipation. The new house wasn't as cosy as it only had a fireplace in the living room, and there wasn't any other heating. We moved in the summer but by the time winter came, Mum was having to get up early to make a fire up to warm the house. She looked like a wild woman, cigarette hanging from her mouth, half of it ash already, sagging ready to drop. In her dressing gown, hair tangled and untidy, cursing under her breath, as she tried holding a sheet of newspaper over the fireplace to encourage the chimney to draw up the flames "For fuck sake! I hate this fucking house! Why did we move here, it's always cold, nothing ever seems to go right. It's alright for Tomas, he's up and fucked off to work first thing and I'm left trying to start the bloody fire!" Our days started miserably. Antony and I wanting to help but not knowing how. I was at Netherhall secondary school now, with Antony not far behind me. We still saw Dad sporadically, Nana and Granddad didn't pressure us to visit him. Frequently they went alone or alternated which one of us would go with them. It was easier that way, making visits only occasional for each of us now. Spencer

113

usually got the short straw. Because he lived with Nana and Granddad, he was more likely to be expected to go. Antony was the one who didn't mind, appearing to quite look forward to seeing Dad. The relationship between Tomas and Antony had worsened, in part because Antony's attachment to Dad irked Tomas. Mum abstained from showing either of us affection, though she was devoted to Shaun. I'm not sure if that was because she didn't feel any affection for us, or if it was to mollify Tomas. He seemed to find us a constant irritation. The atmosphere in the house was turbulent. We couldn't do anything right. Tomas would give us chores to do. Make a cup of tea, that was either too weak, or had too much sugar. Do the washing up, that was never done properly. Tidy up our bedrooms, they still looked like shit pits. Breathe, we did that too noisily. Cough or sneeze when we had a cold, couldn't we "Shut the fuck up and stop sniffing!" or slurping, or wheezing. We became clumsy, afraid to carry a cup of tea or dry a plate. We turned on each other in attempts to be popular and earn Tomas's approval. We still had the weekends, Nana and Granddads. Our haven, the safety zone.

Going to our grandparents at the weekend was the backbone of our lives. I don't know who I would've become if it hadn't have been for their love and support. I know now that they were the sustenance of my childhood. If I hadn't had the love that they gave me, I would have had none. My brothers and I shared camaraderie, we enjoyed times of togetherness and there was a certain amount of loyalty. Antony and I did share some affection but never with Spencer. Spencer was proud, he was the oldest therefore he was in authority and made sure we knew it. It never troubled him when we left to go home on Sunday evenings, and he was happy to have the status quo back to normality. He liked being the only child. When we were there we interfered with his things, and wanted attention. In comparison to our home lives his was

114

very indulgent, which made him seem rather spoilt. Sometimes there were moments of spitefulness. He liked to separate Antony and I, choosing one of us over the other. He would destroy something one of us had made, or ridicule things we did. Nana or Granddad would admonish him for being selfish. Despite the impertinence he showed us, we still held him in high regard. He was our big brother. We couldn't remember the last time he'd come to our house, Mum and he were estranged. Spencer never mentioned her, and he didn't ask after her. Fourteen now, he probably found us an annoyance to have around. When we went to stay, often he'd disappear off to his room, withdrawing and disassociating himself from us. That was unless he had a very specific need that I was especially useful for satisfying.

Sunday mornings I liked get up early and help Nana in the kitchen. If I was in the mood for baking that was the time to do it. Nana would already be there making a cooked breakfast for Granddad, and preparing vegetables for Sunday lunch. She wore a pinny that tied at the hip, and slippers. She'd be smiling, even as she squinted at the lard spitting from the frying pan, as sausages rolled around with their skins splitting and bursting. The radio was on, and there might be a tune from "The Glen Miller Band" playing. Granddad would be outside the back door polishing shoes, mending bicycle punctures, or cleaning out the fireplace and resetting it. The kitchen would be warm because the oven was going already. There was a fridge, but Nana still kept things in the larder. There was a stone shelf that she put the milk and cheese on to keep. "Yorkshire puddings are always better if the milk is at room temperature." She said. Getting an earthenware mixing bowl from the larder for me, she asked "What would you like to make? Fairy cakes or a Victoria sandwich? How about a chocolate sponge?" I'd look around the kitchen to see what she'd been baking. There was always a dessert on Sundays and I knew there would be either a trifle in the making, a lemon meringue pie, or perhaps a rice pudding. Today it was going to be apple pie, the aroma of cooking apples simmering on the stove top infused the room, "Can I make the pastry Nana, and some chocolate fairy buns too?" She laughed nodding her head and set about fetching all the ingredients. She knew all the measurements and would reel off "For your pastry you'll need four heaped tablespoons of plain flour and 3ozs of butter, rub it all together between your fingers until it's like breadcrumbs." I'd concentrate hard to keep the mixture in the bowl, not spilling it everywhere in case she shouted at me. "It's always best to have cool hands, when you make pastry and not overwork the dough" she instructed. Granddad would look round the kitchen door to see what was happening "Is that breakfast ready yet? What's going on in here then?" I'd preen and busy myself so he could see I was making something "Ooooh look at you! What you making then, something nice for tea this evening?" I'd say over my shoulder, "I'm doing the pastry for apple pie Granddad, and I'm going to make buns for us all!" If Antony was inclined he would come and join us, sometimes there would be all three of us lined up at the work counter baking. Spencer would still be upstairs and Antony might be making plasticine figures at the breakfast table. Nana would serve the breakfast on plates warmed under the grill, the pastry making paused, and we'd sit down and eat. Granddad shouted up the stairs "Spencer, breakfast is ready!" We would gather at the table. No one picked up their cutlery until we were all settled and ready to eat. We didn't talk as we ate, because Granddad wouldn't allow that. He would tell us off if we started chatting while a mouthful of food churned around like a cement mixer. When we'd all finished our last mouthful, and placed our cutlery neatly on the plate, then we might chat about how we'd slept or if we'd dreamed, and what the week ahead might bring.

I remember a knock at the back door and Jenny the neighbours grown up daughter waiting to be invited in "Jenny! How lovely to see you, come in!" Granddad hugged her before going back outside to finish his chores "It feels like ages! How are you? Would you like a coffee or a tea?" Nana greeted her cheerfully. I went back to my baking and listened as they chatted. It was nice because Jenny was so friendly. She always asked "How are you Samantha?" including me in the conversation "How's school? Is Mum alright? You're growing up so fast! You're a young lady now." I liked Jenny, she was pretty with long blonde hair and lots of bangles that tinkled together on her wrists. Suddenly I felt ugly and fat next to her. Excusing myself I said "I've had enough of baking now Nana, I'm going to get washed and dressed." Slipping away upstairs I locked myself in the bathroom to stare at myself in the mirror. My hair needed washing, it looked lank and greasy, there were pimples on my forehead and I needed to brush my teeth. Going through the motions, I did the best I could to look presentable, but couldn't face going back downstairs yet. I'd wait until Jenny had gone. It was then I heard Spencer moving about in his room, I'd go and see what he was doing, maybe he wanted some company. Knocking on his door I asked "Spencer, can I come in?" There was a pause, some seconds passed before he came and opened the door "What do you want?" Feeling reproached, I went to turn away "Nothing, it doesn't matter." He grabbed my arm "What is it? It's alright, don't go away. Stay up here." That was better, I felt wanted and realized I'd been too quick to get in a strop. "Can we listen to some music? I'm bored, I don't want to go downstairs. Jenny is here and Nana is too busy talking to her." Spencer had his own LP player in his bedroom and had started a small collection of albums and a few singles that he'd occasionally let Antony and me listen to. "What do you want to play? Have a look and choose something." We were allowed to watch "Top of the Pops" every week at home so I had some idea of what was current in the charts. Wanting to impress him I asked "Have you got any of "The Police" or there's a song I really like called "Going underground". That pleased him, enthusiastic now, he responded "Yeah! I know that one, that's the Jam. I've got that. I'll find it" He thumbed through his collection and finding it, pulled it from the rest. He stopped. I was waiting, there was an odd look on his face. I could see he was thinking, he got up and pushed the door shut "How much do you want to hear it?" He looked at me, there was an urgent look in his eyes. I didn't understand. "I really like it, I want to hear it." I shrugged. Why did he shut the door? I was getting confused. "If you really want me to play it, lay down on the floor." I felt silly now, I didn't understand what laying down had to do with listening to music "Why do you want me to lay down?" I could see he was getting exasperated with me, I was such an idiot. It was so stupid I wanted him to think I was cool, that I was equal to him. Without asking further questions I lay down. Spencer stood listening at the door, voices were muffled from the kitchen as Nana and Jenny chatted. There were tinkering noises coming from the backdoor as Granddad serviced our bikes and Antony must still have been engrossed with the plasticine. Undoing his trousers, Spencer knelt over me, pushing my skirt up over my waist he left my underwear intact but proceeded to press himself against my stomach. I was still, I had never been this close with him. Rubbing and pressing against me, he breathed fast and heavily in my ear, until shuddering, he came to a halt. I was frozen stiff, unable to move. Staring at the ceiling as he pulled himself up and away from me "Get up now, before anyone sees you," he threw a pair of socks at me "here, wipe yourself with these." I was still laying with my skirt up to the waist, raising my head warily I looked down, to where there was a wet pool beginning to dribble down my side "Quickly I said!" he snapped at me, I sat upright and began wiping away the

118

fluid running across my stomach, the smell was repugnant to me, I felt disgusted, nearly retching as the alien odour invaded my sense of smell. "If you ever tell anyone what I did, I swear I'll tell them you're a liar. Do you hear me?" Spencer snarled at me, his top lip curled and his eyes boring into mine "No one would believe you, who would they believe me or you? So you keep this to yourself and never tell anyone, do you understand?" I didn't speak. Smoothing my skirt back into place I stood shakily. "Do you understand?" he hissed at me again, I nodded mutely. He turned to put the single on the player as I left the room. Locking myself in the bathroom once more, I washed myself again. Looking in the mirror at my lank hair and pimples, I felt ugly.

This exploitation and manipulation of me by my eldest brother would continue for the next couple of years.

Chapter 20

Home coming

Dad's expected date of release was summer of 1981. I would be twelve, Antony eleven and Spencer fifteen. There was an amount of speculation at home, Mum and Tomas even asked Antony and I if we knew when he was coming out. Nana or Granddad hadn't told us, although things were afoot and there was an impending sense of something about to happen. Plans were being discussed in hushed tones and preparations being made in secrecy. Nana was looking anxious, as Granddad behaved industriously. He didn't linger to chat with Mum when he dropped us home on Sunday evenings. Change was coming again, we recognized it for what it was, and the adults always gave it away. It could be smelt in the air, they almost gave off different body odours with their new perspectives and attitudes. We knew the signs, we'd seen them before.

Tomas was working as a milk man now. After a string of jobs. There had been intervals where he was unemployed, though they were always short lived. Sometimes he'd do a bit of cash in hand work for a building contractor that lived in the area, he'd be part of the demolition team that cleared sites ready for construction. Nana Sheila came to visit practically every afternoon, much to Mum's irritation. Nana had another dog since Fred had died, she called this one Rupert. Tomas loved taking the micky out of her choice of name. We also had another dog, a "Heinz fifty seven", mostly Labrador mix, called Ben. Every afternoon Rupert was walked to our house, often they would already be there when we arrived home from school, or shortly after us. Mum made her a cup of tea and if she was in a good mood would invite Nana to stay for Dinner, which wasn't often. Nana gossiped about the latest scandals in the neighbourhood and made crude comments about men. If Tomas was there, she would be suggestive and flirt overtly with him. Rupert continually tried mounting Ben and Nana would over-excitedly shout "Look at them Carolyn! Couple of queers, Rupert wants to do Ben up the bum!" She relished Mum's discomfort, Mum loathed her uncouthness, and there were several outbursts. Mum lost her temper and would tell Nana to "Go on, Fuck off! I've had enough of you coming around here!" Tomas would try to intervene "Calm down love, there's no need to be like that." But Mum wouldn't be pacified "No I'm not having it, who does she think she's talking to? You're nothing but a shit stirring slag! Get out!" She'd have Nana by her coat collar and be shoving her towards the front door, dogs barking, Nana remonstrating. Once she was the other side of the front door and the door shut, there was no coming back in. When they were getting along Mum would go and visit Melvyn at Bedford Prison with her. They would take the bus there, making an outing of it, combining it with a shopping trip. Sometimes Antony or I would go with Nana to keep her company. We would be persuaded to go and always treated to something nice for making the effort. It might be a new dress for me, or a toy for Antony. We were familiar with prison visiting procedures now. Mark came to see Mum regularly still, he and Tomas got along well. Mark liked Tomas's sharp sense of humour and Tomas, always the talkative one, enjoyed Mark's company. Sometimes it was Mum and Mark that went to visit Melvyn together. The threesome were close, even now.

I was a solemn child, people commented upon how little I smiled. There didn't seem to be much to smile about. There were moments of fleeting happiness at home, I loved Tomas when he played music and described what the song was about or what the lyrics were telling us. If we watched a film, whether it be a western or a war film, he would give us an explanation of what was happening at that moment in history. He was knowledgeable, an avid reader with an inquiring mind, soaking up information which he would relay back to us, including my Mum. We spent afternoons and evenings listening to him rant about a subject or comically replaying an occurrence that he'd witnessed that day, often jumping up off the sofa to energetically re-enact a scene. When he was like this we were mesmerized by him. The only problem was, his mood could change so suddenly. If he detected a slight of any kind he became a raging tyrant. When he spoke it was best to listen and remain silent, but not too silent, that maddened him too. Antony spent most of his time in his own world, playing with his toys, off out on his bike with other boys, always up to mischief somewhere. Endlessly Antony was in trouble for something, coming in late for dinner, getting letters home from school or back chatting Tomas. When he was out and about, he was up to no good. The police brought him home a couple of times and once came knocking for him because he was suspected of shoplifting. Tomas was furious, though Antony denied it vehemently. Mum raided his bedroom, and seizing clothing, cigarettes and magazines, burnt them on a bonfire in the garden. Every day there was some bone of contention or a new dispute. Tomas could lose his temper frying an egg. It was normal for him to be bare-chested at home. Frying himself a breakfast was a sight to behold. Egg and bacon simmering furiously in the pan, would spurt and spit at him until, in a pique of frustration he'd start swearing at it "Don't you fucking spit at me! You fucking cunting useless piece of shit!" He would brandish the spatula, waving it in front of him as a shield against the onslaught of hot fat. It was like a 'Tomas vs the fried egg' tennis match. Eventually overcome with fury at the outrage of it he would open the back door and throw the frying pan, eggs, bacon and all outside. We would steer clear of him when he was in these rages, it was terrifying to see. Our dog Ben would hide behind the sofa, and if the cat got in the way, as she was fleeing towards the door, she would get a quick up the backside on her journey. Misty was pregnant and had been kicked so many times that her kittens, when they came, were all still born, the last became wedged in her uterus with its face peering out at us. Mum, Antony and I carried her to the vets so that he could remove it. The vet spayed Misty so she wouldn't get pregnant again. Mum had a row with Tomas when he came in from work later, demanding that he never kick the animals again. He laughed mockingly. Slightly abashed he insisted that there must have been something wrong with the kittens anyway.

Our weekends at Nana and Granddad's were different now we were older. Spencer and Antony wanted to do more without me. They liked to play football over at the playing field away from the house and I was a nuisance to them. They complained that I followed them around and didn't know how to do boy's stuff. They liked play fighting, getting over enthusiastic, they would get too rough and Spencer would overpower Antony, causing him upset and humiliation. Four years younger, he wasn't going to win the rough and tumble. Spencer would hold him in a head lock while repeating "Submit! Do you submit? Give up…tell me you submit!" Then legs kicking and fists flying Antony would scrabble against him in a frenzy of movement, to confuse his hold and force him to relinquish his grip. Spencer would giggle fanatically as he frantically tried to pin Antony down to maintain the upper hand. These games were of no interest to me. The few times I'd been subjected to them had resulted in panic and tears for me. This display of emotion labelled me as pathetic, too girly to be able to join in, and a killjoy. These power struggles for dominance happened habitually. It was increasingly difficult to bear the visits, I avoided any chance at being alone with Spencer and couldn't face any physical contact with him. He was scheming and cunning

123

enough to outwit me, managing to engineer unavoidable moments where we were left together. Much to Mum and Tomas's chagrin I was reluctant to go to my grandparents, requesting to stay at home more often. There was also the attraction of having my younger brother. I wanted to spend time with him, enjoying the uncomplicated, easy innocence of his company. Helping him to learn to read, I found pleasure in his budding keenness to learn. That was the panacea I unknowingly needed.

We were only told the weekend before Dad's release. When we went to visit next time, he would be free. Granddad was the one to impart the news. He told us in a sombre voice, unsmiling "Your Dad will be here when you come next weekend, he's coming home. You can tell your Mum and Tomas, but nobody else. He'll be looking forward to seeing you." There were no high spirits, the three of us didn't cheer or jump up and down with excitement. We were glum. That feeling of dread I'd had visiting him in prison for the first time presented itself again. Although we knew it was coming, there had been no warning I'd believed we'd have time to be prepared. This time Granddad did come in to see Mum and Tomas when he dropped us home. We were ushered into the living room, so the adults could shut themselves away, behind the kitchen door, to chat in private. When Granddad left, Mum looked stricken. Tomas was comforting her, his arms around her shoulders, his forehead resting against hers, he said "You don't have anything to worry about love, you have me and I'll never let anyone hurt you." That week little reference was made to the fact that our Dad was coming back.

The following Friday Granddad came once again to collect Antony and me, as he had countless weekends before. In the car we were subdued, not really sure what to say or how to behave. Granddad broke the silence saying gently "Your Dad's at the house, he's pleased to be home and

124

very excited to see you. He's a different person now, being away has changed him. He's going to do the best he can to be a good Dad and stay out of trouble. It won't be how it was before, that's all in the past now. So we're all going to get on with our lives. Be happy to see him. He's waited a long time for this day." Our full attention hung on every one of Granddads words, we watched him speak as he drove. Of all the grownups we knew, when he spoke it was sincere, he was always truthful with us. We trusted that he wouldn't put us in a dangerous situation. If he said Dad was alright, then he must be. Arriving at the house, we hadn't opened the car doors, before the front door was flung open. Dad with Spencer at his side, came striding down the path to meet us, hand in hand I believe now, that at that moment he honestly wanted to start from scratch. He really believed he could be our Dad properly. Antony jumped out of the car, and ran into Dad's embrace "Dad! Welcome home!" Dad spun around in a circle with Antony hugged against him "Awww my boy, that's a proper welcome! Look at me, free! I love you!" I hardly recognized Antony, usually reserved with his feelings, he generally cultivated an air of aloofness. I'd slid out from the back of the car and stood awkwardly, waiting my turn. I was nervous, but fascinated too. Dad was different. Here, outside Nana and Granddads house in normal clothes, he looked handsome. He looked the way I imagined Dad's should look, not like Tomas with flared jeans and shaggy long hair, or any of my uncles with their open necked shirts and necklaces. He looked like a Dad from one of my Christmas annuals. I edged closer, aware that I was supposed to be pleased to see him. I was scrutinizing him, searching, and trying to see inside him. Looking back at me his eyes searched mine, and pulling Antony with him towards me, he scooped me under his arm, so he enveloped both of us "Don't think I'm leaving you out, I've been waiting for this! Don't be shy with me. I'm your Dad! Now we're going to be a family again." Squeezing us

125

to him, I enjoyed the feel of his arm around me, I liked the sensation of his hug. He was my real Dad, but in his jubilation, he didn't see me cringing. Nana was on the doorstep, waving at us to come in, tears running down her face. Granddad shooed us all towards the house away from the neighbours prying eyes. I think they were fearful of being celebratory in the street. We piled into the house "Dinner is sausage and mash, go and sit at the table, we're all ready to eat!" Nana was wiping tears away with a tissue and blowing her nose, Dad grabbed her and kissing her noisily on the cheek, sang "I'll be working my way back to you girl!" She flapped a tea towel at him, shushing him, as he tried to dance her back into the kitchen.

Chapter 21

A sense of humour

Having Dad around was interesting and difficult. All the usual routines we'd had we're broken. Where Granddad had taken us to play rounders, or cricket at a local beauty spot, Dad wanted to kick a ball around at the nearest park. Usually we had sausage and mash on Saturdays at lunchtime, with rice pudding for afters. He shunned that saying "Aargh! That's so old fashioned, it's like being back inside! I reckon we should all have a Chinese take away, there's a new place opened up on the high street." Nana wasn't impressed. They never bought take-away food. Even if we were going on holiday, they'd do a food shop to take with us, sometimes even taking a joint of meat to roast in the caravan for Sunday lunch! We three were excited though, thinking it was really exotic, we all pleaded that we try it, just once. The only time Antony and I had Chinese food was if we went to collect it for Mum and Tomas. Sometimes if we were lucky, we ate the leftovers from their plates. We forgot how safe and confident we were in the traditions we normally upheld at our grandparents. Fascinated by our Dad and his sudden spontaneity. We thought he was cool, and that being around him was fun. He was rash and impulsive. We never knew what he might suggest. We didn't watch the usual TV programmes or the Saturday night matinee. Dad bought home videos, which were often not suitable for us to watch, but if Nana or Granddad protested, he'd yell "Stop interfering! I'm their Father, I decide what's suitable! They're not babies anymore." Looking obviously upset and disapproving, they didn't argue with him, making gasps of displeasure at the TV screen whenever there was violence or unnecessary nudity. Staying up later too, we watched "Tales of the unexpected" or whatever late night movie was showing. I'd be nodding off in the corner of the sofa and Nana would have to nudge me awake, insistent that I go to bed.

Dad began going out. Restless he would suddenly decide to abandon our company and defiantly announce "I'm going out for a bit." Granddad would look at him suspiciously asking "Where are you going at this time? I thought you were settled in for the evening, I think you should stay in. with the children and spend time with them." This made Dad more wilful. He didn't like being questioned. We sat still, poised, quietly waiting for his response, and waiting for a row. "The kids are glued to the TV, I need to go out. I can't stay in the house every night. I'm going to the pub for a pint, I'll only be an hour. I've got to start getting out." When Granddad turned his face away from him and back to the TV without response, Dad slammed out of the door shouting "It's like a fucking prison! I'm a grown man, I've served my time and I'll do as I fucking well please!" He left us feeling wretched, Nana red in the face and tearful, while Granddad reproached her "He'll never learn! That boy is no good, there's going to be more trouble!"

A girlfriend appeared on the scene, Sandra was her name, a bit of a rocker chick. Dad introduced her to us and we warmed to her straight away. She always wore black, with lots of kohl eye makeup, a choker around her neck and glossy black bobbed hair. She was a little bit old for the look, and our grandparents didn't know what to make of her! My Nana liked having a woman around to visit, but Granddad didn't have much time for her. She liked astronomy and read Tarot cards, which was definitely a contributing factor for Granddads indifference to her. I was thrilled because Sandra said she would read my Tarot cards for me but when Granddad heard, he soon put a veto on that, saying "We won't have any of that nonsense in this house, load of old hokum and trickery pokery."

That was enough to deter Sandra from ever mentioning the mystics again. Dad enjoyed the discomfort it caused, upsetting the dynamic in the house was satisfying to him. Any chance of confrontation or conflict with Granddad was entertainment, especially with us and a girlfriend to put on a performance for. Dad had started bringing cans of cider into the house, which he and Sandra would sit drinking, whispering and giggling together, getting louder and more raucous. It wasn't a pleasant sight. We didn't understand what was funny, or why they were laughing. Fondling and nuzzling Sandra on the sofa while we were all present, irritated Granddad especially and Dad would smirk at him boldly, provoking a reaction "What are you doing? Remember children are present. Why don't you go upstairs if you want to be alone?" That was just the excuse Dad was hoping for "Come on Sandra, we're going down the pub. We'll have some peace there." With a flurry of activity, they'd suddenly get up, put on coats and be gone, only a brief gust of Sandra's perfume remained, as she'd swung her coat around her as they left. Nobody bothered to comment now. It was a usual occurrence, and a relief when he was gone.

Now, whenever we went to stay, Sandra would already be there. She had a certain vulnerability, anxious to please, and agreeing with anything Dad said. She looked at him like a dog looks at its master. More and more often, I noticed she had a black eye or bruises up her arms. She was afraid of Dad. We were all afraid of him. Whenever he spoke to me I felt he was mocking me. He would look scornfully at me, and I wouldn't initiate conversation with him. Just like being with Tomas, it was better to speak only if spoken too. One afternoon he asked us if we'd like to take the ball over to the park and have a kick about. These were rare moments when he wanted to actually do something with us. Our outings with Granddad had been upset, because Dad's bidding came first. Stirred by the idea of doing something together outdoors, we agreed unanimously to go. Sandra also came. Dad liked to sport a jumper across his shoulders, which he kept hitching back into position as he ran around in control of the football, selfishly in possession shouting "C'mon! Tackle for it! Try and get the ball away from me, you useless little drips." This jibe motivated Antony and Spencer into action, both surging forward, eagerly trying to show him their footwork skills. How we wanted to prove we were valuable. I had hung back, not wanting to perform for his pleasure. Seeing my lack of interest, he called to me "Samantha!" As I turned, he kicked the ball with all his might, his smiling expression full of malice. The ball soared at speed directly into my face, my cheek broke its trajectory. The impact was so harsh that it nearly knocked me to the floor. I cried out, my hands flying to my face, stinging as if slapped. Sandra ran to me "Samantha are you alright! Oh let me see, come here. Please let me see!" She tried to prise my hands away from my face as I sobbed. I was hurt and embarrassed all at the same time. Dad was in fits of hysterics, laughing so much he'd doubled over in paroxysms of joy, not even trying to conceal his delight at my expense. In that moment, despite the humiliation and upset, I knew I hated him. I wished he was dead. If I'd had a gun I'd have shot him, as a vet might destroy a rabid dog. There would be many times I'd fantasize stalking him down and killing him.

At home with Mum and Tomas, I enjoyed a certain amount of respect as the oldest. Antony wasn't interested in Shaun, whereas I doted on him. I was trusted to be responsible around him, which gave me some kudos with Tomas. He invited me to help with a couple of Saturday morning milk rounds, the incentive being some pocket money, made the idea attractive to me. The last time I'd done anything alone with Tomas was when we'd been at the swings with Ricky. Being alone with Tomas wasn't appealing to me, but I needed money. I wanted to be able to go in to town with Mum and buy myself a new outfit. I was sick and tired of wearing castoffs from charity shops courtesy of Nana Sheila. So it was agreed. Mum tried to prepare me as best she could "It'll be very early, you'll have to be up at the crack of dawn, dress warmly, and remember to do exactly as Tomas says. You'll need to be quick and keep up." She was dubious. I don't think she ever realized the reserves of will power and resilience I had. Up in the early hours, only Tomas and I were awake. Tomas said "Don't bother washing. Get your clothes on and we'll go. You can have breakfast when we're finished, you'll have worked up an appetite by then." We left quietly, going in his car to the dairy to collect the milk float. I was half asleep and uncertain about what my part was to be. At the dairy I waited, while Tomas loaded crate after crate onto the milk float. It was a stark, fluorescent lit industrial unit, lots of concrete and signs about workplace regulations. A few other men similarly loaded up other milk floats for their runs too. Tomas bantered with them "Father Murphy's baptising Paddy, he says "Paddy have you found Jesus yet." What does Paddy say?" The other men groaned and relenting asked "What does Paddy say?" Tomas laughing at his own joke already, chuckled "He says "Father Murphy, are you sure this is where he fucking fell in!" There were guffaws and snorts of laughter as the men prepared to set off. Tomas pulling my coat collar up around my neck, said "We're ready, you'll come up in the cab at the front of the float with me, there isn't a seat for you, so you have to stand and hold on." It wasn't as if the float was designed to go fast, Tomas was making sure I wasn't likely to fall out of the door less vehicle while it was moving. We set off, Tomas driving and pulling over to the side of the road. We worked as a team, he explained that he would pass me the milk bottles, and I would run where instructed, to deposit the milk on doorsteps, inside porches, or beside front doors. This worked quite well, he was short with me at times, because I wasn't as fast as he'd hoped, or I'd head towards the wrong door. So he had to

131

be vigilant with me "No! Not that door, bloody idiot! The next door!" he'd hiss in hushed tones, so as not to wake the whole street. We continued like this, it felt for an age. Somebody had put a note out "No milk today, thank you." Tomas cursed, "Why don't they let me know the day before if they don't want any milk? Save me stopping!" he went on to tell me about one customer who had "Pissed me off so much, I did something to piss them off. I was bursting for a shit, so I crouched on their doorstep, and did it right outside their front door. Then I wiped my arse and left the tissue on top of the pile. Serves the bastards right, they probably thought the cleverest dog in Cambridge had shit on their doorstep and even wiped its own arse!" I did laugh at that, it was one of the funniest things I'd ever heard. It was a reasonably successful morning's work. I saw the dawn creep into daylight, gradually the milk bottles became fewer, and the crates emptied. We took the milk float back to the yard and Tomas gave me my wage telling me "You've done well this morning, you worked hard." I felt magnificent. I hadn't disappointed. He was happy with me.

Tomas fascinated me. When he told a story I was captivated, whether it was funny or aggressive, the way he re-enacted it, mimicking voices and behaviour was mesmerizing. Whenever anybody came to the house he would amuse our visitors, regaling them with jokes and tall tales. We had few visitors that weren't family. Usually callers to the house were either Nana Sheila, Mum's brothers, and especially Mark or an addict friend of the family called Phil, that would pop round occasionally to share some "gear" with Tomas. Mum kept a separate cup in the kitchen cupboard for him, because he had an awful way of foaming at the mouth as he talked. Nobody else ever wanted to use that cup. Wild eyed and nervous, he could talk incessantly, on and on about his old Mum and his cat Blackey. We'd be waiting for him to leave. When Tomas and he were talking it was impossible to know what was truth or a joke. It was very rare that anyone came to call late in the evening. There was seldom a knock on the door was knocked after I'd gone to bed.

Chapter 22

Knock Knock

I liked my bedroom. It was small, with only enough room for my single bed, a bedside cabinet and a tiny chest of drawers with a mirror. There was a built in cupboard in the room, which stank of mildew. Mum washed the walls out once in a while, to keep on top of it, but during the winter months, mould grew like hairy jelly. I wouldn't hang my clothes in there, I had enough problems fitting in at school as it was. It wasn't too much of a problem having limited storage space, it wasn't like I had a multitude of clothes to store. Mum had persuaded Tomas to paint the bedroom for me and he'd done a good job, in pale pink. They'd scrimped together, with some help from Nana Sheila to buy a cheap piece of cord carpet, and that was a duskier pink. Mum ordered some Pierrot doll curtains for me, from her home shopping catalogue. Those sad clown figures were all the rage at the time. At night when I'd gone to bed I spent a lot of time reading, often very late into the night when I should have been sleeping. Tomas seeing the light under my bedroom door would shout out "Turn that light out! You've got school in the morning. Wasting electric all fucking night long! Out now, or I'll take the lamp away!" I'd resort to putting the lamp under the bed clothes to read by, only to discover, that it started to burn through the sheets. Mum was already asleep next door. Usually Antony, Shaun and I would have little discussions with her on her bed before we went to our rooms. We loved those snatched moments when we had her to ourselves. Sometimes, exasperated Tomas would have to tell us to leave her in peace, so she could read. She went to bed early every night to read, while Tomas stayed up until the early hours, often even sleeping on the sofa, if he nodded off. A couple of times, I was desperate for a wee, not wanting to arouse Tomas's attention, instead of going to the bathroom to use the toilet, I would wee into my bedside glass and throw it out the window onto the front lawn. Badly timed, he must have heard the loud splosh of water hit the ground during a quiet TV interval. Having pulled the living room curtains back to investigate, he jumped up and threw the front door open to investigate further. Still unclear what had happened, he shouted up the stairs "What are you fucking playing at up there?!" I opened my bedroom door and peered over the bannister at him, red in the face I said "I don't know what that was, I heard it too, it came from outside, I'd opened my window to see what it was!" Unsure what to make of it and where the blame lay, he was undecided about what to say "Well...shut your window, turn your light out and bloody well go to sleep!" He banged the living room door shut and went back to the TV.

The door knocked. I heard Tomas swearing under his breath. I guessed he'd be pulling up and buttoning his jeans to answer the door. I opened my door as quietly as I could to listen out. Realizing my light might give me away, I switched off the lamp and put my ear to the crack of the door. It wasn't Phil. I heard Tomas exclaim in a surprised voice "Hello! Blimey I hardly recognized you, what are you doing here? You'd better come in." There was more than one voice. It sounded like two men. Tomas had lowered his voice "They're all in bed asleep upstairs, come in to the living room." I could hear them. "Sorry to trouble you mate, but we didn't know what else to do." Then "We only want a quick word." It was definitely two voices. I was curious, I didn't recognize them. Feeling odd, my heart raced unexpectedly. Mum switched her bedside light on. Sneaking out of my room, I tip toed to her door and peeped round at her. She was laying down, but had lifted her head and was straining one ear towards the doorway to hear "Who was that?" She asked me "I don't know, I think its two men, I don't know who they are."

Looking a little startled now she sat up and asked "Pass me my dressing gown." Handing it to her, I was feeling concerned now. She wrapped the gown around herself and pulled the belt tight at the waist. We both tip toed onto the landing now, and leant over the bannister. We heard, muffled voices. They were talking amiably with Tomas and he appeared to know them. Mum told me "Go back to bed, stay there, don't come downstairs. No eavesdropping." As she said this the living room door opened, she commanded me again in a whisper. I was staring at her, she repeated "Go back to bed. Now." I went, quietly pressing my bedroom door shut. Still waiting behind it I heard Tomas advance up the stairs. "Who is it?" Mum asked him. In a concerned tone he said "They're not here to cause any trouble love, don't be afraid. It's Dick's brother Kevin and his mate Chris. They want to talk to you, that's all." I could detect the anxiety in his voice. Mum was suddenly fearful "Talk to me! What about? I've got nothing to say. I don't want to get involved." Tomas was firmly insistent "You must Carolyn. What am I supposed to do? Please come and speak to them, they're not here to hurt you. I wouldn't let anything happen to you." Nothing else was said between them, there was silence for a few seconds more, and then I heard them tread back down the stairs.

I gave it a few more minutes, they had gone into the living room, where the two men were waiting. I was afraid for Mum, I wanted to know she was alright, and I wanted to know who these men were. Again, gently opening my bedroom door a crack, I slipped silently into the hallway and began to descend the stairs. Very slowly, edging my way one step at a time, trying to make as little sound as possible. I only needed to get half way down the staircase to hear vague snippets of what was being said. Mum's voice was distinct "I don't want to get involved, they're good people, they've been good to me." Then one of the men said very firmly and clearly "We promise you

Carolyn, no harm will come to them, we don't want to hurt them. We just want him. He has to pay for what he's done." I knew immediately. They were talking about Dad. My heart pumped madly in my chest. I was rooted to the spot. The furious surge of my brain putting the pieces together, and the sudden hammering of my heart drowned out my hearing. They were talking about hurting Dad, and that, I understood. The voices were muffled again, as they continued talking, voices lowered. I was scared, they were not good men. There was some movement in the room. Startled I turned, treading as softly as I could and I stole back to my room not wanting to hear more. I was afraid. Pressing my bedroom door shut once more, I slid under my bedclothes, pulling them over my head. Laying like this I waited, pulse racing, my heart seemed to be beating inside my head. It wasn't much longer when I heard them leave. Apologies were being made "Sorry to have bothered you, you won't hear from us again. Thank you Carolyn, but we didn't know how else to find him." They left. The front door closed behind them. Mum and Tomas, then came upstairs to bed. When they reached the landing, Mum opened my door and looked in on me. As far as she knew, I was asleep. My light was out, I was tucked in tightly, unaware of the conversation that had passed.

Chapter 23

With Intent

Dad had gone to Sandra's. It was a bank holiday weekend, which meant an extended stay at our grandparents. At least one day of it was going to be spent without Dad to ruin it. Some of the best weekends at Nana and Granddads were spent exploring the cattle market opposite the road where they lived. It was a great place to investigate when it wasn't in use, the empty stalls had an unnerving, spine chilling effect on us that was quite exhilarating. It was only ever in proper use on bank holiday's. That was when it came to life and had a different energy. There would be a bustling market full of brightly coloured stalls selling everything from socks and underpants, to kitchen and home wares. Farmers would bring cattle to auction. This May bank holiday, we made our way to the stalls, which were scattered with straw for the livestock, to be housed there temporarily. So many crammed into the stalls that there was no room for them to turn. Pigs would be squealing their dismay, sheep baulked, wide eyed and panicky, and cows queued to be paraded in a circle around the sale room. Spencer, Antony and I had watched as people bid for cows or pigs and the auctioneer would babble figures to the throng, we'd scan the crowd ourselves to spot who was indicating an interest and placing their bid. The gavel would bang as a sale was finalized. It was rousing. The sales room was a nucleus of activity, buyers eager to broker a bargain, while traders keenly waited to assess the earnings their yield had made. When we were satisfied we'd seen enough at the auction, we'd go and peruse the market stalls, looking for a bargain ourselves with pocket money Granddad had given us. I might buy a skipping rope or a stencil kit for drawing,

138

while Antony and Spencer would be interested in marbles, to compete against each other with. Granddad would buy vegetables and homemade preserves, while Nana stayed at home, relishing the peace and quiet. By mid-afternoon there was a hiatus as the market slowed, stalls depleted. Families began their departure across the litter strewn field. We made our way home, happy with the day's undertaking. Back at home, we were greeted by Nana who was curious to know what we'd bought and what stories we had to tell. For tea she'd prepared sandwiches of cold cuts of meat. We were lucky, a real treat was in store and Nana had ordered breaded ham on the bone from the butcher for us all. Replete we ventured to the living room, where Nana offered us dessert "Who'd like a piece of sponge cake or a bun? You can eat it in here this evening, as long as you don't get crumbs everywhere." She beamed at us generously. The three of us chorused "Me, me, me, yes please!" While she went to cut the cake, Granddad got the fire going in the grate and pushed the furniture nearer to the middle of the room, making it cosier, " Let's get comfortable and put the box on shall we? "The Generation Game" is on in a moment." We positioned ourselves in our favourite spots on the sofa, usually Spencer and Antony at either end, me in the middle, Nana and Granddad always had the armchairs. "Here we are then, a nice slice of chocolate sponge each." Nana came in with a tray, laden with mugs of tea and liberal slices of cake "There's a cup of tea to wash the cake down, only it's very hot. Leave it to cool down a bit." She balanced the tray on the arm of the sofa, to a murmur of appreciation, as she delivered a portion of cake to each of us in turn.

The night was drawing in outside, so Nana drew the curtains as we contentedly relaxed together. Laughing unanimously at the silliness of the programme, as contestants tried to complete the challenge presented to them. Nana was watching us, taking pleasure in our enjoyment, she winked at me. Granddad flicked through the newspaper to see what movie was on TV later, he was relieved to have control over what we would watch, without Dad's intervention. Reading aloud to us "There's "Holiday on the buses" before "The Professionals…" He stopped speaking as a loud rapping came from the front door. We were all a little startled, it might be Dad home from the pub. If he'd been drinking he wouldn't bother searching around for his door key. When the lights were on, and we were all still up. Granddad looked uncertain, hesitantly pulled himself out of his armchair, he went to the crack in the curtains and squinted, trying to peer out through the dusk. Tutting to himself now because he couldn't see who was at the door, I asked "Who is it Granddad?" He ignored me, turning the TV down until it was a murmur. Nana said "Be quiet, while Granddad answers the door, it's probably Beryl from next door." Spencer, Antony and I sighed in exasperation, we were involved in the programme and couldn't hear what Bruce Forsyth was saying. Granddad opened the living room door, switched on the hall light and gently pulled the door to behind him. We all sat quietly waiting, curious to hear who was interrupting our evening and impatient for Granddad to return. We heard the door knob turn, then, just as the locking mechanism released, the door was kicked open with sheer brute force. Granddad yelled with shock. The three of us screamed as Nana sprang to the door crying "Les! What is it? Les!" Full of anguish, outweighing fear, she flung the living room door open as two men burst into the hallway, we ran to Nana, terrified for Granddad, but cowering behind her. Aghast, as we saw them. The forced door gaping behind them, they looked wild, one of them brandishing a shotgun. Nana pushed us behind her shouting "Stay in there! Do not come out!" I was petrified as Granddad shouted at them "You can't come in here, he's not here! I know what you want, but he's not here!" Undeterred one of them bawled at him "We know he's here, you can't hide him, and we'll

140

find the bastard!" Granddad went towards him, about to urge the men back towards the front door "Go on, get out, I'm telling you he's not here, he's done his time!" Nana was trying to pull the living room door closed behind her, pushing us back into the room. The man with the shotgun shoved my Granddad with the butt of the gun with all his might, sending him sprawling along the hallway, his plummet only stopped by the door to the kitchen. I was screaming with terror now, they meant to harm us to get to the ends they wanted. Nana wailed "Leave him alone, get out! You brutes, there are children here!" She left us, to run to Granddad as he sat, dazed and bewildered. He was no match for the two thugs. The stuffing knocked out of him, he grappled at the bannister, trying and pull himself up, Nana at his side. One of the men lunged towards us as he headed towards the living room, scaring the three of us ran back into the room. We cried out in terror, believing he was coming for us. His stare held complete contempt as he regarded us, then flicking his eyes around the room he ascertained that Dad wasn't hiding there. He left us huddled together in the corner as he strode back out to the hallway. Nana and Granddad now too crushed couldn't attempt approaching either of them again. Overcome, Granddad still tried to reason "You're wasting your time, he hasn't been here. We haven't seen him for weeks!" Nana was weeping. She cried "Why don't you leave him alone? Don't you think he's suffered too?!" The gunman headed up the stairs, as the unarmed man sneered "Suffered! He's not suffered! He's going around town bragging about how little time he's served for killing Dick! When we get hold of him we'll shut him up, he won't be bragging then!" We stayed trembled in the living room, too petrified to go to our grandparents, while overhead the gunman stalked from one room to the next, searching for Dad. They believed he must be hiding, that he was in the house, in the wardrobe, or under a bed. Doors were being wrenched open, and beds overturned. Nana and

Granddad cowered in the hallway, unable to intervene or come to us. The unarmed intruder, waited at the bottom of the stairs for his accomplice, glowering malevolently, and prepared to use whatever means necessary to intercept Granddad if he tried to stall their hunt. Finally the man with the gun, thumped noisily back down the stairs, shaking his head "No sign of him. The bastard's not here." They both turned their attention to Granddad again, the armed man glaring intently at him, there was silence. We all waited. What would they do now? Their search for Dad had failed. The armed man strode over to my grandparents, he leant towards them, and through clenched teeth, hissed with hatred "Tell Charles when we find him, we're going to blow his kneecaps out!" Then they left, back into the night, as unexpectedly as they had arrived. Nana immediately ran for the phone to call the police, not even considering there may be any chance they could return.

In the living room, still scared, we waited apprehensively. Nana came in and tried to console us "They've gone, it's alright, they've gone and they won't be coming back. The police are on their way." Granddad couldn't come and face us. He had shut himself in the kitchen, and was trying to gather himself. I blurted out through tears and shock "Is Granddad hurt Nana? Will he be alright? Those men hurt him, I saw what they did to him! Can I see him? Please, I want to see if he's hurt!" But Nana wouldn't allow it "Let him be for a moment, he needs to sort himself out before the police get here. He'll be alright, you've all got to be strong now and show us how grown up you are." Spencer was ashen, frightened, and angry "Will the police catch them? Why are they taking so long!? They'll be long gone by now! They'd better catch them, I'm not staying here tonight if they don't!" I was afraid for Granddad, Spencer was afraid for himself and Antony, always Dad's champion, was afraid for Dad "They won't find Dad will they? Will the police find Dad before they do?" He didn't

142

cry, his jaw twitched with tension, and he scratched at one of the patches of eczema on his arm, which was blistering already. Two policemen arrived, then another two. A patrol car was sent to scour the vicinity in an attempt to apprehend the men.

Nana told us to be good and wait quietly in the living room while in the dining room, the policemen took statements from her and Granddad. They examined the front door, and each room, especially the bedroom, where the wardrobe door had been ripped off of its hinges. We sat waiting. Still terrified, we knew that tonight, our lives had been irretrievably altered again. Nana and Granddad wouldn't ever be the same. Spencer began nervously spouting on "I'll kill them, if I find out where they live, I'll get a gun and I'll kill them! I'm not staying here, they could come back. The police won't be able to help us. How will they stop them?" I listened to him, the fear subsiding. It was ok. Nothing would happen while the police were here with us. I began to think more clearly, my thought processes became lucid again. I knew. I knew who they were! They were the men that'd come that night to Mum and Tomas. Without thinking it through, and without analysing the consequences, I blurted it out to Spencer and Antony "I know who they are."

Spencer's attention immediately focussed on me then. I was very aware that Nana and Granddad were in the next room, in here it was only Spencer, Antony and I. Naively I thought that I could confide in my brothers, that what I said next would only go as far as the three of us. Spencer's eyes bored into mine, he wasn't sure if I was a stupid idiot or if I had something worth saying "What do you know? If you know something you'd better tell me, do you know how dangerous those men are?" I already wished I had said nothing, but I knew it was probably too late to backtrack now. Antony intervened "What do you know Manth? If you know something you must tell us. Don't

143

keep it from us. We're your brothers and you wouldn't let anyone hurt us would you? Do you want those men to be caught? Look at what they did to Granddad tonight, imagine if they came back, it could be any night" I felt guilty and ashamed, because maybe I could have prevented the events of that night. I just hadn't thought it through. What could I have done? Should I have betrayed Mum, or should I have known to prepare Granddad? All I had known was that it was better to say nothing and know nothing, we were always being taught to know nothing. So now I told Spencer and Antony the truth "Two men came to Mum's one night, I was in bed, but I heard them. Tomas came and got Mum because they wanted to ask her where Dad's parents lived. Mum must have told them." Spencer turned to Antony. I could see the look of incredulity on their faces. I was so ashamed. Antony looked at me with loathing and said "So Mum told them, and she still sent us here, knowing that those men were coming with a gun." He broke down and cried. Spencer left the room to go to the policemen, leaving the two of us in despair. Never had there been a worse moment. I felt like a lead weight had replaced the organ that had been my heart. I'd made such a huge mistake, which I wouldn't ever be able to take back.

There was a commotion at the front door as Dad arrived. He was greeted by the silent flashing lights of two police cars and met by an officer outside the front door, who explained the events of the evening. Coming in, he was extremely excitable "What the fuck! Where's my Dad? Dad! You'd better find the cunts that did this before I do! Do you hear me?! Dad!" He pushed past the officer to get to Granddad, the officer tried to quieten him down "Mr Charles. Please. Remember your children are in the house and try to remain calm. They've had enough turmoil already tonight." Dad Looked in on Antony and I, he was completely wired. Anger, fright and hatred flitted across his face. He was extremely distressed. Antony remained

144

seated, only moving to raise his head and look at Dad, who hunkered down on his haunches in front of him. Scrutinizing Antony's face and taking his hand he asked "Are you ok? Did they scare you?" Antony stared back at Dad, listless and silent. Dad stood. Raking his eyes over me, he declared "They'll regret this, mark my words, they'll never come here again. Looking for me were they? Well I'll find them and they'll never look any further!" The police officer was saying "Enough now, Mr Charles, that's enough." As another of the officers came from the kitchen to help pacify him "Dave, come through to the back here, your father is very shaken but unharmed. Everyone is obviously upset. We need to gather as much information as we can to find the men that did this. Now you must remain calm." Dad contemptuously swaggered past them both, seeking out Granddad. He found Nana, Granddad and Spencer gathered at the dining room table, where they had been talking with an officer, who sat at the head of the table, making notes. A police radio crackled as Nana got up to dash towards Dad "Oh Dave! It was a nightmare, they came for you! We were so afraid, thank goodness you're safe!" She wailed, fussing and flapping around him, her face distorted with anguish. "I'm alright Mum! It's you and Dad I'm worried about. Did they hurt you Dad? What did they do to you?" He could see Nana was indignant and afraid but unharmed, while Granddad sat there silently, with his hands clasped together on the dining table. Gravely he spoke "They didn't care about anyone or anything, all they wanted was you. If you had been here they would have shot you. I thought they would never leave." Spencer was seated next to the officer making notes, he was shaking, one of his knees vibrating against the table leg as he trembled "Samantha knows who it was, I've told the officer, and they need to ask her. Go on, ask her!.

I stayed where I was, sitting in the corner of the sofa in the living room. Antony was at the other end, his elbows on

145

his knees and his head in his hands. His crying had subsided, but he remained in that position, not wanting to look at me. I tried to talk to him "I've probably got it wrong. I shouldn't have been eavesdropping, I only heard part of what they said." Finally lifting his head, scowling at me through swollen, red eyes he said "Shut up, just shut up." Now I wanted to cry, my face burned as tears welled in my eyes. The door opened and one of the police officers, stepped into the room "Samantha, we'd like to speak to you about what happened tonight, you don't need to be afraid. Please would you come with me into the next room so that we can have a chat?" He spoke gently and gestured with his hands towards the doorway, signalling me to follow. He led the way to the dining room at the back of the house. We went through the kitchen, where Nana, Granddad, and Spencer were standing with two other officers. They had left the dining room so that I could be questioned, with only Dad in attendance. As I walked past them Granddad turned away from me, while Nana busied herself getting cups from the cupboard for an officer who had offered to make tea for everyone. Spencer stared reproachfully at me, imploring me to tell the truth.

In the dining room Dad was waiting for me, he was sitting at the table and gestured to me to sit beside him, which I did falteringly. The policeman sat across from us as Dad slid his arm along the back of my chair, resting it behind my head. His whole body was twisted in my direction as he leant over me, all of his attention focussed on me. It was completely unnatural and my guard was up immediately. His behaviour was as threatening to me as that of the two men that had called earlier. The police officer crossed his legs, adjusted the note pad in his hand, and rested it on his knee. Peering over spectacles at me he began "Samantha, what happened tonight was terrible. The men that came here and upset everybody had no right to behave as they did. What they did was very bad and we have every right to arrest them for it. Do you understand that?" He peered solemnly at me. I nodded my head, Dad crossed one leg over the other and began swinging his foot. The officer raised an eyebrow at Dad and continued "If you knew who these men were you would tell us wouldn't you?" Again I nodded, without speaking, Dad shifted position, now removing his arm from behind me. He sat back and crossed his arms. "You realize we must stop these men from doing anything else that could harm your family?" This time I whispered "Yes." There was a brief silence between the three of us, as they waited for me to continue, but I wasn't forthcoming. Finally the officer asked "Do you know anything about the men that came here tonight? Your brother seems to think that you said something, which suggests you know who they were." I replied "No, I don't know anything." I couldn't even look at the officer and Dad sat bolt upright "Samantha, tell the truth! Do you know anything about those two bastards?" I whimpered as the officer intervened, sharply admonishing Dad "That's enough Dave. We won't get anywhere with that tone. Now if Samantha says she doesn't know anything, then we must accept that. Samantha you may go. I don't have any other questions for you." I went blubbering back to the kitchen. Nana caught me by the hand as I dashed past her intending to head back to the living room. She pulled me to her and held me, pressing my head against her bosom "There, come here and have a cuddle, it's not your fault. You've done nothing wrong. It's time you children were all off to bed, you're all exhausted. We've all had a nasty shock this evening, but we're alright. It'll seem better in the morning." Bustling now, she nudged me towards the hallway, nodding her head towards Spencer to follow me, with her hand resting on my shoulder she urged me onwards towards the stairs Spencer behind. Reaching the living room, we paused as Nana fetched Antony, who glumly joined us as we straggled up the stairs to bed. Nana tried to lighten our spirits as we went by saying gently "We're going up the wooden hill to Bedfordshire." Usually one of us would respond "Why the wooden hill Nana?" or "Where's Bedfordshire?" Not tonight though, the three of us were exhausted. All we needed was the comfort that the oblivion of sleep would bring. Nana turned down the bedclothes, lay out nightwear for us and reminded us to brush our teeth, saying "Get ready for bed and I'll make sure that Granddad comes to say goodnight before you go to sleep. Nobody needs to be afraid, the police are still downstairs, and there's no way those men will come back here tonight." Spencer and Antony settled down in twin beds in Spencer's room, while I went to Nana and Granddad's room, which I always shared, a single bed lay parallel to their double bed. I wasn't afraid to sleep, because I felt secure knowing they would sleep alongside me.

I lay completely sapped, hearing footsteps on the stairs I waited for Granddad to come. He went to Spencer and Antony first. Their voices were low, muted and subdued. They were worn out too, I could distinguish Granddad's gruff voice gently murmuring concerns and giving reassurances, before the sound of the door swished across the carpet as he pulled it shut. Then he came to me. I was lying on my side and looked at him as he wearily shambled around the double bed to reach me. The light in the hallway fell through the opening of the door into the darkened bedroom, creating a shaft of light that illuminated Granddads profile. He came around towards me, his shoulders rounded and his expression sombre. Sliding his bottom onto the edge of my bed, he sat beside me and put his arm around my shoulders "I love you Granddad. Those nasty men shouldn't have done what they did." I told him, wearily trying to express my concern for him. "What's done is done and can't be undone. We'll have to hope the police catch them. Now it's time to sleep, let's not talk about it anymore tonight. I love you too. Goodnight girl, see you in the morning." Tucking the covers in around me, he bent down and pecked me lightly on the forehead. I watched as he slowly, quietly trudged out of the room, and leaving the door ajar headed back downstairs. Still I lay, fighting sleep, listening to the mumble of voices, Dad's voice louder than any other, intermittently raised then hushed. It seemed I'd been lying awake for a while, straining to hear the police departing and the subsequent tread of my grandparents footfall towards bed. When I did hear the stairs creak, accompanied by footfall, it was Dad. He had waited for the moment I was alone. The police were distracted, continuing their discussion with my Grandparents, and they, preoccupied, were side tracked by questions, as Dad slipped away under the pretence of using the bathroom. Now, he came into the bedroom, the light falling on him as he swiftly rounded the bed, and sat facing me. He knew I was still awake, while I lay frozen, staring wide eyed at him. He leant forwards, arms resting on his kneecaps, fingers locked together. Shoulders slunk low he peered at me in the gloom, sitting quietly at first, simply looking at me as I returned his gaze. Then he began "I don't know, what a commotion eh? All this fuss tonight. You kids must have been terrified. I'm sorry about that. You know I'd never let any harm come to you?" I didn't know that at all, yet I nodded hastily, quickly showing him complete assent. "Imagine if I'd have been here tonight, could you imagine that? If those men had got me, what do you think would've happened eh?" His voice was controlled, quiet, and reasonable. He waited for my answer. Eager to finish this conversation, for him to leave me, I tremulously answered "They would have shot you." Leaning in closer, he smiled at me grimly "Yes they would have. Would you have wanted that? Would you want to see your Dad hurt?" Immediately I vigorously shook my head, I didn't want to think about it, I just wanted him to go away. "Do you understand that if those men aren't caught that they could come after me at any time? Do you realize that they might find me another night?" Now I didn't answer. I was getting confused and I didn't know if I should be nodding or shaking my head. He continued "If you knew something, you would stop them wouldn't you? You wouldn't let them shoot me, you love your Dad don't you?" There was a long pause, my heart raced. I was supposed to answer this question promptly and wholeheartedly "Yes I do." I hated him. He terrified me, even being in the same room as him made me feel nauseous. Now he was becoming impatient, I could feel the tension emanating from him, and it was taking all his will power to keep control of himself "So, if you love me, tell me, do you know who those men were? It's alright to tell me. No one will ever have to know that it was you that told. It'll be our secret, I'm not going to do anything. I'm just making sure they are stopped." I lay still, thinking, scrambling through my mind, seeking an answer that would allay him. It wouldn't come, I could think of no other way to extricate myself from this dilemma I'd dropped myself in. Finally I conceded to him "I do know something, but I don't want to get anybody in trouble." His frustration boiling over, he said "Who would get into trouble Samantha? Who are you talking about eh? I'm not interested in getting anyone into trouble either, all I'm interested in is catching those men." I felt some reassurance. He wouldn't hurt Mum, and he only wanted the men "Mum, I'm worried that Mum will be in trouble." Dad was emphatic "I'm not going to hurt Mum, you don't need to worry about that. Tell me the truth, that's all you need to do. Tell your Dad what you know." My main concern quashed, I believed him "The men came to see Mum, they wanted to know where you were living, they thought you lived here and she told them the address." Now he stood, pacing backwards and forwards in the channel between the beds in agitation "Your Mother told them where they might find me! She knows who they are!" All the veneer of self- control slipped away and he

150

seethed angrily "Your Mother sent those men here! Do you understand that?" I did understand, I'd understood the moment I'd told Antony. I nodded at him " You think you're protecting her, well let me tell you, do you think if she gave a shit about you or your brothers she would have let those men come here?!" I was jolted by the reality of his statement. Shaking, I knew he was right, but was too upset to answer him. I just stared balefully at him. With no further need for coaxing and wheedling, he had reverted back to his true self, the Dad I recognized "I'll have something to say to your Mother, I don't fucking care who it upsets. You can tell her when you see her I'll be coming to visit!" He stalked out of the room, back to the officers downstairs to let them know what had been revealed

Chapter 24

The walls have ears

I dreaded returning home that weekend. I didn't know what reception to expect. Nana had told me on the Sunday morning that the police were going to visit Mum and Tomas. I knew there was no avoiding the fact, that it was me that had informed the police. Granddad drove us home as always. He didn't come in, as he sometimes would, for a cuppa. Tomas came out to meet us as we arrived, he sent Antony and I indoors so that he could speak with Granddad alone. I never knew what was said between them on that occasion. Antony went straight to his room. Nobody admonished me, or initiated a discussion about what I had said.

We resumed our usual weekday school routine. Antony leaving the house without me to meet his friends, I either walking alone or crossing the road to a friend's house to knock for her. It was only a few days later, an afternoon after school, all of us home, when Dad arrived at the house. He had been drinking, but had driven to our house, the alcohol giving him the unrestrained confidence he needed to confront Tomas. Perhaps Tomas was prepared or at least had half been expecting it, because he heard the car pull up outside before Dad even knocked at the door. Tomas had seen him through the window and leapt up off of the sofa, saying to Mum "He's here. You stay here, the fucking cunt's just pulled up. I'll deal with this!" Mum stayed rooted to the spot as Antony and I strained to see through the net curtains if Dad was really outside. He was striding determinedly up to the garden gate, a bottle in his hand. Tomas left us, to waylay him, before he even got to the gate. He threw open the front door and as Dad had stepped on to the garden path we heard Tomas shouting "Don't come any further down that path Charles. You'd better fucking stop right there!" We saw Dad falter, he waved his arms around wildly, pointing the bottle at Tomas "I've got a fucking bone to pick with you. You and your fucking whore! Sending those men around to my parents! They've been nothing but good to you and that's how you repay them, eh?! Well I'm letting you know I'm going to make you pay for what you fucking did." He slurred loudly and wobbled on the pavement. Tomas's voice reverberated with fierce authority as he thundered back at Dad "I'm warning you Charles, if you come any further up that path, you'll fucking regret it. Go on fuck off, it's a pity you weren't there when they came. It's a fucking shame they didn't finish you off! You're no good, you're just a fucking coward that stabs a man in the back!" Dad still refused to leave, and the argument continued. Mum sat, ashen faced and holding Shaun on her lap, as Antony and I watched fretfully, afraid how far this was going to go and whether Dad would enter the house. Dad stumbled further up the path, incensed and shouting "You've got it coming, you think you're a fucking hard nut do you? Well the police have arrested your pathetic fucking little friends! So I'm warning you now, if you ever cross me again, you're dead, you fucking hear me!" With that he started to leave, heading back out of the gate, looking over his shoulder and continuing to hurl insults and threats. Tomas all the time swearing and shouting abuse back at him. Drunkenly spent, Dad threw himself back into his car, engine still running, crunched through the gears, and clumsily sped away. Tomas followed Dad out onto the street and ran bare foot down the road, still hurling profanities at the car as it receded into the distance. We saw him storming back towards the house, fists clenched at his sides. Antony and I quickly sat back down, heads hung downwards and eyes cast in the same direction. We braced ourselves for the barrage that we knew would come when Tomas came back in. As he flew back in he went straight to the phone in the hallway. I thought he was calling the police, but he wasn't. He called my Uncle Nigel "Nigel! Yeah, Charles's just been here, he's off his face and making threats. Yeah! That fucking cunt isn't getting away with this!" Mum was crying now "Leave it Tomas please! Leave it, don't get Nigel involved! Call the police!" It was no use, Tomas was enraged. Pulling on his shoes, he stormed out to the shed. We heard him rummaging furiously around, which was where Nigel joined him when he arrived. As he helped Tomas in his search for a weapon in the shed, Mum pleaded with them both "Leave it! No good can come of this! Please, the pair of you, you'll be arrested!" They found what they were searching for. It was the nail gun. As they stormed out of the house to Nigel's car, we could hear Tomas shouting at Mum "We'll find the bastard if it takes all night. If we have to go to every pub in Cambridge, when we do find him, we'll nail the cunt to the pub door!"

They didn't find him. Wherever he went from ours, it wasn't a pub. He at least had enough intelligence to tuck himself away somewhere. Tomas didn't return until gone midnight, we'd gone to bed. Mum waited up, her light still on until he arrived back. After that weekend I was not privy to many adult conversations for a long time. Whenever people came to visit Tomas would send me out of the room telling our guests that "The walls have ears in this house." I was sent upstairs to my room, while Tomas watched from the bottom of the stairs to ensure I had gone, shouting after me "And shut your bedroom door! I'm watching you, I'll be checking on you!" Nobody directly confronted me for my lack of discretion, but I was made aware via jibes and snide digs, about being a "grass". Whenever I entered a room, when they were talking, conversation stopped and eyes skimmed over me, until the silence drove me out. Where once we would congregate on Mum's bed for a chat, before retiring to our own bedrooms, her door was closed to me now. Antony no longer sought out a moment for time alone with her, and my attempts at closeness with her were stonewalled.

Chapter 25

Name changer

1981

The two men that came to my grandparents were Dick's brother and his best friend. Dick's mother gave a statement to the newspapers saying "Dick's younger brother always felt that when Charles came out of prison, he would get him. We tried talking him out of it but he wouldn't listen. He was a changed man after the day Dick was killed, and I dreaded Charles coming out of prison." She explained how Dick's brother and his friend had become inseparable after Dick's death and that they had vowed vengeance at his funeral "It was an obsession with them, it was eating them up. They had been living for the day Charles came out of prison. Once Charles was out, there was no holding them." Dick and his brother had worked together and were so close that the younger brother was now raising Sammy, his brother's daughter.

In December 1981 the pair had already been on remand for six months when the case came to trial. Charged with possessing a 12-bore shotgun with the intent to endanger life, they both denied having entered my grandparents' house, or having a shotgun. The trial lasted three days. As it progressed Dick's brother eventually admitted to having been to the house. However, he denied that he'd threatened to blow Dad's kneecaps off, or that he had any intention of causing anyone any harm. Admitting that he'd been upset, because he had heard that Dad had been boasting that he had only done six years in prison for Dick's manslaughter, he said that they only intended to frighten Dad. He told the judge "I wanted to make sure Charles kept his gob shut about this bragging he was doing, I was going to scare him." Further admitting "I was going after him for murdering my brother, but I had no intention of harming him." Conceding that he had considered attacking Dad, but would only have fired the shotgun into the ceiling to frighten him. His accomplice also recanted his initial statement, saying that the admissions he first made to the police were confused and inaccurate, because he'd been questioned in the early hours of the morning and that the detectives had not written his statement correctly. The jury returned a verdict of guilty as charged for both men. However, the judge seeming to feel some compassion, freed Dick's brother. Passing an unspecified prison sentence, he said "The sentence should be whatever was required to ensure that the defendant, who has spent six months in prison on remand, should be set free at once." Ordering him to pay costs, he then told the court "The defendant would have gone to prison for one year, if he had not already spent time on remand." The accomplice was acquitted, both men were bound over for two years to keep the peace, and also ordered to pay sureties. They were then ordered to not go within a hundred yards of my grandparents' house. Mum and Tomas didn't suffer any consequences for their part in the events of that night. In the scheme of things it would hardly have affected them if they had. Something far worse had happened since that night and the trial.

What the men didn't know and perhaps wouldn't have cared to know, was the effect that night had on my grandparents and us. My Granddad was never the same, my Nana had to take charge in every situation thereafter. Where she had always been the most docile of the pair, she was now the stalwart, taking charge where Granddad no longer could. Spencer was afraid of his shadow, suspicious of everyone and startled by any unexpected visitor. Antony couldn't forgive Mum or Tomas, believing that they were responsible for having sent the men. I was the stool pigeon, the informer, not to be trusted, the one that had betrayed Mum and Tomas. I was the traitor,

157

because I hadn't warned my grandparents or my brothers. I was in a no man's land, there wasn't even the sanctuary I'd previously had at the weekends, at Nana and Granddad's. I had to centre myself, steady the core of me. I perfected a mask of impassive indifference, telling myself I'd have to learn to be tough. I was growing up. I had to become hardened if I was going to hold my own in this world. There was one slither of good that came as a consequence of the men being released. I did have them to thank, because Dad decided to leave the country for a while. He changed his name and went to Amsterdam to live. We wouldn't see him again for a few years. Nana and Granddad had cashed in a Provident policy that they'd had. It was all the meagre savings that they'd accumulated and was intended for their retirement. They gave it all to Dad, still despite everything, wanting to save him.

Chapter 26

Penance

1981

The men came to my grandparents in May of 1981 and the trial was in December. The chaos that was my family was further exacerbated by this whole episode, and the consequences isolated each of us. Mum was going through the motions of maintaining an ordinary home life. The subject of that night was never broached. Tomas was still working as a milkman, he would already have left for work when we woke up in the mornings. Mum was going through the motions of maintaining an ordinary home life. She got up before we did, still habitually having her cup of tea and a cigarette. Shaun would be awake too, usually curled up in the corner of the sofa watching TV, or waiting for breakfast with us. She made us all breakfast every morning. We didn't often have enough milk for cereal for all of us, but there was usually enough bread to go round. It was the same every morning, two slices of toast and a cup of tea. We were never sociable, in our house, at this time of the day, now even less so. Antony always surfaced dressed, ready to leave for school as soon as he'd eaten. He spent as little time as he could in our company, making only mono-syllabic conversation. I wished I could change everything. If I could have turned back the clock, I would have prevented the chain of events. Mum wasn't horrible to me, she was just non-committal. I ate before getting ready for school and would shout "Bye! See you later" as I went out the door. Occasionally Tomas and I would pass, if he managed to finish his round early. It was more likely though, that we wouldn't see him until we came in from school. At school, even though there was hardly a year between me and Antony, others could be forgiven for not knowing we were brother and sister, so seldom did we

159

interact. He had begun to nickname me "The slug", a name he'd heard Tomas use for me. I made sure there was always distance between us at school, so that he couldn't embarrass me in front of my friends. Once one of his friends cottoned on that we were siblings, asking Antony "So is that your sister then?" To which he'd responded "Yeah, that slug's my sister."

Antony continued to visit our grandparents on a weekly basis, whereas I went less often. Spencer still manipulated me whenever he had the opportunity. That hadn't changed. What with his unwanted attentions and the late night violent visit, my desire to see Nana and Granddad was almost extinguished, yet still not quite. On balance, the environment at home was preferable to the awkwardness of seeing them. The weekends were not so bad. If Antony wasn't there it was just Shaun and me, the household was a more pleasant place. The relief was tangible. Mum could shower Shaun with affection, without damning looks from Antony. He'd started making snide, critical remarks at her expense. Tomas had overheard them on several occasions and reprimanded him. Resentment fermented inside him, his boyhood seemed to be receding rapidly, but. I enjoyed his absence at weekends. The house was less volatile and Mum was more approachable without him. The only one of us who seemed unsullied was Shaun. He was still a delight. Untouched by the guilt of the rest of us, his innocence was a comfort. Mum doted on him, she held him to her and I would see her breathing in the smell of his hair. He was the succour that gave her life purpose. We began a new routine, Mum suggesting it might be nice for Shaun if the two of us took him to Cherry Hinton Hall in his pushchair. The hall is a small house with a park that has a duck pond and play area for children. It was extremely rare for Mum to do something interactive with Antony and me. Shaun, however, inspired her to do things that I was happy to participate in, as it meant contact with Mum by

160

attachment. So we'd take the stale end of the loaf of bread, tie the bag in a knot to the handles of the pushchair, and head off down the road to feed the ducks. I'd be allowed to push him as Mum strolled alongside us. We'd chat about the weather, the houses and the people who smiled as they passed us, nodding hello. At the park we'd give Shaun the bread to feed the ducks and then take him to the playground. Mum would let him run free and chase him. He'd laugh and run from the slides to the swings, free to choose what he wanted to do. I observed benignly, not really participating but enjoying it anyway. The walk home almost always included stopping off for an ice cream. On one of these little outings, as we stepped off the pavement to cross over to the grocery store, I stumbled and fell in the middle of the road. Mum just laughed. She didn't even pause to ask if I was alright and continued ahead with Shaun. I was humiliated, tired of everything, I just sat in the middle of the road as she continued. When she realized I wasn't making any attempt to get up and catch up, she stopped abruptly and shouted "Get up Samantha! What on earth are you doing?!" I continued sitting and shouted back "I don't want to get up! I wish I was dead. I wish a car would run me over and kill me!" Completely flabbergasted she looked around in embarrassment now, as pedestrians paused to see the commotion. She hissed at me exasperatedly "Samantha get up! For goodness sake, whatever's wrong with you?" I was crying, my face as red as a beetroot, I knew I must look an absolute idiot, but I didn't care. By now a car had appeared and was heading down the road towards me. Mum was losing her temper now, and the people passing by had begun laughing. "There's a car coming! Get up now you silly girl!" Finally realizing how ridiculous I looked, I staggered to my feet. Mum was already surging onwards with Shaun, her back ramrod straight, full of outrage, she bristled with annoyance. Suddenly I was painfully aware of the pathetic scene I'd created. I

161

followed her the rest of the way home. We didn't stop for ice cream. It became yet another incident we didn't discuss.

Nana Sheila came to ours virtually every day of the week, within walking distance of her house it was still the route she'd take her dog Rupert for his walks, stopping in to see Mum for a cuppa and a chat. The walk always seemed to coincide with dinner time. Mum frequently complained that Nana seemed to deliberately arrive as she was dishing up, and she would feel obliged to put an extra plate out for her. She felt that Nana should really be cooking for herself and Mark, who still lived at home. Mark was an aloof young man, shy and quiet. I always thought he was quite surly. Nana was still employed waitressing at The Cambridge University arms hotel, while Mark, when he was in work, was usually labouring at building sites. Mum and he were united in their scorn for Nana Sheila, she having no idea that when brother and sister were together, they made fun of her. Mark enjoyed having dinner with us, without Nana. Mum often invited him separately, without letting on to her that he'd been invited.

It was July, the school holidays were nearly upon us again. When the milk round was complete, Tomas would head home via the bookies, to place a few bets. When he got in, he'd ensconce himself in front of the TV for the afternoon. Shaun had his afternoon nap, and Mum liked to lie on a blanket in the garden, reading while she soaked up the sun. Antony and I would come home from school to find Tomas asleep on the sofa, Mum lounging, and Shaun toddling about in the garden. There was a paddling pool for him to splash around in. They were relaxed as a threesome. Mark or Nigel might pop in for a chat with Mum and Tomas, I'd feel ill at ease as the sun made my skin prickle with an itchy heat rash, while they joked about my obvious discomfort. Our house was the meeting point for the family. My uncles and Tomas had clandestine conversations, plotting some little break in somewhere. Tomas suggesting a house that he knew of, that might be ripe for the picking, or Mark wanting to rob a public building of some description. Mostly Nigel listened humorously, contributing information and advice, but wanting to stay out of trouble. He'd already served time himself for committing similar misdeeds. Reminiscing about Melvyn and his exploits, they enjoyed the conspiratorial scheming. Despite Tomas's caution around me, he and Mark didn't quite manage to disguise their underhand activities. Becoming skilled at maintaining poker faced obliviousness to their shenanigans, I was, however, aware of their movements. Excitable, they'd recklessly make plans, thinking I had no understanding of what was afoot. Conversations halted mid flow as I entered the room, unaware, I'd already overheard most of what had been said anyway. I witnessed them digging a hole in the back garden at dusk one evening, away from the gaze of the neighbours. They had some sacks containing shiny goblets and such like, that where too risky to try and pass on. When I asked Mum "What are they burying?" She said "It's just some rubbish and there's nothing else for it, but to bury it."

Mark was only 21. Raised in a family of miscreants he had learned an alternative lifestyle, different from the conventional norm. In the height of the summer that year, two months after the men came to my grandparents, Mark drowned. He had fled from a burglary at 3.30am. Pursued by the police, he'd attempted to cross the river Cam to escape arrest. Frogmen searched for seven hours until they found Mark's body fifteen feet from the river bank. Escaping with a seventeen year old accomplice they had tried to cross together, but Mark had panicked when he lost his footing. Unable to swim, he had nearly drowned his friend in his frantic attempts to survive. The friend was found by the police at the riverside, bedraggled and distressed. He desperately tried to get their help in saving

Mark, who had already submerged. The police described finding the accomplice in a state of hysteria, but with no sign of Mark, they thought it was a distraction technique to give him time to get away. Paying no heed they had said "If you don't shut up, we'll throw you back in." The coroner recorded a verdict of death by misadventure. Nana Sheila was distraught, she was the one who broke the news to Mum.

Chapter 27

The plummet

1981

I was twelve years old when Mark died, Mum was forty two. When the news of Mark's death came she couldn't accept it. In the first few hours she was certain there was a mistake. The evidence all pointed to the obvious, that the body dredged from the river had to be Mark's, but she believed it was somebody else. It could be anybody, one of the numerous people that disappear all the time. Mark must be somewhere else. He was probably laying low. After the dust had settled, he'd reappear. Her conviction was slim. She went with Nana to identify the body, despite Tomas saying she shouldn't. When she saw Mark, that last vestige of hope was extinguished. The shocking blast of grief that swept through her, blew out the dwindling light of optimism. Throughout the years she'd had faith in chance and believed that, despite the odds, her life would improve. She'd been moving forwards, believing that if she had faith, life would correct itself, like a set of scales there must be balance. Ultimately the trauma that she'd suffered would be counterbalanced. She wasn't a bad person, working hard to be a good wife, trying to be a conscientious daughter and mother. Yet she'd let down Edie and Les. She was the betrayer. An awareness of all her imperfections flooded over her. Why had this happened? She'd tried to be a good person, she'd wanted to avoid the cycle of disaster that had been propagated by her parents. Was there no escaping? Mark had been her son more than her brother. She had held him from the day of his birth, and nursing him as her own. The bond was sealed when his eyes had first focussed and found hers looking back at him. Now he'd been cruelly taken from her. She didn't crash spiralling in to the abyss, her decline was gradual. Steady but sure. Melvyn was released under police escort to attend Mark's funeral. My aunt Susan flew back from America, and Nigel swore vengeance upon the officers that pursued Mark when he died. Mark's cremation was accompanied by the strains of Jimmy Ruffin's "Farewell is a lonely sound".

We all wanted a piece of Mum. Nana expected her to be the consoler, she needed to be comforted. Overcome with grief she didn't countenance the depth of Mum's sorrow. Tomas was considerate and kind with her, yet still foremost, she was a wife. While Antony, Shaun especially and me wanted our Mum. So a daughter, wife and mother, she continued to be. Household duties were consistently maintained, cleaning, washing, shopping, and cooking. Attentive to Shaun, she showered him with affection. Antony and I were onlookers, as Mum tried to maintain a hold on reality, we could see her grip slackening. Tears came unexpectedly, at any time and often, as often as Nana was ensconced on the sofa. Her visits had become a twice daily habit. When we came home from school for lunch she was there and when we returned in the afternoon she returned too. The grief was all consuming, Mark's absence the continual theme of conversation. Mum was losing weight, she hardly ate and when she did she slipped away to the bathroom to vomit the meal back up. Tomas took charge and insisted that she see a doctor, he simply didn't know how to help her. She was adamant she didn't need help, and that grief was a process, she would get through it. Eventually she acquiesced, admitting she needed help. The doctor prescribed Valium.

The tablets worked to a degree, Mum was calm, and the most patient she'd ever been with any of us. Previously she'd been emotional, short tempered and volatile. Now she just wasn't there. Physically she got up each day and got through each day. Mentally and spiritually she wasn't there. The fathoms of her grief, which had been so unbearable, were now a chasm she could comfortably plummet to the depths of. That was when the sleep paralysis and visitations commenced. Napping in the afternoons with Shaun, she heard Mark. He called to her, the latch on the back gate opening as it always had, the back door swinging open, as he called her name "Carolyn! Carolyn…" a speech impediment caused him to pronounce his Rs with a W, so she knew it was him without a doubt. Asleep on the sofa with Shaun beside her, she smiled, the heaviness that engulfed her disintegrated with Mark so near. He came to sit beside her and she felt his weight sinking into the sofa. Pins and needles prickled along her body where he sat. She tingled, the hairs standing on end. His lips brushed against her cheek and his fingers lightly touched her skin. The panic set in when she tried to move to greet him. She wanted to turn over and sit up, but was paralysed. When she tried to speak her throat wouldn't respond to the command from her brain. The initial elation that had lightened her heavy heart was suddenly replaced by the terror that her body wouldn't respond, the realization that Mark couldn't be there. She wanted to see him. Wanting but knowing this was impossible she fought against the paralysis, struggling to surface back to consciousness. She awoke, crying out in a strangled voice "Go away! Leave me alone!"

Over the next few years the visitations and the sleep paralysis became a normal part of our lives. We all knew, and it was openly discussed. Tomas, being an atheist, was infuriated and tried again and again to convince Mum that she was ill. Nana thrived on the experiences that Mum related to her, her grief alleviated by the belief that Mark was somewhere, if not in this realm, but between worlds, alive on some other plane. That possibility was better than the alternative. Antony and I were spokes spinning in the wheel that was our home. Outsiders, listening to Mum's experiences, Nana's enticements for more instalments and

Tomas' exasperation, we were just two atoms existing in the same atmosphere as Mum's descent. She slept every afternoon, the combination of the Valium and her fear of sleep at night, kept her in a perpetual state of fatigue. Fighting sleep at bed time, because she was afraid of Mark's visits, she said "He visits every night, waits for when I'm alone, and at the in-between stage of sleep and consciousness, he comes." Even Shaun was party to the knowledge. We heard her some nights, calling out as she struggled back from the realms to the surface. She believed she was experiencing the drowning, unable to breathe herself and gasping for air, she alleged Mark was showing her what had happened. Tomas became fearful for her and, unable to help her, he talked about convalescent homes. We grew afraid too. Of all the appalling things I had faced growing up, the scene I witnessed the day Dad had attacked her and she had walked out, was emblazoned on my mind. I was afraid she would have to leave us. I could bear all of it, but I couldn't bear living in that house without her. The idea that Tomas might have to send her away was terrifying.

Tomas was up with the dawn for his milk round, he didn't know that Mum was so afraid to be alone, that she crept into my bed every morning in the early hours, as soon as he left. She would lie behind me with her arm around my waist, spooning me. This was the closeness I had longed to share with her, the affection I had so craved. But I lay, unable to sleep, listening to her steady breathing as she slept. Completely still, I didn't want to disturb her. I would lie for another few hours like this until it was light. Sometimes, I drifted asleep too. Knowing all the time that this wasn't affection, it wasn't love. She needed me. In those moments I was a port in the storm, and nothing more..

For a while I was sent to stay with Nana. I didn't want to go because I didn't feel any attachment to her. I

168

understood she was grieving alone and that she needed company, but I felt Mum needed me at home and that was where I would prefer to be. I knew there was no use pleading with Tomas, if he told you to do something, you did it. Reluctantly I went, anxious that while I was at Nana's, Mum would deteriorate further and Tomas would have no choice but to have her committed to some institution. That was my understanding of it. I thought he'd send her away to a lunatic asylum. They would shave off all her hair and dose her up with drugs, until she was just a tranquilized shell.

It was the school holidays, I spent all my time with Nana. We went into town on the bus, walked her dog, and did her housework. At night I slept in her bed, the TV switched on until the early hours, as she was unable to sleep. I'd wake up disturbed by it. The days dragged, she was unhappy company and unforthcoming. She wasn't like Nana Edie, she wasn't child orientated. We didn't make conversation and she was silent in her grief. We read books quietly, tidied her garden and chatted to her neighbours over the fence. Bored, I investigated the house when she was distracted, sifted through her jewellery and dressed up in her clothes. Then I discovered her record collection and listened to some of them on her player. That was alright to begin with, she didn't seem to mind. I enjoyed learning about Motown and soul music. Her LP collection was extensive. I discovered Teddy Pendergrass, Isaac Hayes, Barry White and Marvin Gaye, to name but a few. Endlessly I swapped records, listening to one then swapping to another. If I didn't like something within the first few chords, I'd whip it off the turntable and play another LP. Whole afternoons were spent occupying myself like this. My stay finally came to an abrupt halt. I was having one of my obsessive music research sessions, scraping the arm of the record player across vinyl as I was switching albums, when the amplified screech triggered the last straw. Nana burst into the room "Will you shut that fucking racket up?! It's driving me mad, I can't hear myself think!" She stormed out of the room slamming the door. I was stunned and embarrassed, but it was only then occurred to me how annoying it must be for her. I heard her wailing in the kitchen. After hesitating, unsure whether to go and comfort her, I decided to go, but at that moment, her wailing changed into furious screams of pent up anger and sorrow. I went to the kitchen to try and console her, but as I started to head down the hallway towards her, she began beating her fists against the tiled wall in front of her. Screaming, she threw her head back and head butted the wall. Stunned, this stopped me in my tracks as she railed, kicking now and screaming, she hit the wall again with her forehead. Scrambling for the front door, I fled shoeless in my socks through the streets back home.

Scolded by Tomas for not being considerate enough, I felt ashamed. I'd let everyone down. Antony was sent in my place to stay with her, Tomas thought that having him there would give her more solace. Unlike me he was happy to go. Back at home again, Mum refused to be alone.She was afraid to be left, and we were afraid that she might harm herself and doubted her ability to supervise Shaun.

Chapter 28

Parenting

Our lives were so immersed with Mum's grief that the months between Mark's death and the trial of Dick's brother and best friend, seemed to be consumed with the tragedy of his drowning and the impact on Mum's mental state. The subsequent acquittal of the two men wasn't even knowledge shared with Antony or I. For certain, it would have been of consequence for Nana, Granddad and Spencer, yet in our household it wasn't mentioned, and I didn't dare ask what had happened to the men. Our household had been completely preoccupied with the inquest and funeral arrangements. Nana Sheila had also found a medium, who Mum and she were now visiting on a regular basis. They went to see her secretly at first, fearing Tomas' disapproval. I was party to their conversations after the visits and was completely fascinated. I'd never heard of these "special gifts" that only certain people possessed. The only experience I'd had of anything close to this was Sandra's tarot cards, which Granddad had told me were "A load of old nonsense". Mum tried explaining to me that "There are some people who have special abilities, they can feel and hear things that most people can't. They are more in tune with the spirit world, they can communicate with people who've passed on to the other side". I was absolutely spell-bound. It was fantastic. Mum explained that the medium she was going to see with Nana was helping her "The medium can communicate with Mark and is trying to help me understand why he comes to me all the time. I want her to help me and send Mark on his way, he's trapped between this world and the next". In fact it didn't make an awful lot of sense to me, but Mum was convinced. She believed absolutely. Apparently she herself had clairvoyant tendencies that she'd never divulged to anyone before. When she was a child she used to see things "When I was very small" she revealed "I can remember being driven somewhere in a car with my Dad. I was in the back seat looking out of the window. As we drove along we passed fields and woodlands. I saw a figure running at the speed of the car, it was a centaur, half man half horse, keeping up with the car. I saw him and he smiled back at me, before disappearing into the trees." This revelation, a secret shared between Mum and me, made me glow with pleasure. I was so proud that she'd trusted me with it, I couldn't care less if it was real or not. When she talked, I listened. It was a gift that I began to cultivate, she had her clairvoyance and I was a listener. The more I listened and the less I talked, the more I learned. All the times Tomas had taught us to be seen and not heard, simply listening was easy. It had got me into trouble before, but I realized now that people like to talk, if I didn't interrupt they disclosed more information. The trick was to keep my mouth shut and never repeat anything! When Mum finally did confess to Tomas that she'd been going to see a medium, he was upset and disgusted. He wanted it to stop. "Where does this woman live? I want to know Carolyn! I'm not having it. She's taking advantage. It's a bloody outrage, it shouldn't happen! You're not thinking straight, you're upset, and she's making money out of your grief! As for your Mother she should know better!" They argued, she insisting that the medium was helping her to get better, while all the time Tomas paced about the living room, beside himself with anger. Mum claimed that the medium never asked for any money. That she had only ever made a voluntary contribution, which always gracefully accepted. Tomas was exasperated by his failure to persuade her. The desperate hope and determination in her eyes was enough to quash his anger, even if it didn't sit easily with him.

Mum and Nana continued to visit the medium and began attending the Cambridge Spiritualist centre in Thompson Lane. It wasn't a secret anymore, it was something else we didn't talk about. Tomas knew and he tolerated it, but that was all it was, a tolerance. If she mentioned it to him, or wanted to discuss the events at a meeting, he became scornful, mocking her belief and conviction that the centre was a sincere or honest environment. I went with her and Nana a few times. Quite uncertain and apprehensive, I wasn't sure what I'd witness. Mum assured me there was nothing to be afraid of "There will be lots of people there, they're all there for the same reasons as me and Nana. They've lost relatives and are looking for answers, or contact with their loved ones". I wasn't convinced. I'd seen her disintegrating for months now, afraid that Mark would come to her while she slept. When I went to the meeting for the first time with them, I realized very early on that nothing exceptional happened. Mum, Nana and the rest of the flock sat paying close attention to the guest speaker who stood on a platform giving the service. They picked out individuals in the congregation and imparted some vague piece of information that could be applicable to anyone really. Everyone waited avidly for the speaker to select and bestow on them a message from their departed, expectantly holding their breath as the medium scanned the audience saying "I have a message here, it's coming through quite garbled...the spirit is quite excited to be here "Yes, yes. Calm down dear, slow down and tell me calmly!" It's a message for Jan. Is there a Jan here this evening?" Everyone now scanned the audience, searching for Jan. When there was no response the medium continued "Not Jan, just one moment, this spirit is very eager to give this message, it wasn't Jan...but June! June are you in the audience this evening?" Cautiously a woman put her hand up with a doubtful yet expectant expression "My name is June." The medium laughed, sighing with relief that someone had responded "There

173

you are June, now don't be anxious, this is good news from the other side. I have a young woman here for you June, do you know who that might be?" June's brow crumpled as she wracked her brains to conjure up a memory of who she might be referring to "No I can't think of anyone." The medium pressed further "Are you sure June? This is a young woman who looks very similar to you, well when I say a young woman, she might be a teenager. I can see her clearly. She has shoulder length brown hair and she's wrapping her arms around herself to keep warm. Does that mean anything to you?" Still June looked confused and struggled to make a connection. The medium asked "Think now June, perhaps it's not somebody directly connected to you, maybe it's a message intended for someone you know, perhaps a friend of yours who's lost a loved one." Now June's eyes opened wide and she sat erect, as a thought occurred to her "Yes! I've got it, I think I know who it is, my neighbour three doors away. Her niece died when she was only a girl from pneumonia...but that was many years ago." Now June looked uncertain, but the medium quickly allayed that uncertainty "That's it June, she's gesturing wildly at me I can see her here right beside me. She's so pleased and she wants you to pass a message on to your neighbour. Are you ready June?" The hall was tense with anticipation, everyone was on tenterhooks waiting for a revelation of great importance that June must relay to her neighbour "June she wants you tell your neighbour that she's ok, she's not cold on the other side and the infection on her chest has all cleared up. She's very happy where she is. Do you think you could pass that on June?" Nodding her head furiously June smiled and was about to speak, but the medium continued "Make sure you pass the message on and there's one more thing, wait a moment, she's whispering in my ear, her voice is getting fainter now, she's fading away...oh, ok I see. June your neighbour has been looking for a missing sock, you must tell her it's in

174

the washing machine, wedged between the lining of the drum and the washing machine door," June interrupted, holding up her hand she asked "But what was the girl's name?" The medium appearing crestfallen replied glumly "Oh I'm so sorry June, but she's gone, already slipped away. I didn't get a chance to ask in all the excitement. However, you must pass the message on to your neighbour. Please can you promise me you'll do that?" June nodded again, half-heartedly, as the audience all applauded. Mum and Nana gave each other approving glances. They clapped along with the rest of the audience, anxious for the meeting to continue, and in the hope that the next message would be for them. It was like this at every one of the few meetings I went to, none ever challenged the guest speaker, who probably came from another town, and wouldn't be seen again.

My form tutor knocked on the door one afternoon to ask why I wasn't going to school, as I hadn't been in weeks. I answered, while Mum was lying on the sofa napping as Shaun watched children's TV. It was an awkward moment. Oddly I felt exposed without my uniform. I'd been doing housework and preparing the evening meal. He clearly hadn't expected me to be the one answering the door, he talked to me while looking into the house for an adult over my shoulder "Hello Samantha, you can probably guess why I'm calling. Is one of your parents at home? I need to have a brief chat with them." He viewed me as a child, a responsible adult should've answered the door. There I was in a tired red and white checked dress over an off white polo neck top, my knee high socks had slouched down my calves, the seams at the toes hanging off the ends of my feet. My hair hung lankly around my face, it hadn't been washed in a week and dandruff dusted my shoulders. How could I explain to him that my family wasn't functioning properly? How could I make him understand that it was me looking after them, when I was only too aware of the pathetic figure I was? "I'm sorry Mr

175

Knee, I have been taking care of my Mum, because she isn't very well." He surveyed me sceptically, head angled slightly and, taken aback, he looked at me with quizzically "What's wrong with your Mum?" Well that was a whole other conundrum. I had to remember not to repeat anything I heard, or be a snitch "She isn't feeling well, she's been sick and I've got a younger brother. He's only little, so I have to help look after him until Mum gets better." Still dissatisfied he said "I should really speak to a parent, is your Mum at home?" I knew Mum wouldn't want to deal with him. She'd be annoyed if she was woken up and had to come to the door dosed up with Valium "She's asleep, I mustn't wake her up because she doesn't sleep at night." Shifting from one foot to another on the doorstep he swapped his satchel from hand to hand "Well I'll expect you to be back at school by Monday next week. If you aren't, I'll come and knock again, only next time I will have to speak to a parent. Otherwise it'll be the truant officer knocking on the door." Speaking sternly and looking me directly in the eye he searched my expression for signs of deception, I stared back at him almost defiantly "I'll be back at school on Monday, if Mum's better by then." I shut the door. It didn't matter to me, he could think whatever he liked, I wasn't playing truant. I was looking after my Mum and if Tomas was here he would've told him the same. I hated the way adults spoke to me like I was a child. Asking for a parent! I was the bloody parent, I cooked, cleaned, washed, ironed and held my Mum in my arms in my bed in the early hours of every morning, besides keeping an eye on Shaun during the day so that she could rest. I went back to peeling the potatoes. When Tomas came home I told him "What the fuck's he doing coming to the house! Fucking cheek. He can send the truant officer round and I'll fucking tell them. Your Mum's not well and your place is at home to take care of her! What do they think happens in other cultures? It's normal for the girls in the family to take responsibility and

176

keep the household running. Why in Africa, girls as young as twelve are mothers themselves already!" He clenched his fists and paced around the living room as he always did when he was riled "Your place is here, this is where you're needed and you'll do as I bloody well say." I didn't return to school on the Monday. The next time my form tutor called, Tomas answered the door and explained why I wasn't attending. It was agreed that I would have to complete some of my year work at home and Mr Knee would collect it on his way to work.

That was how it was for a few months. Striving to complete school work at home with no idea what had been discussed in the classroom. I didn't see the few friends I had made, spending most of my time in the house. One evening a note was posted through our letterbox, a faux love letter. Two of the girls that lived in my street, who I'd thought were my friends, had decided it would be a hoot to pretend a boy in my year was missing me at school, so much he'd written me a note declaring his love for me. I heard their laughter as they ran off. Tomas delivered the note, dropping it into my lap, he laughed "This came for you. Looks like your so called friends think you're a joke." When I read it, my face burned with shame. It was one of the many times that I took myself to my bedroom and lying on my bed, my face buried tightly into the pillow, the edges folded up around my ears, I would scream into the fibre, the sound muffled to a dull cry. I hated everyone. The rage inside me was so fierce, it felt like my chest might burst open. I wanted to scream at Tomas. He could swear, curse and shout all the time, he said the most awful, hateful things about everyone. From behind net curtains he even criticised the neighbours in the street. He made me feel like a disgusting, fat, imbecile, showing no concern for my feelings. I wanted to tell him how much I hated him, how I despised his opinions and his behaviour. My eyes were swollen and red from crying so hard. My throat raw, my chest heaved with the dregs of the last juddering sobs, I would sit up and seeing myself in the dressing table mirror, I'd be repulsed by my own reflection. This was exactly what I believed Tomas saw. I would never tell him how much he hurt me, and never let him see how affected by it I was. I was torn between pride and fear. Going back downstairs later, in my nightgown, Tomas greeted me as I walked into the room "Oh look out, it's the fucking Virgin Mary! What is that? A phantom pregnancy, or fat?" He sneered as Mum simply gave him an admonishing look.

My periods arrived when I was twelve. I told Mum that there was blood between my legs and in my knickers when I went to the toilet. She flapped around for an afternoon, excitedly telling me I was a woman now. Fetching a sanitary towel from her dresser she told me where they were kept and said I should help myself. It was nice that she was so interested in me briefly, and for a moment, I felt loved. We'd had sex education at school. Mrs Barratt our head of year had shown us how to put a condom over the end of a broom handle. Mum had also been quite forthright and I felt armed enough to know that I couldn't let Spencer continue doing what he was with me. I asked Mum what incest meant, she told me that it was when close relatives like a father and daughter, or brother and sister had sex. I asked her why it was wrong for two people to have sex when if they were related, if they loved each other. Mum tried, as best she could, to explain the morals of it and the genetics. The idea that a baby born from an incestuous coupling would be a deformed monster terrified me. I had to make Spencer understand that what he wanted to do was wrong.

Chapter 29

Storm break

1982

Throughout the summer holidays of 1982 I made every effort to try and recreate myself, consciously deciding to metamorphose. When school reopened for the autumn term, I intended to return as a young woman, not as the awkward and solemn girl that my teachers or schoolmates might expect. Mum knew I was self–conscious about my weight so she'd shared a secret with me that she used to control her weight. She told me that she stuck her fingers down her throat after meals, vomiting up as much as she could, so that she wouldn't gain weight. I thought that she'd gotten to be so skinny from grief and pill popping. Desperate to be slim, I tried it out, and soon, I was vomiting even if I'd only eaten a boiled sweet. My body changed quickly, everywhere became thinner except my stomach, that wouldn't budge. It really did look like a pregnancy bump. Trying to get rid of that too, I started an exercise regime on the hall landing. Morning and afternoon, while Tomas was at work, I did sit-ups, press-ups and various aerobic exercises. Mum joined me and we lay on the landing carpet exercising together, sometimes in fits of laughter. Antony was reluctantly home again. Nana had recovered and sent him back to us, wanting her life to return to some semblance of normality. He would step over us on his way to the bathroom or his bedroom, smirking at our efforts, telling us we were stupid. In the afternoons I joined Mum sunbathing in the garden, while Shaun played with his toys, or napped. Antony had a flick knife, which he threw time and again into the grass. Throwing and collecting it to throw again. One time he threw it and it nicked Mum's leg as it grazed passed her into the lawn. He was immediately sorry, running to her

179

saying "I'm sorry! Are you ok? I Did I catch you? I'm sorry Mum!" She was stunned, the colour had drained from her face. Getting up to grab Shaun she shouted at him "How many times have I told you not to play with that bloody thing?! You meant to do that, you're just like your father!" Taking Shaun she hurried away in doors, slamming the backdoor behind her as she went upstairs to her bedroom. Antony completely dejected shouted at me "What are you looking at?!" Before he stormed out the back gate. Mum, at least didn't tell Tomas about the incident, and later that night Antony sat on the edge of her bed apologizing once more as she explained that he mustn't ever play with knives, or bring that flick knife into the house again.

Tears still flowed often in our house. Mum would cry unexpectedly at the smallest of things. It seemed anything might bring her to tears. Shaun cried if Mum was upset and Antony and I cried with anger, frustration and resentment. Our tears were usually hidden or shed in our bedrooms. Over a year had passed since Mark's death. Mum was improving, not drastically, but in very subtle ways. She was trying to come back to us. One afternoon she accompanied Antony and me, with Shaun, to Cherry Hinton hall. The four of us took a picnic which she had suggested and arranged. We fed the ducks and settled down beside a brook in the shade of the trees. Some of our school friends passed by and stopped to chat, probably intrigued to see us out together. The sunlight dappled through the trees as we harmoniously ate sandwiches together. Mum talked animatedly to us and our friends. We ran off with Shaun to the swings, but when we returned Mum had fallen asleep on the blanket. The effort and the pills had taken their toll. Back at home she went to lie on the bed as I prepared the evening meal for when Tomas got home.

Mum's afternoon naps were as habitual as her morning cigarette. Shortly before Tomas arrived home, she'd rise and splash her face with water to sober up before coming downstairs. He'd told her I was going back to school when term started and that it was time things began getting back to normal. Shaun was going to begin pre-school and she had to pull herself together. When he came in from work Tomas always sought Mum out for an affectionate cuddle, before he'd settle into the corner of the sofa. Betting slips would appear along the arm of the sofa and the TV would be switched to the racing. Sometimes Mum would at least muster enough motivation to make him a cup of tea or if not he'd shout at Antony or me "Is there a drought in this fucking house?! Put the kettle on one of you and make me a cup of tea, and let it brew. I don't want a cup of fucking gnats piss." Either one of us would make the tea, if we had anything in common at all, it was the shaking of our hands as we stepped into the living room to deliver it to Tomas., We knew the moment we set foot across the threshold into the room he would bellow "Watch what your fucking doing! Don't spill it you little idiot. If that goes on the carpet I'll be using you to wipe it up!" We couldn't win, his booming voice jolted our nerves and had us spilling tea every time. I tried not to fill the cup up to the brim in the vain hope that might rectify the problem but then he just shouted "What's this? Get me a fucking ladder, I can't reach the tea at the bottom of the cup!" If there wasn't crying in our house, there was shouting.

Grief comes in stages, Mum had told me. She had, in the first instance, denied the death of Mark and over the past year had succeeded in isolating herself from us all in a dazed bubble. Nana's grieving had developed and progressed much more quickly, while Mum's grief had plateaued. Then unexpectedly her grief welled up in one startling moment. She had risen from her usual afternoon nap, as Tomas had come in from work. I was in the kitchen opening corned beef and baked beans, as Tomas attempted to give her his customary bear hug. He grabbed her breasts, as he openly did in front of Antony or me, and

181

she grimaced, pulling away from him. He noticing her displeasure, was obviously upset and, pushing her away from him said "Don't pull that face at me when I'm giving you a hug!" He angrily stomped over to the settee, threw himself down, and fumbled for the remote to flick through the channels to the horse racing. Mum asked him if he wanted a cup of tea, staring fixedly ahead he ignored her. With that she came back into the kitchen, picked each mug up smashed them one by one. With each shattering cup, her rage grew and the vehemence with which she swung her arm became more ferocious. I stepped back against the work surface, immobilized by her outburst, I was unsure whether to stay put or run. Tomas came running to the kitchen doorway and stopped in his tracks, he too was uncertain, as Mum swept her arm along the worktop, sweeping canisters shattering to the floor shouting "All you do is go to work and come home! It's the same day in and day out, work then home, and when you're here all you fucking well do is sit in the corner of that sofa watching the fucking horse racing!" She screamed and, bunching her fists she grabbed hold of her hair, pulling at it by the handful. I didn't dare move, afraid to draw her attention to me. Tomas tried to step towards her and reach out to her as, she swung herself towards him. Her hair still gripped, looking feral she screamed at him "Don't fucking touch me! If you come near me I'll kill you, I swear I will!" Releasing her hair she wrenched the cutlery draw out and off its track and hurled it crashing to the floor between them, creating a barrier to prevent Tomas from approaching. Cutlery bounced and clattered, until it was strewn all around. His face was ashen with fear and concern for her. Wanting to go to her, his arms and hands still reached out towards her, yet his body was entrenched where he stood. Neither of them were aware of my presence, both so caught up in the moment and the confusion of their emotions, I remained fixed to the surface across the kitchen from them. Mum screamed with anguish, tormented and unable to control the upsurge of grief and rage, she lunged towards the backdoor. As she went Tomas seized the opportunity, he leapt forwards, grabbed her wrists, and he pulled her to him. She struggled wildly, with arms flaying, she tried to beat him away with her fists as he wrapped her tightly to him, engulfing her body against his. Now pressed so firmly against him, she couldn't move. It was like thunder and lightning, followed by the breaking of the storm, as suddenly she was spent, the anger released. Her body relinquished all tension as it dissolved against him. She collapsed, her arms hanging lifelessly over his. Sobs came then. Deep from within her they surged upwards and burst from her throat as ripping vents of sorrow. Tomas held her, kissed her face and stroked her hair, he murmuring gently "That's it love, let it all out. Let it go. I've got you." He scooped her up and carried her away, striding upstairs to lie beside her on the bed, cradling her in his arms. I moved then to the bottom of the stairs to listen as he whispered to her. Antony came bursting in the backdoor and I held my finger to my mouth to silence him as he was about to speak. I didn't need to explain, my gesture was enough to know that there had been an outburst. Antony turned heel and left the way he came. Shoulders stooped, he silently stepped back out of the door and quietly closed it behind him. Shaun sat on the living room floor, the TV continued its steady monotonous drone while he stared, eyes wide with alarm. I went back to the kitchen to begin clearing up the fall out. That night Tomas emptied every bottle of pills Mum had down the toilet and flushed them all away.

When September arrived I was eager to return to school, my prolonged absence wouldn't seem as remarkable since everyone had enjoyed the summer break. I could slip back in seamlessly, or so I hoped. It wasn't as easy as that, there were gaps in my knowledge of the subjects that had been covered in the previous months, and I had to catch up. My school mates were surprised by my new image and made approving noises about it. Where once I'd shaved my eyebrows, I'd let them grow and plucked them neatly into shape. My hair was styled neatly and I wore ribbed opaque tights that had been handed down to me by a trendy cousin. I'd earned a little pocket money babysitting for a couple who lived in our street, which meant I'd been able to buy myself a fashionably styled school uniform, including a loose cable knit jumper that camouflaged my pot belly. The fad of the moment was to wear bold make up in bright hues of fuchsia. Heavy foundation was in, all the better for me to conceal spots and create a mask to hide behind. I shaded my eyelids in a rainbow of colours with brushstroke after brushstroke of eye shadow, over accentuated my cheek bones with heavy blusher, and glossed my lips until wet with lipstick. Occasionally girls got hauled out of assembly for wearing make-up and were ordered to remove it with wet wipes in the sick room. Purely by chance I was always overlooked, maybe because I'd learnt the art of avoidance. If the head master or deputy head appeared to be surveying the queue as we left the assembly hall, I'd ensure I was looking the opposite way, so that they couldn't see my face or, putting myself in the centre of a crowd, to engage myself heavily in a group discussion. There were few subjects I enjoyed, but the ones I did I excelled at. Art was my favourite, my teacher allowed me to stay in the classroom and draw from my imagination, while the rest of the class went outside to draw trees and flowers. When they had to draw still life's in class I would draw and build collage into my piece, adding material in layers to enhance and give it effect. At home I had spent so many nights reading under the covers into the night, that my English teacher thought I was a joy. He always chose me to read aloud and scored my essays highly. One of the essays he'd assigned us was to write a story based around the theme of "Fury". How I enjoyed writing that article, I wrote an account about

Tomas, embroidering it with a tale of smashing his head in with a marble ashtray. I got an A star for that. The teacher I admired the most was my religious studies teacher Mrs Ewan-Smith. She used to bring a kettle to class so that she could make us all a hot drink and sometimes she'd treat us to Danish pastries. Our desks would be rearranged in a semi-circle around her desk. We talked about Christianity, Judaism, Hinduism and Sikhism. When asked what faith we had, I described my Mum and Nana's belief in Spiritualism. Mrs Ewan-Smith loved that, she was enthralled and asked lots of questions, wanting to know what their belief involved. It was in this class that I was to meet Simon Cross. He was a beautiful proud black boy, one of the very few black children in school. He was a Jehovah's Witness, it turned out that he had been one of the children who had sat on the grass outside our house, when Antony and I had insulted them before fleeing the scene. That was seven years ago. Now I was thirteen and here we were sharing a classroom and conversing together about religion, difference, and culture. I was growing up.

A school trip had been arranged to Peterborough ice skating rink, everyone had been raving about it. I'd seen the flyer and overheard conversations, but didn't expect for one moment that I'd be able to go. Knowing there was no point asking Mum or Tomas, and certain there was no way I would be able to pay for it, I'd not bothered even entertaining the idea of attending, until the day of the trip had arrived and they still had seats left on the coach. A couple of my school mates were going and urged me to come "Come on, why not come? You can just get on the coach and give them the money when you have it. No one will say anything once you're on the coach." I was so tempted, surely it couldn't be that simple. With some coaxing I was persuaded to go and ask our form tutor if it was possible, He confirmed that there were indeed still some empty seats and as long as I paid as soon as possible, it was ok if I wanted to join the party. In a moment I'd decided. I wanted to go. At home, they could fuck themselves. I was going and I wasn't asking Tomas for permission or letting them know where I was. I'd grab a change of clothes at home during lunch break and stuff them in my bag, ready for the trip as soon as my last class ended.

I changed in the loos and ran to join the queue that was waiting to board the coach. It was slightly chaotic, rowdy teenagers and irritated teachers. There didn't seem to be much organisation and we pushed and barged our way on board. Everyone nabbing seats with their best friends in a gush of activity. I passed a couple of girls from my form who let me know the seats beside them were allocated already by hastily plonking their bags in the empty space, while haughtily jutting out chins and sucking in cheeks at me. Not that I would've sat with them anyway, silly, spoilt, stuck up little bitches! Floundering and searching around for a vacant seat, a teacher spotted me and waved me impatiently towards a space. As directed I slid in next to a dark haired Italian boy from my year called Peter. Flushing a furious red, I expected him to turn his nose up and curl his lip in disdain at my appearance by his side. Peter didn't do any of that at all. He smiled and said "Hello, you're Samantha aren't you? This is great isn't it? I'm really looking forward to it. Have you been ice skating before?" I'd expected to be ignored, expected indifference or disinterest. This was disconcerting. It took a couple of heartbeats to gather myself and actually respond "Yes it is great, I've never been ice skating and I'm dead nervous, but I can't wait!" I laughed and he laughed with me. He didn't know that I'd never really done very much of anything. I had a Dad that had killed someone, a brother that liked to molest me, my Mum was locked in depression, and I didn't believe I was "normal", but I'd never been ice skating. "Who are you with?" Peter asked me. I felt foolish when I told him I wasn't with anyone, and he looked surprised "You mean you've come on your own? Wow that's cool!" The two boys in the seats in front of us were friends of his that I also recognised. They kept peering through the gap in the seats at us, pulling faces and giggling. Peter stared back at them "Stop being so stupid and grow up will you!" he sighed, raising his eyebrows in mock exasperation he turned his attention back to me "I'll show you the ropes, I've been ice skating before. I'm not great, but I do manage to stay on my feet." I forgot about home, Tomas and Mum. I didn't think about cooking the dinner or what time I'd make it back. I simply enjoyed talking with Peter. He asked me "Your Antony's sister aren't you?" I nodded my head cautiously expecting some negative comment, he smiled and said "Yeah, Antony's really good at football. I've seen him at break times kicking the ball about, he's pretty nifty with his footwork". At that moment I was proud to be Antony's sister. The journey continued and I was completely absorbed with Peter, he was funny and charming, and it seemed he liked me. He told me "When you smile you're whole face lights up and you're beautiful." I smiled even wider and he said "See, beautiful!" I laughed, blushing with embarrassment but loving the compliment. No one had ever told me I was beautiful before. We chatted all the way and when we arrived, I thought he'd disappear in the surge of kids spilling off the coach, but he stayed by my side. As we joined the queue to collect our skates, my nerves were beginning to get the better of me. I fretted internally about getting on the ice and making an idiot of myself. As he moved forwards to exchange his shoes for skates, I lagged back slightly, thinking I'd make excuses to use the bathroom, which would allow him to go ahead and re-join his friends, but he turned and gestured me forwards " Ladies first, you get your boots and I'll follow you." There was nothing for it but to go with the tide. Collecting my skates, I went and found a bench to sit on and began hastily putting them and tying them up. He plonked down beside me and followed suit, not appearing to have any idea that I was a bag of nerves, or showing any sign that he could see my awkwardness "It's so cold! Can you feel it? It's really fresh in here, just like winter." Beaming at me, he blew warm breath between his fingertips and grabbed my hands to pull me up. I took his hands gratefully and stood with as much grace as I could muster, lurching towards him, he still holding my hands stepped backwards at arm's length and tilting his head to one side looked quizzically at my boots. Suddenly he saw the problem and cried "Hey! You've got them on the wrong feet!" I nearly died with shame and felt tears pricking at my eyes "Oh! I errm…don't know what I was thinking, I was in such a hurry to get on the ice." I mumbled with my chin tucked into my chest as I sat back down to sort myself out. Without hesitation Peter was on the floor at my feet untying my boots and holding my calf as he helped ease one foot out of the first boot "Let me do it, I expect you're nervous. That's understandable, here let me." I watched the top of his head as he tugged off my boots and swapped them over, looking up intermittently to smile and laugh cheekily at me. My heart quickened. It was such a cliché, and I was reminded of stories I'd read in girls annuals at Christmas time, yet here I was with a fluttering in my chest. "There all sorted, are you ready? Let's go." Once again pulling me up, I allowed him to take charge and followed his lead. Clumping along to the rink together he stepped on to the ice first and tucked my arm into his "Don't be afraid, I've got you. Keep close to me for support and you'll be fine. When you're feeling a little more confident you can let go of me." I couldn't believe he was only a boy, he was the same age as me and behaved like he really cared about other people. In my world everybody cared for themselves, you had to look out for yourself. Having his evident concern for my comfort and enjoyment was unexpected. All sorts of emotions were running through me, I trusted so quickly. I wanted to feel this trust. Being able to let go and have faith in someone

188

else, was such a wonderful feeling. He pushed off, gliding along with me clinging on at his side. I mimicked his footwork and he nodded at me in approval. The latest chart pop music played in the background over the ice and echoed cheerfully around the expansive rink. We glided along gently together, making our first lap. It seemed quite effortless. I was reminded of time spent over snowy winters, skating along icy pavements with abandon. It was terrific here, the atmosphere was great. Brightly lit, happy people laughing and calling out to each other. Warm clothing, lots of woolly hats and scarves. Our schoolmates called out to us as they passed, wolf whistling and caterwauling. We laughed at them and to each other. "Are you ready to try it alone?" Peter asked me with an earnest expression full of concern, I couldn't swallow my pride and say "No". Instead smiling absurdly, belying how I really felt I said "Sure, I'll give it a go, don't leave me though will you?" Putting his hands on his hips he smiled wryly saying "You don't get rid of me that easily, I'll be right here. So if you need a hand just say." With that he skated backwards a couple of feet giving me some space. I marvelled at his ability to appear so nonchalant and it fuelled my desire to try harder. My arms were still outstretched towards him. I must have looked like a toddler reaching for her Mum. I was left half bent at the waist, leaning in his direction, with my arms outstretched and my fingers splayed, ready to grasp at the safety of his support. Gathering myself together, I straightened up and with my arms now out at my sides, I gingerly pushed off as he'd done before, methodically gliding one foot in front of the other. I did it. "Yeah! That's the way, you've got it! Keep it going, you're doing great. Whoooee!" He whooped as I made my own path on the ice. It was exhilarating, and my heart pumped wildly as I glided along. Onwards I went, probably not particularly elegantly, yet it was joyous. He urged me on and I felt as if I could fly. A group of our schoolmates headed towards

189

me in the opposite direction. They were no more skilled than me and clung precariously to each other as they skidded and careened in my direction. Seeing them veering towards me, in an uncontrollable gaggle, all screeching and pandemonium, I stopped in my tracks and resumed the toddler position, waiting for the impact, arms outstretched to ward them off as the inevitable collision came. They hurtled towards me from one direction, as Peter skated from the other to try and reach me in time. Too late I was swept off my feet and landed firmly on my backside as the group drove into me. We scattered across the ice like pins in a bowling alley. As my bum made impact, the jolt burst all the tension inside me. Laughter burst up through my chest and out of my throat, the group scattered around me laughing too. It was hysterical. We were flat on our bottoms, some on our backs, and the laughter echoed all around the rink. Spectators paused to come over and laugh with us as groups of other skaters came to help gather us up. Peter was there in the throng. He took my hand, and bracing my elbow, helped me up, immediately hugging me and pretending to brush me down dramatically, making seeping motions with his hat and gloves, as if my personal valet. I couldn't remember ever having laughed as much. Coming to my senses, I wiped the tears of laughter from my eyes, as we joined again, skating arm in arm as he sang "You were working as a waitress in a cocktail bar, when I met you, I picked you out and shook you up…" Looking at him I knew it didn't matter, he thought I was ok, he wasn't bothered that I'd made a fool of myself and I didn't feel bad about it. My qualms had been dissolved with laughter. We spent the rest of the evening together, I fell over several times, but he was there, helping me back up. Even he fell over once and it was my turn to help him. Maybe he did it on purpose, I'll never know now.

On the way home, it was dark outside and the lights on board the coach were dim. We were weary, everyone subdued. Satisfied, and worn from the excitement we all settled ourselves with our companions as we headed homewards. It felt perfectly natural when Peter held my hand after being arm in arm for most of the evening. His fingers entwined with mine and he squeezed them gently, holding our hands up he looked at them, smiling at me. I was elated the evening had been a success and was overjoyed that I'd decided to come. The teachers were tired too, slumping into their seats at the back of the bus, from where they were supposed to be able to keep a watchful eye over us all. Having a brainwave Peter gestured conspiratorially to me as he slipped his coat off his shoulders and, swinging it around, he put it over both of our heads. I smiled shyly at him in the shade under the coat, as he leant in to kiss me. Shutting my eyes I felt his lips reach mine. It was a tender, delicate kiss, he lingered and I held it for as long as he remained. When we released we gazed at each other smiling, and without words reached in tandem for each other again. This time the kiss was more fervent. Eagerly we sought each other's tongues and it was deliciously, lovely contact. We felt so comfortable together, and our kissing grew more confident. He whispered to me softly "Are you enjoying this? It's nice isn't it?" I murmured gently in agreement as we continued secretly under the coat, the canopy giving us impetus to become bolder. I felt a whirl of sensations in my stomach and an aching that I hadn't experienced before. The ache was pleasant, as he cupped one of my breasts through my jumper I felt my nipples responding to his touch, and the ache grew. I wanted him to touch me there, where a pulsing sensation throbbed between my legs. We continued to kiss more passionately, as he fumbled with my jumper and t-shirt, trying to free it from the waistband of my jeans so that he could gain access to my skin and hold my breast in his hand. We were completely engrossed in each other when a voice boomed down the aisle between us "What's going on down there!

Take that coat off of your heads this instant and let me see your faces!" It was one of our form tutors, bellowing with indignation at what we might be up to. Immediately we threw the coat off. Peter scrunched it up into a pile on his lap, as he ran his fingers through his hair with his other hand to straighten himself up and I hastily tucked my t-shirt back into my jeans. In the light I could see how flushed he was and knew my face burned as guiltily as his. Looking away from each other, he stared out the window feigning an interest in the cars that sped by, as my eyes scanned the aisle to ensure the form tutor had stayed put, and to ascertain who else had been paying us attention. A few enquiring eyes looked back at me, but no one, including the form tutor really had any energy left to entertain much more interest in us. Eventually after a few minutes, Peter looked bashfully at me, his hand seeking mine again. We continued the journey reticent, afraid we'd attract more attention. When we finally arrived back we held each other briefly and agreed to meet at school the next day. Kissing innocently this time, he was met by his parents and I ran home in the dark. It was only then that I considered the consequences of my actions and begin worrying about what would be waiting for me when I got home.

It was 9pm by the time I burst in the front door. Mum, Antony and Shaun were already upstairs in their bedrooms as usual. Tomas sat in the living room watching TV. When he heard the door he called out "Samantha?" I braced myself, telling myself to act natural, he didn't know what I'd been doing. He wasn't God. He wasn't an all- powerful all- seeing being. Breathing in deeply, I opened the living room door and tried to be insouciant as I casually said "Yes?" I don't know who I thought I was kidding, I'd just behaved totally out of character and arrived home 5 hours late, without explanation. He was sitting in the corner of the sofa with his belt and trousers undone to allow his belly to escape. He didn't look away from the TV at first as he said "What time do you call this?" I replied "I don't know." He turned his head to look directly at me then "What do you mean you don't know? What the fuck have you been doing until now?! We were relying on you to prepare the dinner!" His face was white with anger and his eyes bored into mine from across the room "Well, what do you have to say for yourself? Answer me!" Now I knew I had to have a plausible answer, something that he wouldn't expect might alleviate his anger "I went ice skating after school, there was a trip and I was invited." I said proudly. He was stumped for a moment, but only a moment. Looking incredulous, then screwing his face up in disbelief, he spat out "What are you fucking talking about? Fucking ice skating! What's that got to do with anything?" Determined to hold my own, I stood calmly in the doorway and explained steadily "There was a trip to the ice skating rink in Peterborough. They had some seats left, so I decided to go. Only I didn't have a chance to let you know. I had to make a decision there and then." This really perplexed him. I could see the questions forming in the furrow of his brow before he asked them "Well didn't you need some money for that? Why the fuck didn't they ask for our permission?" he asked the questions slyly seeking to trip me up, but I was prepared "They said I could pay it back when I can and they have a permission slip that mum signed at the beginning of term for any school trips." He processed what I'd said, but was unsure whether I was telling the truth. "How are you going to pay them back? You haven't got any fucking money!" This was the tricky bit. I began to feel uncomfortable, and squirmed a little "Granddad will give me the money if I ask him." I knew that would irk him, but it was all I had. "So you went without any money and you think you can just rely on your Granddad to bail you out! You're a cheeky little cunt, your Mum and me were worried sick about you. We had no idea where you were, or if you were coming back. You could've been abducted for all we knew! I ended up having to cook the diner when I came in from work! From now on you come home straight after school, nowhere else. No visits to friends, straight home! Do you fucking hear me?!" I knew it was coming and here it was, like a tidal wave that you watched approach, helpless to prevent, certain to be drenched as it broke over you. "Yes." I replied. The format was always the same, the outcome so predictable. Turning his attention away from me now, he flicked through the channels on TV with the remote control "Go to bed, and don't go bothering your Mum, she's trying to read her book. Leave her in peace." I left the room, closing the door behind me, I treaded silently up the wooden hill to Bedfordshire, as Mum would say. After all I didn't want to disturb her, especially when she'd been so concerned for my whereabouts.

The romance with Peter was short lived. In the harsh reality of daylight I knew it wasn't sustainable. True to his word he kept trying to catch up with me at school while I kept trying to avoid him. He eventually managed to snare me in the corridor between lessons "Samantha! Wait a minute will you? How are you? What's going on? Are you ok?" He tried to take my hand in front of the other kids, and I pulled away. He looked hurt as tactfully I tried to make excuses "I'm fine, I've just been busy. I haven't had a chance to try and catch up with you. How're you?" He pulled away in response to my coolness saying "I've been worrying about you? I want to see you. Can we go to the cinema or something on Saturday? I need to spend some time with you?" I could've cried and I didn't know how to say no, or make up a pretence that would be suitable. So to hide my discomfort in that moment and for the sake of avoidance I lied and told him "I'm sorry if I seem different, it's school. I can't be myself here and I really want to see you too. I'd love to see you on Saturday." Our schoolmates streamed around us, heading towards lessons. Taking stock of Peter and me in the corridor having some kind of heart to heart they smiled knowingly at us, continuing on their way. It was so awkward, I didn't want to talk about it there, in the middle of school. I also knew I wouldn't meet him at the cinema either. I wasn't allowed out and I had no money. His friends began tugging him by his shirt sleeves and pulling him away. Swept along he called back to me "I'll meet you 10 o'clock outside the Victoria!" Smiling, happy again he waved at me as I stood watching him disappear into the melee. Saturday morning came and I simply didn't turn up. At home I watched the clock reach 10 o'clock and wondered if he was there waiting. Somehow I knew he would. I knew I could have been sure of him. On Monday back at school he ignored me. He began flirting with another girl in our year, a pretty blonde girl. She was popular with all the boys. Always spotlessly dressed in the latest fashion, she glowed with confidence and had many friends. It was obvious to me that she was loved. She'd probably never known a moment of hardship. Peter and I hardly ever spoke again after that. Whenever I was in their presence, there she was, hanging off his arm.

I'd liked him a lot. Yet I knew there was no chance of us having anything together. How could I be his girlfriend? I was spotty and ugly. My brother liked to do stuff with me. I vomited up any food I ate. I didn't have any pocket money and wasn't allowed to go out. I was expected to cook the family meal every evening and mind my Mum. I'd had one evening of escapism away from reality. It would have to be enough. I held on to the knowledge that Peter had liked me. He'd told me I was beautiful. I held on to the hope that there would be other boys that would find me attractive. One day I'd be free.

Chapter 30

Granddad's decline

1982

Only months after the men had come to the house and terrorized us, Granddad had a stroke. He fell and was rushed to hospital. I didn't see it, but I saw the aftermath of it. There was lots of confusion, as Nana had usually been reliant on him to take the lead. He was the one that held the reigns in the household and we had all looked to him to set the pattern of our weekends. Always so constant, steadfast and reliable, we'd taken him for granted. Driving to pick us up on Friday evenings, keeping us occupied, walks in the woods, cricket and rounders. He'd made our swords and shields for play acting, mended our bikes, picked us up and soothed our woes when we'd fallen. He'd been so capable, our practical, logical failsafe. Tomas had to take us to Nana for the first time ever. Granddad had been allowed home, but wouldn't be able to drive. When we arrived he was sitting in the garden. He didn't get up to greet us and looked faraway in thought. Antony and I didn't know what to expect, we approached him hesitantly, unsure how to initiate a conversation or acknowledge his condition. Turning his head towards us as we neared he didn't seem to focus on us. Half-heartedly he raised his arm to signal his awareness that we'd arrived. Antony dropped back awkwardly, leaving me to approach him "Hello Granddad, how are you? We're really sorry you haven't been well. We've been wanting to see you and it's felt like ages. It was terrible news and we've been so worried about you." He barely responded to me. His jaw tensed angrily and he stared ahead, down the garden, at the two apple trees he'd planted years ago, so that one would fertilize the other. Still sitting, he motioned at the garden and said "I'm alright. It's a bloody nuisance is what it is. I have to get the grass cut with the …Um…Er…What's name…what's it called? Oh you know the blasted thingamajig what's name!"   His speech was noticeably slower and slightly slurred. Nana had warned us that he couldn't remember the words for some things and that it made him frustrated and angry, she said he would improve with time. It was horrible, I wanted to recoil from him, I felt terrible because it scared me. I didn't know how to respond to him and he seemed so angry. There was nothing in his limited actions or general behaviour that was intimidating, but the aura that surrounded him, the defeated slump of his shoulders and the bitterness that cast a shadow in his eyes, conveyed anger and disappointment to me. For the first time I felt afraid of my Granddad, not because I feared what he might do or that he might harm me. I was afraid because I had no idea how to reach him. I didn't know this man before me, who was now so weak and feeble. Before I'd always looked to him to set the agendas, he'd control the pace of our weekends and we'd abided by his rules. He'd been the dynamo that had helped us thrive throughout the other parts of our lives even when there had seemed to be no hope. Now I was afraid. How was I going to repay him? How could I instil hope in this man who'd inspired hope in me? It was like finding a bird in the garden with a broken wing and knowing I didn't have the skills to mend it and fearing it would never fly again. Antony braced himself and forcing false bravado hunkered down to his haunches, telling Granddad "You don't need to cut the grass. Don't worry, I'll get the lawnmower and do that, if you stay right here and keep an eye on me I'll manage it. I've seen you do it often enough, you've taught me everything else I know."

Nana was emotional, she'd get teary eyed while trying to maintain the semblance of normality. Preparing the lunch as always, but flapping and worrying about what Granddad was doing and whether he was alright. Spencer was angry. He railed about how that night, when the men had come to the house, had been the catalyst for everything going wrong. His behaviour suggested that he wore the trousers in the house now. He'd pick arguments with Nana, which resulted in tearful outbursts from her while Granddad would shake his fist at Spencer with frustration and the lack of vocabulary to express his anger at the boy's disrespect. Spencer had got a dog called Simba, it was a Sheltie. Granddad accidently spilt boiling water on him while trying to carry the kettle from stove to work surface. Spencer was furious and the dog had to have treatment. Even the poor dog began to mistrust us, he'd startle easily and shy away from Granddad who'd say "Bloody what's name, getting under my feet! Bugger off!" Spencer would tell him off for cursing at the dog "Don't talk to him like that. It's not his fault you're bloody useless!" Then Nana would cry at Spencer "That's enough Spencer! How dare you speak to Granddad like that?!" Our Grandparents house, once a haven had become an unhappy household.

Nothing is sacred. I've learnt that. Women always claim that there is no dignity in womanhood. When you become a Mum, all modesty goes out the window the first time you have a check-up with the gynaecologist and it's never regained once you've given birth. That notion, that dignity is destroyed is perhaps universal, or maybe it comes with age to us all, male or female. The stroke had affected Granddad in many ways, not all obvious. His moods were altered, and his concentration was poor. As his physical capabilities improved, he could walk. Ambling around the house, he'd attempt various domestic tasks from changing a plug, or the hoover bag, to setting the fire in the grate, or tacking a loose piece of stair carpet back in place. Countless times he'd forget what he'd been doing or give up from sheer frustration, totally bewildered by his own lack of coordination and humiliated at his inept proficiency. It was horrible to see. He lost his temper with

Nana and again, she would cry. She'd always been cheerful previously, eager to accommodate and entertain neighbours and friends. Her sensitivity was betrayed now by his shortness with her. Tears came easily and often, which annoyed him even more. Eating was now difficult for Granddad. He had trouble swallowing food properly, which meant mealtimes were miserable. The stroke even affected his ability to empty his bowels, it seemed he'd spend ages in the toilet sitting on the loo trying to have a shit.

Sunday morning was still the day I was encouraged to help Nana in the kitchen to do some baking. Doggedly she persisted with the traditional Sunday roast. I'd make scones or cakes, while Antony and Spencer would do the gardening, or wash Granddad's defunct car. We had the radio on, as we always would. Listening to David Hamilton's music line up and jovial babble it felt like normal. Nana was happy, humming along to the music and chatting to me. Granddad came from the shed through the back door, and taking the newspaper, went upstairs. There was a hush between Nana and me as he went. She followed him to the bottom of the stairs calling after him "Are you alright Les?" He mumbled under his breath, treading upstairs tiredly. Clicking her tongue with a Tut and shaking her head, Nana came back to the kitchen "I hope he's alright, he's had terrible constipation." I didn't know what constipation was but imagined it might be similar to the flatulence she sometimes had "What's constipation?" I asked her. Becoming a bit sheepish, her cheeks flushed a little "Oh dear, it's nothing really. Well it just means when it's difficult to go to the toilet." She started drying up the dishes on the drainer, briskly preoccupying herself with the task. I wasn't satisfied "What do you mean difficult to go to the toilet? Can't Granddad go to the toilet properly?" She got redder, and waving her hand at me, said "Since the stroke he has trouble going, that's all. It takes him longer and he gets irritable." I imagined him sitting on the toilet reading the paper and compared the thought to Shaun, when he'd been potty training. Nana said "Oh, he's been up there a while. I'll pop and check if he's alright." Putting down the tea towel, she pulled the kitchen door to behind her, went to the bottom of the stairs, and called up to him "Les! Are you alright up there?" I heard a muffled response as he answered her and she said "Do you need a bar of soap!?" Relenting he snapped back at her through the door with mournful shame "Yes! For god's sake, why not let the world know!" She bustled back into the kitchen and rooted around in the cupboards, producing a bar of soap she laboured up the stairs sighing and breathing heavily. I watched her struggling to help, physically and emotionally. Scooping up the scones I'd cut and placing them on the baking tray, I brushed them with milk. Pausing I listened as she tapped on the toilet door and whispered "Les…Les, Here you are." I could hear the bolt on the door slide back, the door opening and slamming again as he snatched the soap from her. It was curious. When she returned to the kitchen her bust heaved from the hasty trip back and forth. "Nana? Why does he need soap?" I asked. She tried to ignore me, pretending she hadn't heard the question, I tried again "What was the soap for?" Turning around she put her hand on her hip, and red faced, replied "It's for his bottom of course." I tried not to laugh, biting my lip I still pursued the question "For his bottom, why does he need soap for his bottom? Has he messed himself?" Nana was embarrassed. Finally she explained "Soap helps if you're constipated. You have to put a little up your bottom and it makes your business slip out." My jaw dropped, I'd never heard such a thing, sticking soap up your bottom. Seeing my face she started laughing, I said "He's up there putting the soap up his bum?" I was laughing now and tears of laughter were running down her cheeks "Yes, it'll make him pooh!" She laughed even harder, I'd never heard her say "Pooh" before. Another thought occurred to me "But what happens with the soap when he's finished with it?" Still crying with laughter she said "Well he'll rinse it off of course." Wide eyed now, I cried "Urrrgh! He'll just rinse it off and put it back in the bathroom? That's disgusting!" Now she was doubled over laughing and holding onto the work surface "Yes, he'll put it back for everyone else to use." I couldn't believe it, about to remonstrate about how awful that was and vow never to use their soap again. She waved her hand at me, her laughter subsiding she said "No, no of course not. When he's finished he'll wrap it in a piece of tissue and throw it away." Looking at each other the hysterics started again. She came, and putting her arms around me, she hugged me. We swayed together in her embrace until the laughter subsided. Then we continued where we had left off, my scone making and her drying up. When Granddad came down, neither of us spoke, or raised an eyebrow as he went through the kitchen back out to the shed. When he'd gone Nana winked at me.

Throughout Granddads decline, Antony remained a constant visitor. He visited unfailingly, while I was torn between seeing them and staying away. I wanted to see Nana, but found Granddad difficult to cope with. I dreaded seeing Spencer and found excuses not to visit. Even so on the occasions I did visit, Spencer still devised ways of getting me alone to intimidate, menace and pressurize me to allow his interference to continue. Allowing it to begin that very first time, was all the ammunition he needed now, to forever hold that over me. Threatening to tell Nana and Granddad, he coerced me into complying with his demands. Time and again, I had to lift my skirt, roll down my knickers and allow him to lay on top of me. I was so afraid he would tell them that I'd asked him to do it. He sickened me but I hated myself.

201

Chapter 31

Caught

1982

Allowing Spencer to use me the first time was my biggest mistake. In truth I didn't understand what he wanted when it began, but even so I felt stupid for not preventing it. I should've learnt my lesson the second and third time. It's an age old story, probably repeated in many households up and down the country, and in all likelihood, in many cultures around the world. Grandfathers, fathers, uncles or brothers taking advantage of the innocence of young boys and girls within their family. It's an unpleasant thought. Lots of brothers and sisters maybe experiment with each other at a very early age, investigating each other's bodies, especially if they're unsupervised, but this usually goes no further. Many a mother will deny knowledge of abuse by an older family member towards a son or daughter. Acknowledgement of ones failings is equal to admitting blame. Better to deny all knowledge. Sometime even blaming the child, and preferable to admitting their own shortcomings. My Mum, was too involved in her own grief, and the oblivion of her depression blinded her to my troubles. I probably sound matter of fact about it. My way of dealing with it and the consequences of my tolerance of Spencer's abuse, is to accept what happened then and place the memories in a little compartment in my mind, where it's labelled as "Shit that happens in human nature." Reflecting on what happened between Spencer and me now, I can see reasons, causes and effects for his behaviour and, indeed, my docility. For a long time the images of what he did, what I allowed and the impact of it haunted me. I've had to come to terms with that.

Spencer's modus operandi was to get me alone. If I wasn't upstairs, alone already, preoccupied in some silly role play game, he would find a reason for me to join him upstairs. Failing that he'd whisper in my ear to meet him, or gesture with eye movements that I'd better do as he was signalling. I knew the drill, if I didn't do as he'd asked, whispered or gestured he'd tell Nana and Granddad how I'd initiated physical contact with him. He'd warned me every time "If you don't do what I want, I'll tell them how dirty you are and what you made me do." Or "If you ever tell on me, I'll say it was you that started it. You took your knickers off and showed yourself to me. They'll hate you then." So I complied. It was easier that way, besides I had a coping mechanism for the actual act. I switched off, emptying my mind and allowing myself to be absent from what was happening. Another useful technique I'd learnt was to imagine my body as a shell. What was on the inside of the shell was something else. My spirit. No one could touch my spirit. While Spencer lay on top of me, jerking up and down, frantically trying to spend his frustrated arousal, only my shell was there. My spirit was elsewhere. After he climaxed was the difficult bit to deal with. The mopping up, while avoiding eye contact with him. The smell that always made me retch, and the sense of revulsion at myself for letting it happen, yet again.

Our Saturday evening ritual at my grandparents eventually returned to some semblance of what we'd had before the men came. It wasn't ever quite the same and I wasn't to know that there were not to be many more Saturday nights, together. To be honest, now we were growing up, it wasn't easy to keep us all entertained together and having us all settled in one room, was no longer such a common occurrence. One of us always had some other distraction pulling us away from the family sit down. Spencer was the one most likely to spend time in his room, listening to music, or reading. It wasn't odd for him to separate himself from us.

We were all together in the living room for once, our grandparents each inhabiting their favourite armchair either side of the fireplace. We'd finished watching "3-2-1"one of our favourite shows. It featured "Dusty Bin", which was literally a dustbin dressed up to look like a person and was the consolation prize if the contestant lost. When it finished Spencer announced he needed the loo. His eyes flashed pointedly at me. Glowering briefly, I knew it was the signal for me to follow him. I never tested him to see what would happen if I didn't follow. I was always obedient, afraid there would be consequences if I rebutted him. Doing as he'd taught me previously, I allowed a little time before leaving the room. I wasn't to arouse suspicion you see. Antony might follow us if he thought he was missing out. I can almost laugh at the very implication of that now. Only almost.

Spencer was on the landing waiting, watching out for my reluctant appearance on the stairs. He needed to make sure of my compliance, and that no one else had followed me. Seeing me heading upstairs he went on into his bedroom, to wait for me. Treading the stairs heavily, I wearily made my way to his room. I paused in the doorway, my stomach knotted with angst. I didn't want this, like some twisted "groundhog day" I knew what was coming. Standing at the doorway I resisted entering until he hissed at me "Come on! Hurry up." Finally, striding over to the door he grabbed my wrist and pulled me over the threshold, pushing the door closed with his other hand. "Don't!" I said "Anyone could come. You mustn't Spencer. It's wrong." There was no misunderstanding, we both knew what he wanted me there for. Smirking at me he told me to "Shut up stupid. No one's going to know, because we're not going to say anything." He drew the curtains and started undoing his trousers as my bottom lip trembled. Wringing my hands together I pleaded "Please, I don't want to. I hate it. It makes me feel sick." I didn't want to look at him, but in an effort to convey how serious

I was, I dared to look him in the eye "I don't want to do it anymore. I'm scared what could happen." He wasn't interested, he'd already decided that was what he wanted. My consent was unimportant to him. He had the power, whereas I believed I had none. Sniggering softly he said "Alright, alright. This'll be the last time. Just once more and we'll never do it again. How about that? I promise." It was a promise he'd made last time and the time before that. The first time he'd said it I believed him. That was the one and only time I'd willingly participated, believing that would be the end of it. By now I knew it was only another tactic to make me relent. I still stood, unresponsive, making no attempt to submit to his persuasion. His voice wheedled as he explained "I know I've said it before, but really, I promise this time. I'll only do it this one last time. Never again. You don't believe me, I understand. Honestly I cross my heart and hope to die, it's the last time." Very quietly I replied "I don't believe you." The tension seemed to seep into the room from the pores in his skin. His bedroom smelt of him, it rankled me. My dislike for that smell was akin to the nausea I felt at the smell in the butchers, on Wulfstan way. His eyes were fraught with desperation and his skin had an ever so slightly sweaty sheen. He was getting annoyed with me now, there wasn't time to waste. He wanted to get things moving, satisfy himself and return back downstairs before they wondered what we were doing. "Listen, just lie down on the floor. You're not doing anything wrong. I won't touch you. I'll only lie on top of you, you can your knickers on. I'll be quick." I wanted to leave the room, but didn't have the courage. I knew how spiteful he could be, the times he'd played "Chinese burns" with either Antony or me. He'd twist the skin around our wrists so tightly with his hands, until the pain made us scream at him to stop. The times an innocent play fight had concluded with him holding a cushion over my face until I thought I might suffocate and had to bang my fists against his sides until he released me.

Still denying him, I shook my head, resolutely rooted to the spot. Then he turned ugly. Screwing his face up, his top lip curled as he told me "If you don't lie down on the floor like I've said, I'll call them upstairs now. Do you understand, stupid? I'll tell them how you followed me up here and started showing yourself to me and asking me to touch you." I wanted to cry and run back downstairs. I just didn't know if he really would shout after me, but I was too scared to try it. He could see my resolve crumbling and continued pressurizing me "Who do you think they'll believe? A tell-tale tit like you? Always whining and complaining "Nana Spencer hurt me". He mimicked me "Or would they believe me? Lie down, or I'll call them up here now!" I lay down on the floor. It was always on the floor. My white knee high socks had slouched to my ankles and hung off my toes. I lay as rigid as a board. My shoulders braced up supporting my neck as I felt the hardness of the floorboards under the thin carpeting underneath my head. He was on me in an instant. His trousers undone, he'd released himself at the fly and only pulled them down far enough to allow enough freedom for his swollen penis to make contact with the warmth of my skin. I stared beyond him, over his shoulder and up to the ceiling. Despite his promises he fumbled around, tugging my skirt up and pulling it roughly over my stomach, in his urgency for self-gratification. The skirt bunched up and around my waist at the thrusting movement he generated, as he frantically sought to find a pace that would relieve his frustration. I was trying to find that emptiness, to leave my body the shell, and let my mind wander somewhere else, remaining untouched. Then I felt him grabbing at my knickers. He was trying to get them down. I couldn't find the emptiness, my mind felt trapped by my body. I had to struggle. Squirming, I tried to wriggle away. My head baulked against the hard floor beneath me, as I cringed at the closeness of his face to mine. My legs splayed out underneath him, I desperately tried to seek an escape from his weight. The sudden writhing motion seemed to excite him further, as he frantically scrabbled with my knickers, trying to prise them down between us, despite the pressure of his body on mine. I didn't know if my struggle stimulated him, or if it fuelled him to ejaculate in a frenzied attempt to make the onslaught complete. I will never forget was the sound of the bedroom door opening and a gasp of horror. There Granddad stood, taking in the scene before him.

Spencer leapt up and off of me in a mad scramble. Hastily pulling his trousers up around his waist and fumbling to do them up, he yelled at me "Get off me you dirty bitch!" It was too late, as Granddad, in disgust, lurched away from us downstairs crying "I saw what you were doing! I know what you were up to! The pair off you!" My heart thundered in my chest, as it pumped furiously. I sat upright and the blood seemed to rush from my head. I felt faint with dread. Pausing to glare accusingly at me Spencer screamed "You're a dirty whore! You made me do it!" He ran after Granddad, while I sat, still stunned and completely unable to decide what to do. I was utterly confused. There was nothing I could do. The worst had happened, nothing that preceded it had been this bad. Nothing would ever be this bad again. I had to go downstairs, but the thought of it terrified me. In that moment I was completely alone. There was no turning back this time, it had happened. Time wasn't going to stand still, however long I sat there. I got up, and with quavering legs, made my way downstairs.

There the commotion was in full swing. Nana had been in the kitchen, putting the kettle on to make a cup of tea. Granddad had come upstairs, I assume, to use the toilet during a programme intermission. Curiosity must've made him wonder why we were in Spencer's room with the door closed. Now he was furiously pacing around the kitchen, railing at Nana "I saw what they were doing, up there….in the bedroom. The two of them together. They were up to no good!" Nana was startled, he'd come flying down the stairs and into the kitchen in a rage. Spencer, hotly behind him, was shouting too "Don't listen to him. I don't know what he's talking about! He's gone mad!" Nana was flustered, looking from one to the other, she didn't know what had happened. I stood in the hallway, not bold enough to venture forwards, but able to see and hear clearly, as Granddad and Spencer argued. Nana, absolutely flustered, tried to understand what was supposed to have happened. Antony had run to the kitchen doorway to see what the commotion was all about, he kept looking backwards at me and towards the turmoil in the kitchen. He too was at a loss to understand why this ruckus had broken out. I moved forwards, using Antony as a shield, I stopped behind him. Granddad saw me. Stretching out his arm, he pointed at me and said "She knows what I'm talking about! Her and Spencer….doing things together and what's name! It's wrong all wrong!" Understanding dawned on Nana's face as she finally registered what he was accusing us of. Looking at me, the embarrassment was obvious from her expression, as she asked "What is he saying? What have you and Spencer been doing?" Everyone was silent as they waited for my answer. Antony turned around at the doorway to see my reaction. Standing in the hallway, the smell of Spencer's semen still in my nostrils, I felt ghastly. I was sure I must look filthy. Answering Nana I lied "I don't know what he means". Breathing a great sigh, as she turned to Spencer with a heaving chest and asked "What were you doing?" Immediately he was reproachful, saying indignantly "We weren't doing anything! I don't know what he's talking about. He's gone mad. We were sitting in the bedroom talking that's all. He flew into the room and started shouting at us. He's bloody crazy, he's lost it!" Granddad continued pacing around the kitchen shouting "Lies, Lies, all lies. I saw them. Disgusting, they're no good". He ripped open the backdoor and stormed out into the darkness. Nana pursued him, we heard her calling his name and then the hushed sounds as she tried to pacify him. Antony looked from Spencer to me and said "What were you doing?" Spencer marched over to him and holding up his fist said "Mind your own business. It's nothing to do with you. You can keep your mouth shut or you'll get a thumping." It was my turn next "And that goes for you as well, keep your mouth shut, or you'll be hurt too." Antony was about to follow Nana and Granddad into the garden, but Nana appeared in the passageway outside. Stepping back indoors she shooed Antony in "Upstairs, come on…all of you. Time for bed. That's enough for one night. Granddad's upset. You all know he's not well. He's not thinking properly and gets easily confused since his stroke." She herded us upstairs, enabling Granddad to avoid us when he came back in. Antony complained "Why do I have to go to bed? I haven't done anything wrong!" Spencer was only too happy to extricate himself, thundering up the stairs ahead of us, still protesting his innocence. He waited for Antony to catch up with him, before shouting at Nana "I hate it here! I don't want to be here anymore!" Then slammed his bedroom door to emphasize his point. With my brothers out of the way Nana took my hand and led me to her and Granddads bedroom, where I still slept in my single bed parallel to theirs. There she turned and grasping my forearms she said very softly "You mustn't let what Granddad said upset you too much. I know how it sounded, but please try to forgive him. He's made a mistake. You must remember that he's not been very well and his mind gets muddled." She squeezed me to her and I was suddenly overwhelmed by the familiar smell of her "Yardley" face powder. She must have thought I was so upset by Granddads tirade that I could neither respond to her words or her embrace. I just stood there limply in her

209

arms. I wanted to hug her, I wanted to tell her the truth. Instead I felt like a liar. I let her believe that there had been a misunderstanding, I allowed her to think Granddad was wrong. Worse than that, I'd said he was wrong. There was nothing I could think of to say. Anything other than the truth would only propagate the lie. She drew the curtains and turned down my bedclothes as I changed into my nightdress. I heard movement downstairs and the sound of Granddad muttering to himself. Climbing into bed I longed for sleep. Nana tucked me in, kissed my forehead and patted my hand, then wished me goodnight.

Sunday morning came. I hadn't heard either of them come to bed and both of them were already up. If their bed hadn't been disturbed I wouldn't have known they'd slept. I dreaded going down for breakfast. The sunlight filtered in through the curtains. It should have been a lovely morning. I could see both sides of their bed had been used, both sets of pillows had indentations and Nana's stash of tissues had slipped out from under her pillows in the night. The covers were thrown back, the bed still waiting to be made. It looked as if they'd been in a hurry to escape the room. Swinging my legs to the floor, my nightdress had hitched up to my waist in the night. I surveyed my thighs, white, blotchy skin and the slight down of hair visible along my shins. Quickly I yanked my nightie back down to cover myself, feeling ashamed at the sight. I crept out of bed silently to use the bathroom and inspect Spencer's room to see if they were awake yet. His door was open and there was no sign of either him or Antony. They must be up already. I used the toilet and scurried to the bathroom to wash, in the hope that I might get dressed before anyone saw me. I wanted to be prepared. I needn't have worried, nobody came upstairs. I should've realized that there was no chance anyone would venture upstairs to risk being caught on their own with me again. As I dressed, thoughts raced through my mind "What would happen now? Would Granddad say something to me when I went down? Would he have convinced Nana last night? What would I do? Would he tell Mum and Tomas?!" It was unbearable. I wanted to die just die there and then on the spot. For a hole to open up in the floor and swallow me. Anything was preferable to facing them all. It was no use, my imagination wasn't going to save me. Bracing myself, I went downstairs.

It was bizarre really. Thinking back, it was as if nothing had happened. We followed the same Sunday morning rituals. Spencer and Antony in the garden, Granddad in the shed, Nana cooking a fried breakfast in the kitchen. The matter wasn't discussed, in fact, it was never mentioned again. The only difference was Granddad. He never made eye contact with me again, never smiled at me, or spoke directly to me again. I lost him that weekend. His relationship with Spencer deteriorated drastically too. I hardly visited after that. At least the molestation by Spencer ended. Granddad's health declined severely as he was diagnosed with cancer and within months he died. Dad returned from Amsterdam for the funeral, Antony attended along with the rest of the family, while I stayed away. Sometimes I read silly little quotations about life. Quips such as "Don't regret the things you do, regret the things you didn't do." If only it was so easy. I will always bitterly regret the way I lost my Granddad.

Chapter 32

Wasters and Fraudsters

1984

Not all was doom and gloom. I wouldn't describe it as happiness, yet there were moments of humour and laughter interspersed between the shit. Little snippets come to me occasionally. One that often comes to my mind is of my Mum on the back of my bike. I told her I'd give her a "bunk up". She sat on the saddle as I stood, peddling us down the road to the off-license. I was fifteen and she was still not much more than a young woman herself really, at only thirty five. It was Friday night. Tomas went drinking with my Uncle Nigel and their mates regularly at the end of the week. If Mum had a spare fiver she'd ask Shaun, Antony and me if we'd like some sweets from the "offy". Usually, Antony and me would cycle down and pick up some chocolate, crisps and "Tizer" to share. This time she'd said she'd come with me. I was so pleased because it was such a rare event for us to do something on our own. It was a warm summer's evening and she was in a good mood. It took ages as I waited for her to get comfortable on the saddle. I couldn't believe she'd actually agreed to it! She clung onto my waist, gripping my t-shirt so tight that it pulled at my back. Each time I pushed off and managed to wobble a couple of yards she kept crying "Wait a minute, wait a minute, stop! Oh, hold on, I'm not on straight, let me catch my breath!" She laughed so hard, every time I started to cycle her nerves got the better of her and she said "What will people think of me? I'm behaving like a kid, I'm supposed to be your Mother. They'll all think I'm a right one!" Her laughter was infectious, I couldn't keep the handle bars straight because she had me laughing so much. We both had tears rolling from our eyes. Her legs were spread wide either side of the bike as she had nowhere to rest her feet while I peddled. We were weaving all over the pavement and I had to pause over and again, to regain composure. It was a haltingly long journey. When we finally made it to the shops, she almost fell off the bike trying to get her leg back across to join the other one in a standing position. She was so nervous, clumsily clambering off and trying, but failing to be sensible. Her laughter was uncontrollable. Other people did see her and smiled openly, enjoying the comical scene we made. I loved her so much then. We walked home, talking along the way. Antony and Shaun were waiting eagerly when we got back with our haul of goodies. I knew that when they were both in bed later, I'd sneak down and watch "Auf Wiedersehen pet" with her, and she'd make us a milky coffee, it would be like it used to.be

We all spent a summer holiday with Nana and Spencer, in a chalet in Clacton. She had convinced Mum and Tomas to make it a family break for us all after Granddads death and showing some compassion, in a rare instance of benevolence, they agreed to make it happen. It was a rather peculiar holiday. Nana packed enough food to feed an army and cooked Tomas and Mum a fried breakfast every morning. Tomas came to the breakfast table bare chested and bare foot, only in his jeans, which made Nana blush and flutter around the table. He teased her as she shooed him away, it was good humoured fun that had us all smiling. She made us sandwiches to take to the swimming pool for lunch and cooked our evening meals. There was a mutual respect between the three adults who seemed easy in each other's company. If there was any antipathy it was between us siblings. Spencer was invited to join Mum and Tomas in the evenings when they went for a drink in the clubhouse, while Antony, Shaun and me stayed back, locked in the chalet with Nana. She tried to entertain us with the card games we played when we were younger. Antony wasn't having any of it, he demanded to know why Spencer was allowed to go to the clubhouse and not him? I didn't enjoy being locked in either, it wasn't like any other holiday we'd had. Antony really began acting up and climbed out of the window. Shaun started crying for Mum, while I was trying to placate Nana as she got more and more upset, she tried explaining to us that they were including Spencer to help him deal with the death of Granddad. Tomas was making an effort to find some common ground with him. None of that made any difference to Antony. Always usurped in Mum's affections, he couldn't understand why he was being left

213

out. As for me, I didn't understand why we were sitting in the chalet on a lovely summers evening and hadn't all gone out together? Our family never seemed to be able to get it right. Over the course of the holiday Mum recuperated well, Nana treated her like the daughter she'd never had, while Mum thrived on the motherly attention she'd not experienced as a child herself. The holiday was an odd gathering. Each of us dealing with our own grief in disproportionate ways.

For a short while Spencer came to stay with us. He'd finished school eighteen months ago, but had been pretending to leave the house every day for work. When in reality he wasn't working, he'd been going into town or hiding in the library. Nana had appealed for help, so he came to us. Finally Mum had to face the fact that she was his Mum and had to respond to Nana's plea for help. Tomas believed he'd sort him out, he got him some work on various demolition sites, in a gang he was foreman to. Spencer left the house early in the mornings and came home covered in dust at the end of the day. He was exhausted and unhappy. After having such a soft, coddled life with our grandparents, this was unlike anything he'd been used too. Never even having stayed a night at ours before, suddenly he'd been thrown into our lives and had to adjust to the way we lived. He was very wary of Tomas, unused to such forthright outbursts, he'd never encountered anyone as blunt and direct as him before. Our grandparents were gentle, passive people, always dignified. Tomas was dramatic, passionate, a fierce half Irishman, with a mouth that could talk the hind legs off a donkey and turn the air blue. Sometimes the disdain was as obvious in Spencer's face as the fear or fake admiration he wore like a mask. I and probably Antony too knew it was all a sham. This artificial state of bonhomie in our home was unsustainable. The amenable geniality came to a halt as soon as Tomas discovered Spencer was lying to him too. Skipping days at work and making excuses all

214

the time. Not a person to suffer fools lightly, Tomas declared "He's not staying here. I know he's your son Carol, but I'm not putting up with a waster and a liar living under my roof. He can go back to his Nana's and she'll have to deal with him." It had been only a few weeks, but he was only too happy to go home to Nana. She despaired of him, yet graciously she still thanked Tomas for trying.

The household returned to normal. Antony, Shaun and I went to school, Tomas went to work and signed on. He was doing the demolition work cash in hand and signing on the dole in his lunch break once a fortnight. Not that it made our fortunes any better, Nana Sheila bought our clothes from the Salvation Army shop, while the larder and our bellies were never really full. The end of each week was always a struggle. We came home from school for lunch, because we had no money. Tired of the trek backwards and forwards we asked if we could take a packed lunch like Shaun and Tomas said "No you fucking can't. You greedy bastards eat all the fucking pack up before it makes it to your lunch boxes! And you'd better not touch Shaun's packed lunch stuff either." He reminded us "When you're buying the food you can eat all you like, but while I'm putting the food on the table and paying the bills, you'll do as I say." Usually followed by "You'll see. When you're sixteen, you're out! You can pack your bags and find out for yourselves." So we walked home at lunchtime and if we were lucky, Mum might have cooked us eggs or beans on toast. On a bad day I'd go without, while Antony would resort to melting margarine to pour on Weetabix for the lack of milk. To be fair to Mum she didn't eat, but she always had her cigarettes, no matter what. When she told us that Tomas was in trouble because he'd been caught working and signing on, we honestly couldn't work out where the money had gone. Tomas swayed between embarrassed bravado and hot indignation, pacing about the living room angrily "They can take me to court! What are they going to do? They can't get blood out of a stone! Let them send the bailiffs round, we've got fuck all. They can take the fucking sofa we got from the charity shop, if they think that's worth anything, Ha! It's falling to bits, they can have it. The TV's not ours, we pay for that with a fucking fifty pence metre!" On and on he moaned. He was right of course, we had nothing "I'll do some time if I have to, I'll even fucking offer. They can pay to keep me for a couple of months at Her Fucking Majesty's leisure! The break would be good, believe me!" He had his day in court and was fined the court fees and the sum he had fraudulently claimed. His name appeared in the local paper "Shamed", as the government had said benefit fraudsters would be, in their new initiative to stamp out false welfare claims.

The Mod revival was still in swing and our musical tastes were already influenced by our parents and Nana Sheila, who were familiar with the likes of Martha Reeves and the Vandella's, Mary Wells, the Skatalites and The Four Seasons. Antony embraced the new wave of Mod bands "The Jam" and "The Who". He identified with their "angry young men" image. His wardrobe started increasing subtly, now it comprised of a fish tail parka, Fred Perry t-shirts, desert boots, and Levi jeans. Styling his hair differently, he was apparently re-creating himself too. Girls and boys at school were noticing him, boys wanted to be like him and girls just wanted him. They weren't the only ones to notice his new look, Tomas noticed too. He wanted to know where the new clothes were coming from, and although Antony could convince him a few times that a friend had given him some cast offs. It became all too obvious that Antony frequently had very new, different clothes. We all wondered where they came from. Nobody's fool, Tomas deduced quickly that Antony was shop lifting, an accusation that he denied furiously. He wouldn't confess and Tomas warned him that if he proved to be lying there would be serious consequences. When

Tomas was out, Mum went and searched Antony's room. She found a haul of new clothes, shoes, and men's perfumes. Confiscating the lot, she didn't tell Tomas, but even so, Antony was incensed. The animosity between them grew. He avoided being at home, spending more and more time out with his group of friends. It seemed we only saw him at mealtimes and when it was time to come in and go to bed. He didn't do homework and arrived home late so many times, that it caused another bone of contention. There were many evenings when, already dark out, Tomas waited for Antony to arrive home. He'd get back, red faced and panting, where he'd realized the time and he'd run to try and make it only a few minutes late. Tomas would meet him in the hallway, as he tried to get through the front door and upstairs, without conflict. There would be a confrontation, yet another argument, as Antony back chatted and Tomas "clipped him around the ear". I would hear it, the arguing and the scuffle, that ensued as Tomas lunged for Antony and he tried to duck the inevitable slap. Lying in bed, I was thankful that it wasn't me. Mum would be in bed reading, as Antony ran upstairs, across the landing and to his room, banging the door shut. It segregated him firmly from us all.

Chapter 33

Drop out

1986

Mum was working. She'd got a job on the check out at the local Budgens, a street away from where we lived. It was ideal. Our household felt a little more prosperous, there was food left in the fridge the day before the weekly shop and the pre-pay gas meter didn't run out before it was topped up. I had an after school cleaning job at my old primary school. The chemist had become my favourite shop, I could buy my own tights, deodorant and sanitary towels now. I'd turned sixteen and was preparing for my mock GCSE exams. We had Careers advice classes at school and I'd decided that I liked the idea of becoming a nursery teacher, or a Nanny. It was a notion partly fuelled by my belief that I'd had an influential hand in teaching Shaun to read, write and do simple arithmetic before he started school. When I was asked what I wanted to do or what I thought I was good at, they weren't easy questions for me to answer. All I knew and had been raised to know, was how to be a housekeeper, a wife, or a mother. Mum hadn't inspired me to believe that women could be achievers, the circumstances of my childhood hadn't brought me into contact with successful women. I only knew Mum, my Nanas, a couple of aunts, or the girlfriends of my Uncles. Each of them only appeared to be useful as house wives or as chattels to their men. They didn't actually strike me as having any awareness themselves, that they might have become anything else. In my wildest dreams, I imagined being free of everyone. I would get a job, leave home and simply be free. I didn't care what the job was or how much it paid. If it was enough to leave home that would do. Only now with exam time imminent, did I fully realize that I'd wasted time. I'd not prepared properly and hadn't truly appreciated the importance of education. Now, when I researched what my options would be, with the results I could reliably expect to achieve, I saw my limitations. Trying to combine what skills I thought I had, with the qualifications I might have, I saw clearly how limited my options were. I also knew, there was no chance of further education. Tomas's words rang in my ears "When you're sixteen you're out." Well I was sixteen and intuitively I sensed the time I had at home was limited, both by my design, and Tomas's. It was completely apparent to me that no one was going to support me through college. I'd toyed with the notion of becoming a nursery nurse, imagined doing an NNEB course. Really I knew that was an impossibility. Combined with this certain knowledge was my lack of self –belief. English was my favourite subject and the exam was divided into two parts, a written test and an oral test. There was the rub. I was terrified that I would have to sit across from the examiners and read aloud under their scrutiny with my lisp. It crippled me. I was so afraid that they would laugh at me when they heard my S's sound like F's and I knew so well from experience, that when I was stressed or nervous, the impediment was worse. I didn't know what would happen, I believed an answer would come.

There was a vacancy at Budgens for a general assistant on the shop floor, with some till work. Mum pressed me to apply. I was uncertain, I wanted to take my exams, but she insisted that it was an opportunity not to be missed. She highlighted the positive aspects of the job, its closeness to home, how few skills were necessary to apply and in conspiratorial tones, the benefits of working together. It did appeal to me, it was an escape route. I could avoid the embarrassment of lisping through my English exam. I was convinced enough to ask Mrs Ewan-Smith if it would be possible for me to leave school without sitting my exams. It was only supposed be a consideration at this stage, but meanwhile unbeknown to me, Mum had already arranged an interview. Mrs Ewan-Smith was incredulous that I'd even consider leaving school without sitting my exams, then equally upset that I might be serious. She tried persuading me to wait, even suggesting that my parents might have to pay for exams that I failed to sit. I still thought it was all a hypothesis and attended the job interview, thinking I had choices. For the very first time, I had options. I was going to take a little time, to figure it all out and decide what was best for me. I should've known better by now! I was offered the job. The manager asked Mum to relay the news to me. It was a foregone conclusion. She made it clear "Even if you sit your exams what will you do? You won't get enough grades to go any further and even if you did, how will you support yourself through college or sixth form?" Perhaps, seeing she'd been too harsh, she added "Women don't need to have careers, you'll get married and have children one day and then that will be your priority. Take this job and have some money. Enjoy yourself while you can." It was meant to soften the advice, but successfully, she had tapped into all my insecurities, whether knowingly or unintentionally. My choices dissolved along with any resolve I'd had. When I told Mrs Ewan-Smith my decision, she cried at me "Why?!" Then, flushed with anger and embarrassment, I could see the bleak acceptance in her face as she acknowledged to herself that she knew exactly why.

Within the week, I had left school. Swapping the anxieties of exams for the apprehensions about starting work, learning the job, fitting in again, and meeting new people. I was leaving behind childhood and entering the world of adulthood.

Chapter 34

The Hamsters wheel

1986

In some ways going out to work was similar to the structure of the school system. I had another uniform, there were new rules and regulations to abide by. There wasn't a register but there was a clocking in machine. I was expected to behave with courtesy and politeness with customers. There were phrases used in the work place that I'd heard at school such as "Team work" and "Punctuality". I wondered what was so remarkable about leaving school. I thought it would be liberating, but it felt like I'd swapped one institution for another. The manager wasn't far removed from a headmaster. Though a day felt much longer at work, I missed the diversity of school. I'd stack a cage full of stock and send it down in the lift to fill the shelves with. My sections were cereals and pet food. While picking the price labels off dog food cans, in order to mark up at a higher price, the manager came to make sure I was scraping off all evidence of the previous price, clasping then unclasping his hands repeatedly in an attempt to seem efficient. With a stiff smile he muttered brusquely through clenched teeth "Make sure there's no trace of the old pricing and try to put the new label exactly where the old one was." Then flicking his eyes up and down my beige and white Gingham pinafore "Do your top button up. Oh, have you got any flesh coloured tights? I'd prefer it if you wore them rather than black ones". Without waiting for an answer, he strode away to inspect the deli counter. If I was on the cereal aisle I could see Mum at the tills. She would lean over, wave and smile at me, mouthing "Are you alright?" I'd nod back at her. Maybe it was reassuring knowing she was there, it brought us together to a certain degree. Having the same workplace in common had opened up new avenues for discussion. Yet for her, it seemed enough, and probably in comparison to what life had dealt her so far, it was. It wasn't enough for me though. She said I was lucky to have left school and walked straight into a job, while many people continued in further education only to face unemployment, or that lots of young women were married and pregnant before they knew it. Her outlook wasn't entirely pessimistic, but seemed quite narrow even to me. If she was right the best I could hope for was to meet a man, get married, and have children.

When I got my first pay packet I felt better. That little brown envelope contained enough money to pay Mum and Tomas for my keep, but still leave some for my essentials, catching a bus into town, and buying a new outfit or some make-up. To begin with it was sufficient. I made friends with a couple of the other girls, they saw my reserve and made an effort to draw me out of myself. There was one girl in particular that I was fascinated by. She was exceptionally pretty with long flame red hair and big blue eyes. Her name was Michelle, she had delicate fingers decorated with several gold rings and her skin was like porcelain and absolutely flawless. I watched her surreptitiously, afraid she'd see my interest. I wanted to be like her. She worked on the till next to Mum's. I'd see them nattering to each other, laughing intermittently when they weren't serving customers. When there were customers, she giggled and chatted with them too. It appeared effortless for her to be sociable, cheery and bright. The customers liked her too, remembering her from previous visits, they called her by name. Taking my time to eke out the hours in the day, I would stack cereal on the shelves, laboriously making sure to rotate stock and line them all up evenly. All the time I watched Michelle, studying her make-up, her hair and her clothes. If I tried being like her, I might fit in. People might notice me. I was going to have to learn to be a people person. Give more than one word answers when customers spoke to me and try to initiate conversations with other staff members. I started applying my make-up differently and styling my hair in a new way. Instead of burying myself in a magazine at break times I just clung to a cup of tea and forced myself to make eye contact. It did make a difference. Pretty much anyone who came into the staffroom said "Hello". Another girl called Kerry asked "How long have you been here now?" She was also a fashionably attractive girl, popular with the male members of staff. I didn't really like her very much, but she seemed to like herself just fine, which made me envious. How do you get to like yourself so much and be so confident? Deciding to let her know I wasn't fazed by her obvious comfort in her own skin, tilting my chin, I replied haughtily "I've been here four weeks now. How about you, have you been here long?" I could see the laughter in her eyes as she noted my tone, before saying proudly "I've been here since I left school. I'm nineteen, so that's 3 years in another couple of months. I haven't seen you before, d'you live around here?" Already feeling uncomfortable, I'd been put on the back foot by her seniority. "I live down the road, I grew up in this area." She laughed mockingly about to ask another question, when the staff room door creaked open and Michelle came in "Who fancies a coffee? I'm making?" Looking around the room she seemed to see me for the first time "Would you like a coffee, or do you prefer tea?" Sitting erect, pulling my shoulders up and trying to look more together I forced a smile "I'd love a cup of tea, that'd be really nice, thanks" Busily putting the kettle on Michelle asked "Sugar, no sugar? Stand a spoon up in it or show it the tea bag?" I laughed as she gestured with a spoon and a mug "Two sugars and not too strong please." Turning towards Kerry with a stern voice she said "Haven't you had your half an hour? You went on your break at ten to, you'd better get back down on the shop floor before Mr Barratt notices." Kerry wanted to protest, but Michelle stood her ground, staring at her and she got up reluctantly, brushing past me in a huff, and flounced out of the room. When she was gone Michelle said conspiratorially "She thinks she's something special, don't take any notice of her." I was so relieved to know someone else had picked up on it I gabbled "Who does she think she is? I don't think she likes me very much!" Concentrating as she poured hot water from the kettle into our cups she waved the spoon around with her other hand as she talked "Kerry doesn't like competition, she doesn't like it because you're young and pretty." My face flushed as the blood rushed up from my neck to the roots of my hair. She said I was pretty. Fortunately she didn't notice or chose not to comment on my red face as she continued "Don't say a word to anyone, but she fancies Mark on the deli counter. He's already got a beautiful girlfriend, but that doesn't stop her from trying it on with him." Putting a steaming mug in front of me on the table she said "I'm Michelle by the way and you're Carolyn's daughter, what's your name again?" "Samantha". I said..

We became friends. I left for work in the mornings with a spring in my step, knowing I'd see Michelle. Previously the days ahead had seemed daunting, I'd thought my life was hopeless, that I'd given up education for a treadmill of repetition. Now I could see that this wasn't the case, there were other possibilities. The simple act of getting a job and making a friend, within the past few weeks had made drastic changes in my attitude to life. I wasn't a child anymore and the recognition that change could come so quickly, came with my realization that I could make things happen. I knew that each day was a new beginning and that I had to embrace it positively. The course my life would take was uncharted. I didn't have to accede to the status quo. I may have inherited the foundations my parents had laid but I could shape my future. I had a clear understanding of my limitations, yet I knew, I would have much more than they allowed. Making plans with

Michelle to meet outside of work, I dressed as any young woman would. Wearing brand new clothes that I'd bought with my wages, walking to the chemist on the high street, I lingered with relish, choosing hair dye, tights, body spray and make-up. After work, at the weekend, we'd drink in pubs. It was a challenge for Michelle to get the drinks in at the bar, all the time nervous someone might notice I was still underage. We raised a glass together when the drinks were served without a second glance. Another victory was staying under Tomas's radar. I'd stay over at Michelle's and he was no wiser to our activities. He assumed we were painting our nails, sitting in her bedroom and listening to "Wet, Wet, Wet" while talking girl talk. Indeed, sometimes, that's all we were doing. Michelle lived with her Nana. She had a lot of freedom, there were no men in her household to answer to. I would take a change of clothes to work with me on Fridays and walk home with her. She'd cook the three of us a meal, something simple with oven chips, then, when we'd washed up, we'd take it in turns to shower using her bedroom to dress, put on make-up, while in the background, albums played on her LP player. Fascinated by her, I'd taken up smoking, even imitating her bad habits. When we were sitting on her bed, sharing a cigarette, painting each other's nails with the same varnish, while talking about fashion, it didn't feel bad. In fact I'd never felt happier.

That was how I met Kevin. There was a free disco every Friday night at "The Dog and Pheasant" on Newmarket Road, It was a stone's throw from Michelle's. I had died my hair jet black and it was cut in the latest style, very short, almost boyish, but for the long fringe I'd kept. I'd seen similar styles on recent pop stars and studied how coquettishly they could flick it away with a toss of the head. Painstakingly I'd mastered the technique of applying a rainbow of eye shadows, in a manner I'd adopted since school. Wearing a little pair of yellow patent court shoes and a pretty skirt and top I looked older than sixteen. When we walked into the pub there was an immediate stir of interest from the lads that were there. One of them recognized Michelle and made a bee line towards her straight away. He was boisterous in a merry, slightly drunken way. She liked him. The disco music was loud. Cupping her hand to my ear, she explained in a loud whisper "He comes into Budgens sometimes to buy his lunch, I serve him at the till. He's really nice!" He was happily playing the clown, dancing around us with a pint in his hand. There was a dance floor, lit up in flashing neon colours, reminiscent of "Saturday night fever". It was still early and people were in good spirits. The evening just beginning, they'd had a couple of drinks, their inhibitions were loose and the dance floor was in full swing. Clutches of girls danced together, busily eyeing the competition every time the doors opened, while similarly, young men appraised them and fooled around in comical attempts to draw attention. Girls tried to behave demurely, fluttering shyly seductive glances as the men postured and posed for effect, glugging back bottled beer with almost Viking like gusto, or staring obviously over pint glasses as they sipped thirstily. Michelle's friend was still dancing around, making an effort to impress her with some basic footwork, as his pint sloshed over the rim of his glass. The group he was with had been watching him from the bar and one of them broke away to come and retrieve him. Wearing a simple white shirt and blue jeans, he was dark haired, moustached and a bit older. Approaching us, he gestured to our clown "Oi, Andy, I've got another pint in for you!" Grabbing an opportunity for some back up, Andy put an arm around the interloper's shoulders, and pulled him towards us "This is Michelle, I know her from the place where I buy my lunch every day and this is her mate." He looked expectantly at his friend. His eyes beseeched him, willing him almost telepathically to distract me, so he could have Michelle to himself. The friend seemed a bit fierce to me. Nodding his head at her, while his eyes swept over me, he took another swig of his pint, before asking "What's your name then?" Despite my nerves, I smiled at him, telling him "I'm Samantha, what's your name?" Leaning in at an awkward angle, with his head cocked so that he could hear better, he shouted over the music "Did you say Amanda? I'm Kevin". I laughed and shook my head at him, unsure if he was teasing, or if he really hadn't heard "Samantha!" I shouted back at him. Michelle and Andy had moved away and she looked engrossed in whatever he was saying. I felt a bit out of my depth, inadequate and unsophisticated. Kevin came closer. Looking quite earnest he asked "How old are you?" His brow furrowed sceptically as he analysed me. Not wanting to reveal I was underage, tilting my chin as I challenged him "Guess. How old do you think I am? He observed ma as I did my best to appear completely at ease. Inside I didn't really enjoy being so scrutinized so closely, but at the same time I was flattered that he thought I was worth the attention. "I reckon you're eighteen...." He hazarded but seeing me shake my head he guessed again, "You're not older that's for sure. Seventeen then…" Again I shook my head, not wanting to lie, but also too afraid to tell him I was only a kid. Wide eyed with disbelief, he asked "Are you only sixteen?" When I nodded he laughed out loud and started to walk away, turned once, did a double take, then walked back to his friends. Foolishly I was left standing on my own beside the dance floor. Looking for Michelle I wanted to warn her that I'd made a mistake and let on that I wasn't old enough to drink. I could see Kevin at the bar, he was still watching me. I stood still, not wanting him to see me running after my friend, desperately wanting him to think I was confident enough to hold my own. Fumbling around in my handbag I dug out a ten pack of Silk Cut and casually lit a cigarette. The occupation with my hands and the act of smoking, calmed my nerves. I'd just ignore Kevin, he could sod off.

He didn't know me anyway. He might think I was a silly kid, but I probably knew more about life than he could ever imagine. Perhaps he saw the air of dejection, or maybe he felt sorry for me. Leaving his friends at the bar once more, he came back over. Curiosity had got the better of him "Please tell me you have finished school at least?" he said Well, I thought, he hadn't told the landlord my age, and he'd decided to come back and speak to me so he couldn't be all bad "Yes of course I've finished school, Andy told you. I work with Michelle at Budgens. I left school in May, I go out to work and I think that gives me the right to have a drink on a Friday night if I want to. I'm nearly seventeen. Well in four months, anyway." This made him laugh, but not mockingly. Smiling and nodding his head he agreed with me "You're right. Tell you what I'll even buy you a drink, what you drinking? Where's your mate? I'll buy her one too." He held his pint up in a toast towards me, as he beckoned over Michelle and Andy.

He bought us all a drink. Mine was a Bacardi and coke, it was the only drink I knew really. It was Mum's drink. The only time we had alcohol at home was at Christmas. Tomas always got a bottle in for her as a special treat. There was the occasional "Snowball" for me and Antony and sometimes Mum let me have a sip of her Bacardi. That's why I quite liked it. After a few drinks I forgot to be self-conscious and began to enjoy the night. We danced, cheesy disco music played, and Kevin, dancing with exaggerated moves and flashing eyes. He was quite earnest really, trying to be cool, but funny, while all the time I could see the yearning for approval behind his display of confident self-assurance. Strutting around me to the music like a peacock, I couldn't help laughing at him and liking him for being able to laugh at himself. I don't remember how much we drank that night, one glass was replaced by another in my hand. I didn't feel drunk and the mood was carefree. In that nice place hovering between sober and inebriated my inhibitions gone, my guard was down. I was just plain Jane, Samantha. The act forgotten, Kevin could see the real me. He liked what he saw and he made it obvious. The group of young men he was drinking with were celebrating, one of them had just become a father and so they were wetting the baby's head. Kevin and I were on the fringes of the group. They were getting rowdier, toasting the new dad and singing loudly. Arms around each other, they waved their pints around sloppily as they chorused, before downing shots of whisky to add to the drunken euphoria. We were apart from them, more interested in finding out about each other in a space where we could make ourselves heard over the din they were creating. Other groups in the bar laughed with bonhomie at the raucous merry makers, joining in the toast for the emotional new dad. Some, however, looked irritated at the intrusion to their get together. Looking on we noticed the annoyed glances that were thrown towards Kevin's friends and smiled knowingly, as our eyes met, both registering the unrest that was growing on the outskirts of the celebrations. Kevin put his pint down and gestured that he'd be back in a moment, he strode over to his friend the "Daddy", who was looking absolutely overcome by it all. I could see Kevin telling him it was time to call it a night "Time for you to go home I think, you're done in mate. You'll be in for it in the morning if you don't get back, the Mrs won't appreciate a hung-over dad breathing boozy breath all over the new sprog!" There were weak appeals of disagreement from some of the group and the daddy wavered uncertainly, swaying backwards and forwards, intoxicated, uncertain whether to stay or go. Seeming tearful with the combination of overwhelming emotion, exacerbated by alcohol, he staggered in the direction of the toilets, brushing clumsily past one of the other group members that were disgruntled with the noisy revellers. Further displeased by the lack of apology, the man from the other group swung round, glaring furiously at Kevin's friend as he blundered onwards, distracted by the urgent need to either relieve his bladder or vomit. Kevin made his way back towards me, I told him "The group over there look as if they're brewing for trouble. I thought one of them was going to follow your friend to the loos to start something." With a calm, steady gaze he said "I've got my eye on them, don't worry. Nothing's going to happen, they're just pissed off because we're having too much of a good time. The night's coming to an end and we'll all be leaving soon". Scanning the bar, Michelle and Andy were nowhere to be seen, I guessed they were outside, getting some space. I was also was thinking about calling it a night "I'm going to find Michelle, I'm staying at hers tonight." With a nod of his head he took my hand. Leading the way he made a path through the throng. Heading in the direction of the exit, he wanted to make sure I found Michelle. We found her outside in an embrace with Andy, it wasn't clear if they'd been kissing, or if they'd huddled together for warmth, maybe a bit of both. Kevin called over "Oi Oi, put her down!" She pulled away from Andy laughing, as he only half- heartedly relinquished her. The four of us were saying our goodbyes and making plans for when we might meet again. We hadn't noticed the new dad exit the bar from the double doors at the other end of the pub. Absorbed in our farewell, we hadn't seen that he'd been followed by the disgruntled man he'd brushed past earlier. We only realized when the sound of an argument caught our attention and turning to see what the fuss was about, recognized the two of them. Too drunk to really respond the new dad swayed giddily on the side of the kerb, the other man shouting abuse at him "You! You fucking ignorant bastard, should be more fucking careful and watch what you're fucking doing!" He stabbed pointedly at his chest, forcing him backwards on to the road. Regaining his composure, the new dad managed to set himself back on the path, apologising pathetically with a slurred voice "Sorry mate". We'd ceased talking now, watching the scene ahead of us with uncertainty, not able to tell what would come next. Kevin had already stepped forward to intervene, but I tugged at his arm. When he looked at me I silently shook my head. Frowning, my eyes pleaded with him not to get involved, believing that it wouldn't amount to anything more, surely the confrontation would go no further. How could anyone rationally blame a drunken man, out celebrating the birth of their first child, for a clumsy mistake? Despite all I'd witnessed in the past I still didn't have enough sense to read the situation, to understand that there are plenty of irrational people in this world who think illogically. Michelle on the other hand saw clearly what was happening. Shaking off Andy's attempts to hold her back she stormed ahead of us shouting "Leave him alone! What do you think you're doing?! His wife's just had a baby you idiot, he's had too much to drink." Before she could reach them the man had already swung his first punch into the stomach of Kevin's friend. Michelle screamed "No, no, no!" as she ran fearlessly towards them. The assailant was about to throw another punch to the side of his head as the new dad, doubled, over vomiting in to the gutter. Michelle grabbed the arm of the aggressor and hung off him as he tried to swing his next blow, just as Kevin strode over to intervene, Michelle was thrown viciously to the ground. Everything happened so quickly. Running to her aid, I felt helpless, uncertain what on earth to do. She was crying uncontrollably in a heap on the floor, as Kevin laid into the attacker. Suddenly, Andy shouted "The Police!" as sirens blared and a Police van screeched to a halt at the side of the road. It was a complete fracas. Another police car pulled up as Kevin and the man scuffled. I tried to console Michelle, while Andy ran alongside one of the police men, trying to explain what was happening, and the new dad was slumped onto the kerb holding his head with one hand, and clutching his stomach with the other. Two other policemen grabbed Kevin by his arms and dragged both him away and the other man away. Michelle got up and started shouting after them "It's not his fault! It's that other one! He started all of this. He's a nutter, just came out here and punched that man over there for no reason!" She was beside herself, as a female officer came towards us. Holding up her hands and waving at Michelle to pipe down, she pressed us back and away from the scene, saying "It would be best if you kept the noise down and got a grip of yourselves now. We need you to calm down. We'll deal with this. You'll have your chance to make a statement in due course." It was no use, Michelle was hysterical, sobbing and crying, and furious with indignation at the unfairness of the whole thing. Meanwhile I tried ineffectually to persuade her to listen to the police officer "Michelle, please listen to what she's saying. There's nothing we can do. You have to let them deal with it". Angrily she shook my hand off her arm, as she persisted in arguing with the officer. While this was happening Kevin was dragged into the back of the police van, thrashing and flailing against them and remonstrating the whole time "You've got it wrong! It's him, I was trying to stop him!" Leaving Michelle, I ran after Kevin shouting "It'll be alright! You'll see, they'll find out the truth, I'll make sure they know!" I didn't know if he could even hear me in the melee. I only hoped my words had reached him and he would calm down knowing that I'd give witness to what had really happened there. The van doors were slammed shut as a handful of officers tried to pin Kevin down, as he fought irately against their efforts to restrain him, one big bundle in the back. The scuffle continued, I could hear them as they thrashed around, bumping and banging against the sides of the van. My heart raced with panic and fear. What was to become of Kevin? He had only tried to break up the fight and now he was being carted off like a thug. The sounds in the van died down, as it pulled away and sped off into the night. The other man was handcuffed and led away to the police car, as the female officer still tried to reason with Michelle. Another policeman was hunkered down with his arms across the shoulders of the new dad. The female officer then asked Michelle and me for a statement of what had occurred, this seeming to give her some solace as she gathered herself together and tried to relay what had happened between heaving sobs. It was surreal. I couldn't get my head around it. I felt quite calm, having managed to remain composed throughout most of the incident, but, I didn't completely understand how it had unfolded, or why. The reactions of all involved seemed so disproportionate to the actual events. I didn't know if it was because I was desensitized, years of overexposure to aggression or cruelty had made me strangely immune. I just knew that if I behaved dramatically it wouldn't help, I had to think and analyse the events of the night in order to evaluate what it was all about. Michelle was given a lift home in yet another police car. I decided to walk to the police station with Andy in the hope that we might be able to see Kevin, or at least get some information that would reassure us he was ok.

The brawl and ensuing scene cleared. Michelle safely on her way home, all was silent. Only Andy and me were left, walking to the police station at Parkers Piece. He was able to see it as clearly as me, and we talked about what had happened, as we strode in unison. In the time we took to get there he told me more about Kevin, how he believed he was a decent man, and that he hadn't known of Kevin ever getting into trouble before. In confidence he said "He likes you a lot, anyone can see that. He's a good person. You mustn't let tonight stop you from seeing him again, trust me, Kevin doesn't mess around. There was a girl he was seeing a couple of years back, I think he even asked her to get engaged. She cheated on him and he hasn't had a serious girlfriend since then. If you like him, please be kind to him. Don't hurt him." The more we talked, the more I liked what I heard. For me the whole evening had taken an awful turn, but I didn't blame Kevin one iota, in fact I admired him for stepping in to defend his friend and Michelle. My interest in him grew. At the police station we queued to be seen amongst a melee of other Friday night revellers that had been caught up in some disturbance of one kind or another. Exhausted by this point, I was fading fast, wanting to know Kevin would be alright and wanting sleep too. More was revealed to me as Andy asked the officers on duty to make sure that Kevin had his inhalers "He's an asthma sufferer you see, has been since he was a kid, gets it quite bad. So please, I just want to make sure you know and that he's got some medication". They assured us they'd make sure he was fine "He'll only be in overnight, he'll be cautioned or charged, but we'll do all we can to make sure he's well looked after". In one evening of meeting Kevin the tentative attraction to him had blossomed into a respect and admiration, that wasn't all that familiar to me, regarding men. I'd seen him use aggression, but somehow, I already knew it wasn't a common trait within him. Satisfied there was nothing more we could do we were ready to leave. Before we left Andy wrote down Kevin's phone number and pressed into my hand, insisted I that I promise to call him. It was the early hours of the morning, and Andy, wanted to see me home safely. He hailed a cab, telling the driver "Get her home will you, here's the money. Make sure she's safely in the house before you drive off!" He banged on the cab roof as the driver pulled away, waving to me through the rear window as I watched him recede into the distance. The cab driver asked me for an address and, instead of going back to Michelle's, I gave him Mum and Tomas's. I wanted to go home to my bed.

That was one of the first nights I arrived home late. Tomas grilled me the next day. Question after question "Why didn't you stay at Michelle's last night? What happened? Were you even with Michelle last night? Where were

234

you?" It would have been easier if I'd gone back to hers, but I'd wanted the comfort of what I knew. I really hadn't wanted to go back and have an endless post-mortem of the night with Michelle, when I was so completely bushed. Now I'd raised Tomas's suspicions, I felt I was under a microscope. This was to be the beginning of the end of my childhood under his roof.

Chapter 35

Dirty stop out

After that first controversial night, I had qualms about contacting Kevin, whether to see him again, or leave it to fate. My head was telling me to leave him alone, while my gut feeling was to trust my intuition and see him again, at least once more. The piece of paper with his phone number on it was in my purse, over and again I told myself to ring and then chickened out. Finally, in the afternoon, I made an excuse to take a walk down the road, so that I could call him without Mum or Tomas overhearing. I made the call and he was home, seemingly quite stoic about last night's events. When he asked to see me again, it was his steadiness that convinced me to say yes. He came to pick me up with his brother Colin, in a well-kept, shiny black Ford Capri. I was impressed that he had a car and could drive. Too nervous to come and knock, he sent his brother to meet me, but I was already out the front door and heading down the path. The net curtains at the living room window twitched behind me, as I met Colin at the gate and he walked me to the car. I knew Tomas was watching from behind those nets, distracted from channel four and the horse racing. There'd be questions later. As I got to the car, Kevin got out to open the door for me, the small act of courtesy touched me. He drove us to a pub called "The Hoofers". It had previously been "The Racehorse", but had been modernised to appeal to a younger more hip crowd. There were high booths, with shiny red PVC seating and bar stools, and a huge TV screen playing MTV. The bar itself was long and spot lit, with an impressive array of optics. It turned out to be Kevin's local, being only a couple of streets away from where he lived with his parents. It was early still and Colin found us a booth then promptly went to the bar to buy us a drink. I think the arrangement had been discussed before they collected me and I warmed to Kevin even more. He wasn't as full of self -confidence as he'd first appeared. Perhaps it had only been Dutch courage any way. The fact that he'd bought his brother along for moral support made me feel more assured, that I'd made the right decision in coming "Are you nervous? Because I am!" He laughed, clasping his hands together on the table in front of us. I sat beside him, glancing shyly at him from under my fringe, trying to flick it casually out of my face, in what I hoped was an alluring way "Yes I am a bit, I suppose that's normal really. D' you come here often?" I felt stupid then, knowing that was a very clichéd line to use even as I said it. He laughed at me "Wasn't that meant to be my line last night?" I just blushed. Biting my lip, I told him "I thought you didn't like me, when you first came over. I thought you were making fun of me." I wanted to gauge his reaction, weigh him up. With a cheeky smile he feigned contrition "That was only me messing with you, I was interested, but when you admitted how young you are, it scared me off for a moment." Colin appeared back at the table. Looking amused, he gently placed my drink in front of me with a flourish "A Bacardi and coke for Madame, and a half for the Bro'" he stepped back and bowed comically "Now I'll leave you lovebirds to yourselves, I'll be at the pool table. If you get bored, feel free to join me!" With a twinkle in his eyes, he left us to our own devices. Kevin clenched his hands together nervously in front of him and cleared his throat. We both started to speak at the same time and stopped short, then laughing at ourselves "Sorry, go on you first" he said. "I was wondering what you do, where you work? How old you are? If you have any other brothers or sisters? All that kind of stuff. Where to begin I guess" I asked him earnestly, trying to appear comfortable. I wanted to ask the right questions and learn enough to figure out if he was an alright person. He sighed, like it was a relief, easier to answer them, than ask them "Well let's begin with my family. It's big! My Mum remarried when I was a kid, so I have a step-dad and he had five children from his previous marriage, they're my step brothers and sisters. She had the four of us, that's me and two brothers and a sister." I whistled in awe, and rolled my eyes to the roof in mock astonishment. Which made him smile "I work for a roofing company as a felt roofer, I'm the pot man, which means I make sure the pitch, which is the thick black tar in the pot, is ready for laying the roofing. It's very hot and you have to be careful, it can be dangerous." I rested my chin in my hand as he talked, listening attentively. I'd never heard of "pitch" before or even considered how a roof was laid. It explained why he was so tanned and weathered looking "I thought you were a gypsy! That's why you're so brown" I teased him. It struck a familiar chord with him "It's funny you say that, they all say Mum must've had a fling with the milkman at home. Yes I'm tanned from being on the roofs all day long, but we're all dark haired with brown eyes. We get that from my Mum. Who do you look like? Your Mum or your Dad?" I wasn't prepared for that question, it wasn't something that'd ever come up before and I'd no idea who I looked like "Neither I think. People did say I looked like my Nana when I was born". The conversation was flowing easily enough, I suddenly remembered he still hadn't told me how old he was "So how old are you?" I smiled at him, head cocked to one side cheekily waiting for an answer. He sighed ruefully, arching one eyebrow, he admitted "I'm twenty three. I was putting off saying because it's a bit of an age gap and I don't want to scare you off." He waited for my response "Whewee!" I whistled exaggeratedly "You're that old!" He looked genuinely crestfallen for a split second and realizing it was a concern for him, I quickly backtracked "Not really. I mean... I suppose I'm surprised you're that much older than me. It doesn't bother me, actually it's quite nice. I guess I'm lucky you're not already with someone, although it does worry me that you might think I'm too young." It was a deliberately leading question, which he picked up seamlessly "I was with someone, but she let me down. I'd even asked her to get engaged, but it didn't work out. She was younger than me too, but I don't think it makes much of a difference. She met someone else. Yes, you're younger too, yet there's something different about you. You seem older than you really are." His forthrightness was lovely. Of course, I already knew, because Andy had told me. The fact that Kevin freely volunteered the information himself, endeared him to me even more. "Well I don't feel like a kid. I've had to grow up quickly. I'm the only girl in my family and I've three brothers. I have a step-dad, like you. He's a bit of a tyrant and my Mum has had lots of problems, so I've had to help out a lot at home." He looked sympathetic and was about to say something, but I cut him off quickly with another question "Whereabouts did you go to school?" I wasn't ready to go down the road of my childhood with him on our first date "Ah! Now if you live over that side of town I'm guessing you went to Netherhall, which means I'm your rival. I'm a Coleridge boy." It was true, I remembered a clash at Cherry Hinton Hall on a lunch break once. A tribe of Coleridge girls had come to gang up on a girl in my year, who'd been seeing one of their boyfriends. He was the two timer, but she was the one who paid for it when they carried her by her arms and legs and flushed her head down the toilet. Admittedly, some of the Netherhall lot secretly relished the scene. Our toilet dunked girl was known to be easy with the boys and many of the girls disliked her for her unfairly earned popularity. "Oh! I thought Coleridge was where all the ruffians went, that explains it! Especially after last night." This comment from me finally brought us around to last night. Kevin was serious now "Last night was a mistake that should never have happened the way it did. I don't usually go around throwing my weight about, but I couldn't stand aside when my friend was being attacked and your mate was knocked to the floor like that." He was upset, I felt I'd offended him "I don't think that's who you are. I was as shocked as you. I was afraid you'd get hurt, that any of us might have. It could've escalated badly…" pausing, sighing deeply I continued "What happens now? Did they press charges? It sounded like they'd trapped a wild animal in the back of the van, when they arrested you." I wasn't joking now. The atmosphere had changed, our jovial flirtatious banter was replaced with anxious concern "The way they treated me was completely unnecessary. Once they'd got me in the van there was four or five of them, all trying to force me to the floor. They wanted to overpower me. It wasn't needed at all…" hesitantly he tugged his t shirt from the waist band of his jeans, pulling it up far enough for me to see two bite marks on his side, up around his rib cage. My hands flew up to my face. Gasping in horror, I exclaimed "They did that to you?!" It was a ridiculous question, he obviously couldn't have bitten himself. "Yes, while they were trying to "restrain me", as they put it. I was trying to fight them off, because there was no need for them to behave as aggressively as they did. I was handcuffed, I couldn't do anything and still they treated me as if I needed a good beating." I didn't know what to say to him, it was disgraceful. I'd been dismayed when I'd witnessed their strong arm tactics with him as they'd bundled him into the back of the van, but I hadn't fully comprehended what was happening "What on earth will you do? They can't get away with that kind of behaviour, surely that's not normal. There must be procedures for making a complaint!" I was indignant on his behalf. Taking my hand he stroked my fingers and said calmly "They've charged me. Apparently they think I'm guilty of an affray and assaulting a police officer," I gasped incredulously as he continued "I'm waiting to hear when my court date is.

But I'm not just going to just accept it, I'm going to get legal aid, get some defence and show them the bite marks. They're not getting away with this."

My attraction to Kevin grew. His determination and conviction to fight against the unethical practices of the people we expect to protect us and uphold the law, filled me with admiration. He was a fighter, a survivor. I believed his spirit mirrored mine. I don't know if I was naïve, easily swayed by emotion, or whether it was his resistance to the police and his subsequent vulnerability, I wanted to support him. I'd witnessed how he'd been overpowered and manhandled, almost gratuitously. There was something awkward, a little helpless about him, which I could see he tried to conceal with bold, typically masculine actions. There was more to him than that, it was exposed in small glimpses in the moments between eye contact and conversation. He wanted to be loved and so did I. That afternoon we talked at length. Already I was eager to see him again, while apprehensive about what the outcome would be when he went to court. Having nursed only two halves of bitter, so he could drive me home, we said goodbye to Colin and called it a night. Parked outside my house we said goodnight. We still hadn't kissed. As I looked at him, he faltered slightly. Unsure how forward to be, he leant in and kissed me gently on the lips. It was such a brief, delicate, fleeting thing that I pressed in to his lips a second time. Encouraged by this response, his kiss became more daring, our lips parting to explore each other's mouths with our tongues. My heart raced. A familiar sensation throbbed in the pit of my stomach, I was excited but cautious at the same time. There was chemistry between us. We separated reluctantly, both aware that one of my parents might have heard the car engine and already be peering from behind the drawn curtains. I said goodnight once more, as I opened the car door and stepped out, he grabbed my hand one more time and kissed my fingertips before releasing me into the night "Ring me soon" he whispered.

There were no mobile phones then and although we had a phone in our house, it was out of bounds to me. Not that I would've chosen to make a personal call in earshot of Mum or Tomas anyway. Kevin had driven away as I'd slipped in the front door. It was like slipping from a wonderful dream into the reality of harsh daylight as Tomas shouted through from the living room "Where have you been?!" My shoulders slumped, I heaved a huge sigh and braced myself for the interrogation "I said "Where have you been?" "Don't stand out there in the hallway hiding. Come in here where I can see you and answer me when I'm fucking talking to you!" I let my bag drop to the floor at the foot of the stairs and, blinking at the brightness of the hundred watt bulb in the living room ceiling, stuck my head around the door "I went for a drink with some friends that's all". Tomas was already fumbling with the TV remote, seeking the volume button, so that he could hear my mumble more clearly "Who was the bloke that came to meet you then? He got out of the car and came to the gate." I rolled my eyes "Don't roll your fucking eyes at me! Answer me, because he was wearing a wedding ring and you got into a car with him!" He sat upright, tugging his jeans back up around his backside, where they'd slid down unaided by a belt. "That wasn't who I was seeing! It was his brother, waiting in the car!" It was humiliating. Who did he think I was? Some silly little trollop? Still dissatisfied, he continued "Why didn't he get out of the car and come and meet you then, eh? What's wrong with him? Are you lying to me girl?" He was ready to jump up now if I gave him any lip "No I'm not lying. That was Colin his brother. Kevin was in the car. He was a bit shy about coming to knock for me and asked his brother to come for support, that's all" I was trying to placate him, though not really wanting to give him much information, when I didn't know what was happening yet.

242

"You be fucking careful! Getting into cars with men and disappearing into the night. People will think you're a cheap slag. You'll get yourself into trouble. I'm warning you, watch yourself and I don't want fucking Bruce Lee knocking on the door either". It was in reference to Colin, because he'd worn all black, including black canvass espadrilles. The trademark costume of the Kung Fu legend. Again Tomas had successfully belittled and sullied me. I wanted to scream at him to mind his own damn business. In one sentence he'd conveyed where I stood, how he saw me, and all the worth he could imagine anyone else seeing in me. As always, all I could submissively say was "Ok. Goodnight Tomas." Happy with that he said "Goodnight. Don't fucking wake your Mum up, banging up the stairs with all your weight."

It didn't matter tonight though. I'd met someone. Someone who had principles. He'd lit something up inside me. I felt like an oil lamp that had been muted to the dimmest glow and he'd just turned a dial that had allowed the flame to leap to its fullest capacity. I could've brightened a whole room with the happiness bottled safely inside me. Lying in bed, I couldn't sleep. The evening replayed over and over in my head. Our conversation ran around on a loop. The way he'd held my hand at the last moment, as I left the car, was a gesture that had only ever existed in my imagination, before that moment.

Chapter 36

Light fingered, heavy heart

Now, I saw Kevin as often as possible. I'd phone him from the phone box on the corner of the road, just outside Budgens. I'd call him after work and he'd arrange to come and meet me. One afternoon, he surprised me by turning up unexpectedly, while I was working. Engrossed in the mundane task of filling the cereal shelf, I became aware that someone was standing nearby watching me, only to discover it was Kevin. He'd been observing me unhindered for several minutes, before I realized. It became routine for him to pop in and buy his lunch, just so he could see me at work. At weekends he'd pick me up and we'd go to a bar in town. He took me to the cinema to see "Karate Kid" twice. The first time we were so close to the screen, I had a crick in my neck for the rest of the evening. Another time he asked me to go and watch banger racing with him and encouraged me to bring my brother Shaun along too. Well aware by now, that I was seeing someone, and that it seemed to be an ongoing thing, Mum and Tomas had cautiously agreed that Shaun could come along. It was all going quite nicely. I was" courting", as Nana and Granddad would've called it, albeit closely scrutinized by Tomas. I was pushing the boundaries, finding it more and more difficult to leave Kevin at the end of each date and getting home later and later. Tomas had already lectured me several times. So desperate to see more of Kevin, I'd even stolen a racing bicycle I'd seen, leaning against the side of a house along our street. I now had a means to get to the other side of town to visit him, under my own steam. I told both him and Tomas a friend at work had lent it to me. Kevin believed me, but Tomas eyed me suspiciously "It had better be borrowed, if someone comes knocking on this door saying you've nicked that bike, there'll be trouble!" I swore solemnly it wasn't stolen, scooting off down the road in haste, cycling at a breakneck speed to see Kevin as soon as possible. Cars bibbed their horns at me as I clumsily ran red lights, stymied the flow of traffic at roundabouts, and cycled in the wrong lane. Frantic to get away from Tomas, anxious to be with Kevin.

Kevin invited me to meet his parents on a Sunday evening. How amusing Tomas thought that was "Getting serious then, if he's taking you to meet them, it'll be a proposal next!" I blushed with embarrassment, half wishing that it might be true. Joan, Kevin's Mum, was a short, rotund woman. Stocky and stern, she didn't mince her words. Bringing up nine children doesn't allow much room for frivolity. There was nothing frivolous about Joan. Almost her first words to me were "How old are you?" Kevin had already primed me, suggesting that perhaps it'd be better to tell her I was already seventeen. It didn't seem too much of a lie, my birthday was only a few months away. Bill, his Step-dad was softer, more amenable. He kindly pulled a chair out at the dinner table for me, which was heavily laden with cold meats, salads and thick slices of bread. They'd put on a proper spread to greet me. Bill was quite tall, with a paunch and a balding pate. He was still dressed in post office uniform "I've not long got in from work. I'm a postman for the Royal Mail" He smiled at me, pushing his glasses up his nose, it was a habit that I soon came to recognise as a trait he had "Do you like working outdoors then?" I asked innocently, racking my brains for little snippets that I might make conversation with "Oh! No, no! I work in the sorting office now. I used to do the rounds, not anymore though. Too old for all that, I like to be in the warm these days." He chortled merrily. Kevin smiled at me, pleased that Bill seemed to be taking a shine to me already "Samantha works at Budgens Dad, she's lucky to have a job in the warm too". Grabbing my hand, under the table, he squeezed it hard. Joan pushed the door open with her bottom as she came in backwards, carrying a mouth-watering fruit cake on a cake stand. With a proud flourish she deposited it in the centre of the table. On cue, Kevin and Bill sighed appreciatively, Kevin touching Joan's forearm, said "Mum bakes cakes, she's a proper cook, there's never any shop brought cakes in this house. Her angel cake is the best. My favourite." Blushing proudly, she replied "Well it's a fruit cake today, we had angel cake last Sunday. Samantha don't be shy, grab your plate and tuck in, get yourself some ham or do you like hazlet?" I didn't even know what "hazlet" was. I did know this was hospitality. An effort had been made for me. Joan and Bill had gone to all this trouble just to please me. In awe of Joan, I was also slightly afraid of her. She was certainly the matriarch in this family. The afternoon was pleasant, lots of food, copious amounts of tea and inconsequential chatter. Other family members arrived uninvited, but welcomed anyway. Colin with his pregnant wife, Kay and Kevin's sister Diane, with her boyfriend Mark. It was quite overwhelming, but warming too. They had come, keen to meet me, but behaving as if it were only coincidence that they happened to drop in during my visit. The house was a hive of activity, impromptu guests, eating, tea cups chinking, plates clattering and cutlery scraping, as cakes and sandwiches were consumed. I observed it all, in the heart of it all, but internally on the periphery. My family was so different, it was fascinating to watch. Kevin flicked through a home shopping catalogue, showing me the jewellery pages he asked me "Which watches do you like the look of?" his brother and sister nudged each other, giggling. Colin sang "It must be love, love, love! He wants to spoil you with a new watch already." It was overwhelming, their easy acceptance of me and Kevin's generous spirit. I picked out a pretty watch, not really believing it would ever materialize.

On my next visit the watch had arrived, Kevin gave it to me eagerly. He strapped it to my wrist on one knee, as Bill joked "It'll be a ring next, you'll see. He looks like he's proposing already!" That whole afternoon I kept glancing surreptitiously at my wrist, as the watch glinted attractively on my arm. Catching my eye, as he'd seen me admiring his gift again and again, Kevin smiled meaningfully at me, his eyes conveying how much he wanted me to be happy. Joan and Bill had agreed I could stay overnight "You'll have to sleep on the sofa and Samantha, you can have his bed" Joan stated plainly. We'd spent the whole evening waiting for them to go to bed so that we could have some time on our own, it was a test of endurance, Joan knowing we were waiting for them to turn in for the night and reluctant to leave us, while we, determined to outlast her, sat it out. Finally, her head nodding on to her chest and jerking awake, she relented. Saying goodnight grudgingly, she gave Kevin a stern, knowing look as she closed the living room door behind her. We smothered our laughter and I whispered "I thought she'd never go to bed!" Kevin put his arm around me and we snuggled closer, no need to be self-conscious now, our chaperone gone. Intending only to watch the TV in each other's arms, in unspoken unison we flicked through the channels until we found a western, and both tried to concentrate on watching it. It wasn't long before we were kissing, gently at first, tentative little kisses, fluttering on foreheads and brows. Then more passionately mouth to mouth. The kisses became hotter, wetter, more searching and filled with need. His stubble rasped against my face, and I soon became sore where the moisture from our kissing, combined with the proximity of his skin to mine, irritated me. I didn't care, I felt alive. My heart raced and my pulses throbbed in time to the beat. His hands roamed under my jumper. Grabbing hungrily at my breasts, he tweaked and caressed my nipples. Groaning gently he pulled my jumper up, so he

247

could see what hid beneath and greedily smothered my breasts with kisses, sucking my aureoles and burying his face in between them. My hands ran up his back, under his shirt, and I parted my legs so that his body could fit in the space between my thighs as he seemed to engulf me with his mouth. Encouraged, his hands ventured up my skirt and along my thighs, as he continued to kiss my breasts, then my mouth again. So aroused, my body seemed to respond of its own accord, my back arched as I pushed upwards against him, inviting him to explore further. Urged onwards, his hands reached the waistband of my tights, and he tugged at it needily. I lifted my bottom to allow him access, enabling him to drag my tights down, as I aided him by lifting one leg up and out from the stocking leg, the other leg left in place, so our need would waste no time. Still kissing as I fumbled with his belt buckle, he chuckled breathlessly, now his turn to lift his weight upwards so that he could undo his fly to free himself and allow contact with me. We didn't pause to consider birth control, a condom was the last thing on our minds. He entered me with care, but even so it still hurt. The excitement became discomfort as he whispered "Relax, don't tense up, it'll be worse if you do". Easy for him to say. He pressed onwards, pushing into me as my thighs quivered and my buttocks clenched. I felt such a burning sensation, it stung. Once he had fully entered me he sighed, pausing briefly, I felt him shudder as he began a slow motion. Back then forth his hips rocked, as he gently moved above me. The stinging sensation had lessened, it was bearable, but still uncomfortable. I didn't feel physical pleasure anymore, my enjoyment was rooted in the knowledge that he desired and wanted me. I clung onto him, pressing my fingers into his buttocks, pushing him inwards to me, whispering "Yes, yes" into his ear. My knees knocked rhythmically against his sides as he rocked against me. I thought "How long will this go on?" All of the passion I'd felt during the prelude to this had disappeared, now I longed for it to end. He climaxed quietly, gasping against my cheek as he trembled against me. His rocking motion stopped abruptly, as he thrust into me with one final judder. I waited, panting gently, listening to his pounding heart beat in time with mine. He was gentle, kissing me again and brushing my hair away from my eyes. He didn't pull away immediately, instead, withdrawing, he lolled alongside me, using his pants to staunch the wet flow between us as he wrapped me in his arms and pulled me closer to him. We lay together on the sofa, my tights tangled around one leg, and my skirt rucked up underneath me. He had hiked his jeans back up, but his shirt was askew, buttons undone and crumpled. "Are you ok?" he asked me, kissing the side of my face "Yeah, I'm fine, a bit sore" I whispered. He smiled and squeezed me against him "It'll get better, it's uncomfortable at first, but I promise it will get easier". I was silent, not sure what to say. Did he think I was a virgin? Did he think this was my first time? What was I supposed to say? Maybe I should say "Well, urm…excuse me, you see, this isn't my first time, not really. My brother has shagged me before, only I don't know if that counts or not…" I said nothing. He thought I was pure and new, wholesome and clean. He believed I was his and he was mine, my first. I wanted him to continue seeing me as this lovely, fresh young girl only touched by him, none before. So I kept my mouth shut and let him believe. "I'd better straighten myself out, we're lucky your Mum and Dad didn't catch us" I smiled at him shyly, suddenly aware of how exposed I was, emotionally and physically. He held my hand, helping me up, we tiptoed to the doorway. He led the way, listening out for any movement from his parents' room, before leading me down the corridor to the bathroom. Switching on the light he said "Everything you need is in here, there are clean towels in the cupboard, have a shower if you like". He fussed around me, finding a clean towel and pulling the shower curtain back. "I'll fetch a duvet and some pillows from my room and turn in, before they get suspicious. When you're ready go and get in my bed. I'll be thinking of you sleeping there, wishing I was with you". We embraced again, he held me tightly and kissed the top of my head "Goodnight, love you" his hand held mine as he lingered in the hallway on the way back to the sofa, I saw his smile fade away in the dim lighting as he receded into the darkness back to the living room, and heard him call softly again "Goodnight". I closed the bathroom door as quietly as I could. Looking in the mirror I saw myself, flushed with excitement, a red rash evident along one side of my face, hair mussed up and eyes glittering back at me. So this was what it was to be with someone, to share yourself with another and to belong. Kevin wanted me. He had said he loved me. I wanted to be that so desperately, wanted to belong to somebody and have them belong to me. Taking a brief shower, towelling myself dry I swiped the towel across the mirror to find my reflection through the steam one more time. It was me I saw, it was me this was happening to. Warm and sleepy from the shower I snuggled up in Kevin's bed, safe.

Tomas was getting more annoyed with me, I had arrived home late again on the Sunday. It was so difficult to leave Kevin, I wanted to be with him, and leaving him was a terrible wrench. Again there was a show down, Tomas waited up and confronted me "How many times do I have to fucking tell you? If you're not home by midnight, I'll lock that fucking door and you can stay out all night." Again I mumbled insincere apologies. Unconvinced he shouted "Do you hear me?! Next time the door will be locked. My house, my rules!" Too tired to respond, I slunk upstairs to my room, exhausted. I had to get some sleep before work the next day. Not even bothering to wash my make up off, or brush my teeth, I wearily changed into my nightclothes, collapsed into bed and slept until the alarm woke me. None of it mattered. Tomas's tirades, the daily drudge at work, or the uncertainty of the future. All I cared for was the next time I'd see Kevin, I was in love. There had been a shift in our feelings, what had at first been light hearted and teasing had changed. Now it was heavier, more urgent. We were hungrier for each other, he was my oxygen and I was his H2o. I'd stolen the bike so that I could cycle to his house and see him more frequently, wanting him to think me independent of him, while in fact I needed him more and more. He was my drug. Wanting to buy him a present to reciprocate his generosity I dipped into the till at work. There was a small silver chain and pendant I'd seen, it was a St Christopher and I wanted to buy it for him. If fate allowed for an innocent desire to give somebody else a small pleasure, I thought. If the balance of the scales allowed for a minor deviation from right and wrong, I wouldn't get caught. I would get away with it, because I wasn't a bad person and I wasn't hurting anyone. That's how I rationalized it. Mum and Tomas got their rent money. I could afford the necessities, my toiletries and a trip into town to buy some new shoes or a blouse, but that was as far as my wage stretched. Any date with Kevin was funded by him. I simply didn't earn enough to subsidise a social life. It embarrassed me that more often than not, he paid for the cinema, or drinks, or entry to the nightclub. It was difficult to have time alone at his parent's house and I certainly had no intention of inviting him to mine. The only alternative was to go to the pub or some such place to be together, where we could kiss and hold each other unobserved by Joan or Bill.

Work was mundane, shelf-filling or working the tills was increasingly mind numbing. Michelle was still friendly, but now distant with me. Since I'd met Kevin all of my spare time was spent with him. Michelle had grown tired of trying to make arrangements to do anything with me. She'd quite quickly given up on me. Too absorbed with Kevin, I was blind to anything, or anyone else. Mum had, at least, got through to me, insisting I visit the local family planning clinic and started taking the pill. I did feel free to admit to her that I was having sex. Usually impassive towards me, she was interested in ensuring I didn't come home with an unwanted "bun in the oven". I trusted her with all the details of mine and Kevin's burgeoning sex life, seeking advice and reassurance. She was my only point of reference on the subject. It also gave me another angle for some form of bonding with her. I was still trying, somehow, to feel her love. That brief glimmer of unity between us proved short lived. Working side by side on the checkout one morning, I was called into the manager's office. Mr Barratt wanted to have a private chat with me. He had pulled a chair up opposite his desk and gestured at me to sit facing him, as he peered over his glasses at me "Do sit down Samantha, this won't take long". He was brusque, and immediately, I bristled. I recognized that tone, had heard it enough from Tomas when something was amiss "Samantha, do you have any idea why I might have called you in to my office?" he asked, leaning back in his chair and rubbing his chin with one forefinger, I could hear the PVC straining in the backrest behind him. "No, not really, is it to do with my work?" I squirmed, unsure whether to cross my legs, or rest my hands on my knees, wanting to sit on them to hide them. "Well, I'll get to the point my dear. There has been money going missing from one of the tills. The till that you are registered to. What do you suppose that means?" He stared at me, arching an eyebrow and peering down his nose through his spectacles. Now I really squirmed. Fidgeting, I changed position, my eyes searching the ceiling for an answer "I don't know Mr Barratt, do you think I stole that money? Is that what you're saying?" I didn't have an answer, I was trying to buy myself time. He harrumphed noisily, clearing his throat, his cheeks flushed pinkly, the veins filled with blood "Can you explain to me why your till might be short? I'm not making accusations, I'm looking for reasons. Now I can't pinpoint when that money may have disappeared, if it was under your operation, or somebody else's. Perhaps you could help me." Sweat ran down my spine, and I knew the colour had drained from my face. I was scared, terrified what to say, afraid because my Mum was the other side of the door, wondering what was going on. Afraid, because everyone would know my shame "It could be all sorts of reasons, Mr.Barratt, I mean there have been times when it's been busy…and I've made a mistake at the till, an over ring, instead of calling for help, I just carried on. That's happened a couple of times, because when we're really busy, you don't always come straight away and you get annoyed with us when we call for assistance. Or maybe I've given someone the wrong change…and not realized, I don't know, two ten pound notes stuck together, it could be that." Even as I talked, I saw the colour rising in his cheeks, his jaw tensed and his nostrils flared. Still I gabbled on "Sometimes when there's a long queue of customers I get flustered and can make mistakes…" before I could finish the sentence he cut in sharply "Are you admitting that it's you?" Flustered now, I stammered "No! That's not what I was saying, what I'm saying is that I don't know. I'm trying to think of how the till might be wrong, that's all!" He stood up and paced the room. Hand on hip he turned towards me "Listen, I could call the police, if I have to, I will. They will be able to have a look at all members of staff, do background checks. If anyone has a history of this sort of thing I will find out. However, it's such a small amount of money I don't think it warrants such drastic action." His voice dropped an octave and calmer, he rubbed his hand across his forehead as he sighed heavily "Samantha, all I'm asking is that you tell me the truth. Did you take any money from that till? It would be better for you to be honest, just tell the truth and nothing more will come of it, do you understand?" He appeared so plaintive, I couldn't hold his stare, and looking away, I remained silent. "It will remain between

253

us, we all make silly mistakes. You're young, you've lots to learn. Perhaps you did it once and regretted it straight away, was that what happened?" He was so reasonable, almost fatherly. I wanted to tell the truth, believing I'd been an idiot. I thought he'd sympathise with me, maybe give me a metaphorical slap on the wrist, tell me never to be so stupid again "There was one time. It was only once, but I didn't take any money from the till, I swear. A customer gave me two ten pound notes stuck together and she didn't realize what she'd done, so I put the money in the till, but I took the extra ten pound when no one was looking. That's all Mr Barratt, I didn't steal it though!" It was no use, already shaking his head, both hands on each hip now, he looked at me with disdain "That's enough. You've said enough for me to know that you are not trustworthy. I'll fetch another member of staff to accompany you to the staff room, collect your things and leave. You're dismissed." Striding to the office door he opened it and called an older female member of staff over "Mrs Rathmore, please escort Samantha to the staff room to collect her belongings and make sure she leaves the premises". As I sidled past him, led by Mrs Rathmore I couldn't look, but knew anyway, that Mum and the other women at the checkouts had stopped to watch me. There was silence, a hush had descended over the whole store. Even the customers could sense that something was amiss.

Mum met me at home, Tomas was already ensconced on the sofa watching channel four racing. She handed me my little brown pay packet, what money I was due had been given her to forward to me "Do you know what she's done?! Here…" She flung the pay packet at me. Tomas was the one awe struck for once, head turning from her to me until he knew all the details "I have never been so ashamed in my life! She's been sacked, the stupid idiot. Stealing from the till, that's what she's been up to!" Exasperated, she gasped noisily as she caught her breath "I would never have thought it of you, you're no better than your Father." She slumped onto the armchair behind her, shaking her head from side to side as she held her face in her hands and moaned through her fingers "Oh the shame of it!" My face and neck burned bright red. Flushed as though licked by the flames of hell. I stuttered foolishly "They've got it wrong, it's not like that! I only took ten pounds!" Now comprehending this latest drama, Tomas picked up where Mum had left off "So you've lost your job because you've been thieving! You're nothing but fucking trouble. How do you think your Mum feels? She's the one who has to go back there to work every day!" He raised his fist to me then, holding it near my face. I shied away, squeezing my eyes shut as it trembled, clenched tightly millimetres from my cheek bone. He had never hit me. | This was the closest he'd ever come and it was only by the thinnest reserve of self-control, that he didn't strike me this time "Go away, go on! Get out of my sight before I give you a fucking good hiding!" He bawled in my face. I turned and ran into the hallway and upstairs to my bedroom. Shutting the door behind me I pressed my back against it and slid to the floor in a heap. Shoulders and chest heaved, heavy silent sobs as I buried my chin into my chest and just cried. Snot and tears soaked my clothes, as I tried but failed to staunch the flow with the sleeve of my top. They despised me! God, even I despised me. I was pathetic. This wasn't going to do, there had to be something better than this. I wished they could understand me, even a little. I wished that they might have a little mercy, maybe a small degree of sympathy for the mess I'd got myself into. It was clear to me, no one was going to help me. I would have to sort this out. I needed another job and quickly. This was down to me and me alone. Internally I laughed at the idea of "helping myself." Look at where that had got me! There had to be more than this, how was I ever going to escape this house and Mum and Tomas? An awkward, uncomfortable resentment reigned between Mum, Tomas and me. Tomas told me

"You can't stay here unless you pay your way, we're not keeping you. If you don't get a job you're out." As simple as that, spoken from behind the sports section of the newspaper, which he shook the pages of vigorously to emphasize the certainty of his statement. Mum didn't speak to me at all, she gave me contemptuous glances, turned away with disdain when I made eye contact with her. Didn't they know how desperate I was to leave? No one was more determined to get another job than me. I didn't want to live here anymore, it wasn't a home to me. The reality was I didn't know what to do, Kevin didn't yet know I'd lost my job and when I told him, he might well decide I was a waste of space too. Perhaps they were right, maybe I was useless, a drain on everyone else. Only the smallest kernel of self-belief still survived inside me.

When I saw Kevin, I told him the truth. He didn't respond straight away, he digested and considered all that I'd told him, one of the things I admired most about him. Unlike Tomas, Kevin wasn't reactionary, still, I waited for him to say he'd rather not see me again. He actually looked me up and down, appraising me, narrowed his eyes sceptically, then smiling said "What are you like? That was a stupid thing to do wasn't it?" Glumly, I nodded, solemnly picking at the bobbles on my over worn jumper "You won't do anything as daft as that again will you?"

He asked sternly "Never, I wish it'd never happened!" I gulped, holding back embarrassed tears. Then he growled "Come 'ere you silly thing!" He folded me into him, hugging me tightly to himself. Rocking me from side to side, he laughed "It's alright, we all do stupid things. Don't beat yourself up about it. Things are going to be alright, and you've got me on your side, remember?" By now he knew some of my family background. I'd opened up and revealed enough, to give him a fairly clear picture of what my home life was like "You will find another job, it's really not the end of the world and it could've been a

256

whole lot worse." His kind reassurance gave my tears release and I cried into his shoulder as he held me tightly. I'd expected recriminations or derision at the very least, but he showed me concern. There was no reservation or doubt, he simply loved me and provided the comfort I needed at that moment.

Joan and Bill were out for the night, we had the place to ourselves. Kevin cooked some weird meal out of a box from the freezer called "rissoles" which we jokingly called "arseholes" and the evening was spent blissfully making love, snuggled up together and talking wistfully about our future. It was already an unspoken understanding that the future was something we both wanted to share together. He was considerate, caring and loyal to me and seemed to see some promise in me that was invisible to anyone else. The night drew in, the shadows drawing in across the walls and ceiling of the living room, creeping stealthily along with the knowledge that night was arriving and so I should make my departure. I didn't want to go. Hoping that Kevin wasn't paying attention to the time, I side-tracked him, not wanting to hear his reminders of the necessity to arrive home in good time, and not wishing to add fuel to Mum and Tomas's despair of me. Chatting animatedly to distract from his awareness of time, interspersed with kisses, I scraped all corners of my mind for topics of discussion to keep him talking. It was the early hours of the morning when he finally insisted "Enough, we must get you home. You'll be in trouble as it is. Besides Mum and Dad will be back soon". I reluctantly gathered my things, silently moving to the hallway and slipping into my coat. He stopped me, tugging my elbow and pulling me around to face him so he could hold and kiss me "It doesn't matter what they say, you'll leave them soon. We'll be together and they won't have any hold over you then. Just a while longer, you can do it, hold on in there." His words perked me up. I could do it. If he was honest and I had his love and support, I could definitely do it. He drove me home, but we needn't have worried. The door was locked to me, all the lights were out and everyone had gone to bed. Knowing Tomas's habits very well, I knew this was staged. Always late to bed, he usually stayed awake until the early hours. No doubt he was watching through a crack in the curtains, congratulating himself for acting out his threats. It didn't matter if I banged, kicked, or screamed at his door, I knew I wasn't getting in. He would have heard the car pull up, the drain cover echo as I crossed it on my way up the garden path, the gate swing closed, spring loaded, and Kevin's car as it idled. Thankfully he always waited to ensure I was safely indoors before he left. I rapped the letter box, a futile attempt as, with the door locked and the darkness inside as effective as a mortise lock, it was obvious no one was coming to let me in. My pride wouldn't let me knock again. I was uncertain, should I wave at Kevin and pretend all was well, let him drive off into the night and sit on the doorstep until morning or should I let him see how little I was valued? I tip toed across the noisy drain cover, quietly shut the gate behind me and leant into the driver's window as Kevin wound it down "What's wrong?" he whispered, reaching for my hand. "They've locked me out. They've gone to bed and I can't get in." I didn't want a scene, Tomas bearing down the stairs threatening me or Kevin "Can't you knock? Won't they come down and let you in?" he asked. Having not met them, if he had, he'd have known the answer already. "No. If I knock, Tomas will ignore it, it's to teach me a lesson." Trusting my judgement, but also feeling my reluctance and pride he didn't insist, he didn't force me to knock them up. I wasn't coerced into an awful confrontation. Telling me to get back in t the car, he drove me away. He took me back to his parents, insisting they put me up for the night. He understood, without need for articulation, that I'd had enough, enough control, abuse and expletive laden dictatorship under Tomas's regime.

That night I slept in Kevin's bed, his arm tucked around me. He told an indignant Joan "Samantha is sleeping in my bed, with me tonight. Not on the sofa."

Chapter 37

Farewell is a lonely sound

Waking up the next morning, the light was filtering through the curtains, not quite drawn fully, a shaft of dust motes flittered, teeming in their own minute cosmic belt, created by the early morning sunlight. It spilled directly across our pillows and faces. Searching out Kevin's gaze, he was already smiling with sleep crusted eyes at me. I'd slept restlessly, plagued throughout the night with worry. Scooping his arm around me, he squeezed me "Time to get up. You can stay here, I'll make you a cuppa." Kissing me, he scooted out of bed, pulling on jeans and a t-shirt purposefully he left the room. I didn't know what he was thinking, we hadn't talked about last night. I didn't know what I was going to do today. Obviously I'd have to go home, Tomas would be waiting for me to show my face. It was hopeless, and I couldn't begin to explain to Kevin how difficult it was. I didn't want him to be burdened with my problems, or even have to admit to him how troubled my life really was. It was a sham, I wanted him to imagine I was together, that I had my head screwed on and had some direction. What on earth must he really think of me? A jobless, unwanted little idiot, going nowhere, with no potential. Even worse than that, he might think I needed him, that I had no capacity for independence or resources to improve my situation. He came back with a steaming mug of tea. Placing it on the floor beside the bed, he sat down beside me "We're going back to yours this morning. Have your tea and take a shower, then I'll drive you home." There was something unspoken, he was matter of fact. I wasn't sure what was happening, he was as affectionate as always, but he was also different. There was a set to his jaw, a determined look that I couldn't interpret "I'm nervous, I know I have to go back, it's stupid but I really wish I could stay with you. Impossible I know, but when we're together I'm happier than I thought I'd ever be. Going back there is like being sent to prison" I looked at him squarely, without tears this time "I wish we could make a life together, the way we want it to be, without anybody telling us what we can or can't do. Where to sleep, or when it's time to leave". I got up, dragging the bed sheet with me and wrapped myself in it. He opened the door, checking the coast was clear so that I could scurry to the bathroom without being seen by Joan or Bill. As I closed the bathroom door he still stood, framed by the sunlight in his bedroom, watching me and smiling gently. I showered, the water rinsing away some of my melancholy, I felt revived, more able to face the day. Standing on the bathmat I towelled myself off and tucked it around me. I was about to clean my teeth with Kevin's toothbrush when Joan knocked on the door, calling "If you've finished with that bed sheet, I'll have it for the wash please!" Startled, I didn't understand the necessity for the sheet right this moment, but, eager to keep the peace, I obliged, opening the door enough to pass the crumpled sheet, bundled up in a ball, to her. She snatched it hastily, with a Tut and an admonishing scowl of disapproval as she bustled busily, along to the kitchen. Kevin had come to the hallway to see what she was about, having heard her knocking on the bathroom door. He called after her in astonishment "Mum! Really! There's no need for that!" She ignored him. I shut the door, puzzled. What on earth was that about? Was today wash day? I had no idea, it was a bit unsettling and slightly embarrassing. The whole scenario was awkward, my impromptu overnight stay, no nightclothes and Kevin's command that I was sharing his bed. When I returned to his room, he was waiting for me, uneasily apologising "Sorry about Mum, she's a bit old fashioned, Salvation Army and all that. She doesn't think it's right you sleeping with me. Don't let it bother you. I don't care what she thinks, all I

261

care about is you". I wanted to believe him, hoping he cared as much as he said. He showered while I dressed. Plenty of time for Joan to load the washing machine, after she'd been in such a rush to retrieve my bed sheet. However, when we walked through the kitchen, she made a point of holding the incriminating sheet up to the light and proceeded to examine it thoroughly for my benefit, inspecting for spoilage or stains. It was unbelievable, I was so embarrassed. I knew it was my spoilage she was looking for. Looking at Kevin beseechingly, my eyes wide with horror, he gestured to me to keep walking, waving me onwards to the hallway to collect our coats. There I covered my mouth with my hand, gasping "What was that? What was she checking the sheet for? Fucking hell". He shook his head at me, as astounded as me. Shrugging his shoulders, he laughed, an awkward, uncertain laugh. We left, without saying bye. In the car we could talk, unhindered by Joan. "I'm driving you home, it's going to be alright. Let's just play it by ear. We'll see what happens when we get there ok?" In the driver's seat, he turned his body towards me and rested his hand in mine. "Please, just drop me off, don't come in. Let me deal with it, it won't help if you try talking to Tomas, he'll only get more annoyed" I pleaded, anticipating that Kevin would think the situation might be resolved with a reasonable chat "Trust me, I know Tomas, it won't make matters any better". Kevin listened and watched me intently, he was studying me, searching my face for confirmation of honesty, and satisfied I was being truthful he agreed "If that's what you want, but I'm not leaving until I know you're alright, do you understand. If he starts having a go at you, I won't stand by and do nothing." I nodded, knowing very well that Tomas was unlikely to have a slanging match on the doorstep with me. No that was not how it would unfold. He wouldn't leave the comfort of the sofa, I would at least be inside the house before the onslaught began and by that time, Kevin should hopefully

262

be on his way. I'd wave him on as I entered, closing the front door behind me.

I hadn't counted on my access being barred. Not by Tomas, but by Mum. When we arrived the trepidation crawled stealthily up my spine, I couldn't let Kevin see how scared I was. It wasn't that Tomas was violent, but his ability to strip away any self -esteem I could muster with words, was brutal. All throughout my childhood he'd attacked me verbally, viciously quashing any sense of my own self -worth at every opportunity. I'd learnt to brace myself, prepare my poker face and present him with emptiness. I'd learnt to pretend, presenting to him that unaffected stance, while inside me, each swear word, every name he called me, each dissemblance of any potential I might have, dissolved and shrivelled away into the core of my being, hidden and protected from his ignorant, thoughtless jibes. Kevin squeezed my hand "Go on, I'll be right here, I'm not going anywhere until you give me the signal all is ok". Breathing deeply, I gulped in oxygen to sustain me against the suffocation that awaited. I didn't look back. Once again I opened the spring loaded gate, and trod the noisy drain cover, knowing it was the alarm to them indoors, that I approached. Even as I knocked, the door was opened before my hand even left the letterbox. It wasn't Tomas, but Mum. Opening the door just enough to shove a suitcase through, she thrust it at me, gripping the door with her other hand, to ensure my entry was blocked. I was about to speak, but with one last hostile glare, she slammed shut the door. It was a surreal moment, it felt like a physical blow. If she'd slapped me across the face I couldn't have been more stunned. Mum was throwing me out, she'd planned it, prepared a suitcase, packed my things and kept it by the front door, ready for this moment. I stood, unable to act, undecided what to do. There were no choices, always stuck in this nightmarish cycle, the choices were made for me. The weight of the suitcase was taken from my hand, it was Kevin. Holding both the case and my hand, he led me back to the car. I couldn't speak, shocked and utterly forlorn. Mum didn't want me. My head spun, I was descending, shrinking, I was a child again, six years old crying through a letterbox with bleeding hands. Kevin didn't question me, didn't tell me what I should do, the silence was unbroken. He drove us away. We parked in a pub car park along the way somewhere, it didn't matter where. It was somewhere to recoup. A moment to absorb the shock. We had no intention of leaving the car, we needed to speak to each other before facing anyone else. He leaned over, grabbed me and hugged me to him in a bear like grip "Let it go, come on Samantha, let it out or you'll burst". I howled, cried like a blubbering baby. It just came, surging out of me like a stream bursting its banks "I can't believe it! I can't believe it, my own Mum! She doesn't care about me, she'd packed my things, had it waiting for me." My words were barely intelligible, garbled through heaving breaths for air and mucus clogged nostrils "What am I going to do? I haven't anywhere to go, no money, nothing. I'm shit, that's all I am, a piece of shit!" Kevin shouted at me "You are not shit! Don't ever say that, I never want to hear you say that again. Of course you have somewhere to go, you're with me! We'll sort it out, you'll see. We'll sort it out."

He took me back to his, spoke to his Mum quietly, out of ear shot, as I sat on the edge of his bed, trying to make out what was being said. It was very hushed, the house was peaceful, even though here I was, an unexpected, uninvited lodger. There wasn't an argument, nobody raised their voices. Joan came to see me, as I sat looking every bit the girl I still was, shoulders rounded, arms limp, my hands upwards, rested loosely in my lap. She stood looking at me briefly before speaking and when she did, it was evenly "Will your parents not have you back? Isn't this just to teach you a lesson?" I looked at her through swollen, red eyes and shook my head. "You can stay here for a little while, but only until you find something else. This isn't a guesthouse. Kevin is my son and I'll allow it for him, but you'd better sort yourself out... and soon." She walked away, her verdict given. As it happened my stay was brief, Kevin made sure of that. Scouring the local ads for rooms to rent, he spent evenings ringing around landlords, railing at Joan for moaning about the use of the phone "Do you want us to find somewhere to live? Then I need to phone around!" Of course, she didn't want him to find somewhere else to live, he was jeopardizing his relationship with her to rescue me. Joan made it as obvious as she possibly could, in all her actions towards me during my stay. Mealtimes, she dished up Kevin's dinner, only to scrape half onto a side plate for me at the dinner table. She didn't need to remind me, I knew I wasn't contributing and I was taking Kevin away from her.

Within a week he found us a bedsit. We hadn't even seen it, the landlord was hesitant about letting us rent it because it was only a small room with a single bed, but Kevin persuaded him to let us decide if it was suitable or not. We loaded up his car with my suitcase and boxes of his things. Joan made a last ditched attempt at reconciliation and went through the airing cupboard, digging out bedding and towels we could have. Bill persuaded her to give us an old set of saucepans, some chipped crockery and an incomplete cutlery set. The car was loaded, we carried things out to it, pausing to smile and hug each other on each trip to and fro. A sense of excitement was building, Kevin was happy, not in the least concerned. His choice was made. I was his choice. Leaving was difficult, Joan and Bill came to the door to say goodbye. Bill found Joan's grief amusing "He's not going to the other side of the world, for goodness sake. He'll only be a stone's throw away" he said, banging Kevin on the back a little too vigorously. Joan admonished me, wagging her finger in my face "You look after him, don't let me down." Kevin cuddled her gently "We're going to be fine. Stop worrying Mum, I had to leave one day and we'll be back every weekend for cake!" She started crying quietly, stepping away and back into the living room to hide. It was a sad moment, witnessing the sorrow a Mum feels when her child flies the nest. I had heard nothing from Mum or Tomas, they didn't know Kevin's address and couldn't have contacted me even if they'd wanted to. I had disappeared from their lives.

Chapter 38

Home

The car drew along the kerb outside the terraced house on Mill Road, bedsit land of Cambridge. Mill Road was, and remains a cultural hot bed close to the centre of town. All walks of life, from all ethnicities and backgrounds live there. Students, young families, old couples, Italians, Indians, Africans, West Indians, drop outs and drop ins. There is an abundance of shops, hairdressers, charity shops, take a ways, restaurants, and mini marts. A variety of pubs on the street, and scattered among the many streets branching off Mill Road, thrive, frequented by this diverse community. Stepping out of the car it was the first time we saw where we would be living. The front door had coloured glass segments, there was a bay window in the front and two bedroom windows above. It was situated at the quieter end of the street, away from the hub of the shopping and nightlife Mill road was best known for. Kevin looked at me for my reaction, I smiled and he reached for my hand. We stood on the tiled front stoop as the landlord came to let us in. Leading us down the long hallway and upstairs to the first room at the top, he opened the door to a back bedroom. We followed him and entered the room ahead of him, expectant, cautious, but excited. There was a window that overlooked the back garden, a built in cupboard and a single bed. Peering out of the window we surveyed the garden, I looked at Kevin, needing reassurance that he was Ok with this. I got it as he beamed back at me broadly.

Gradually we made the room a haven. We got a little fridge and used the top as a counter for our kettle and toaster, so we could store fresh food and have breakfast in our room. We painted the wood chip walls with a fresh coat of paint, brought two small armchairs, a coffee table and a portable TV. Kevin put up shelves and a mini music system. It was the beginning. Our home, a safe place. His brothers and sister came to visit and we saw Joan and Bill regularly. We argued occasionally and made up passionately. We loved each other, there was no name calling, spite, hatred or sorrow. I had thought I was falling, but I was wrong, I wouldn't let that happen. This was where my beginning would be.

Epilogue

An appeal

November

1997

It was a Monday four days before my birthday, I would be twenty eight and my daughter was seven. She was looking for Wally with Tomas in her "Where's Wally" book. I was with Mum in the kitchen, talking to her while she washed up their dinner plates. A cigarette smouldered in the ashtray, while an air wick air freshener intermittently squirted an overpowering scent of artificial lemon into the room. Kevin listened to the news, waiting patiently for a cup of tea to be offered. Winter was on its way, the nights already drawing in. The living room curtains were drawn, Mum didn't need much encouragement to out shut the world beyond the windows. The gas fire burned and Tilly their Yorkie snoozed on the hearth rug. There was a quick, short tap at the front door, and then Nana Sheila let herself in without waiting for an answer. The house suddenly came to life, her dog Bilbo was greeted by Tilly in a frenzy of tangled ankles and dog lead, while Bilbo circled Mum and Nana in an effort to sniff out Tilly's back end, Tilly trying to shield it by hiding behind Mum. Tomas shouted "Tell that fucking dog to sit down for fuck sake! What's going on? What are you doing, walking the dog after dark?" Nana was excited, she was on a mission, something couldn't wait until tomorrow "I had to come and see you straight away, I thought you needed to see this Carolyn." She handed Mum a newspaper, it was already opened and had been folded back to a particular page. Mum's face drained, the paper trembled in her hand as she slowly sat, sinking into the armchair. My daughter, Katie, went to her and slid into the seat beside her "What's wrong Nana?"

The headline read "**Woman calls for help to solve riddle**" Dick Gilchurch's daughter Sammy had placed an appeal in our local evening news. She was searching for Dick's ashes. The article read "A young woman is appealing for help to solve a twenty three year old mystery and find her father's remains. Samantha Gillingham 25, wants to find the ashes of her father, Richard Gilchurch, who was stabbed to death when she was a toddler. Ms Gilchurch believes that Carolyn Pride, her father's girlfriend at the time of his death, arranged his funeral and cremation. Now she wants to find out where they are, so she can give him a fitting memorial."

20899956R00159

Printed in Great Britain
by Amazon